THE
RUGBY FOOTBALL INTERNATIONALS
Roll of Honour

THE RUGBY FOOTBALL INTERNATIONALS
Roll of Honour

BY
E. H. D. SEWELL

The Naval & Military Press Ltd

Published by
The Naval & Military Press Ltd
5 Riverside, Brambleside, Bellbrook
Industrial Estate, Uckfield, East Sussex,
TN22 1QQ England

Tel: +44 (0) 1825 749494
Fax: +44 (0) 1825 765701

www.naval-military-press.com
www.nmarchive.com

In reprinting in facsimile from the original, any imperfections are inevitably reproduced and the quality may fall short of modern type and cartographic standards.

ALPHABETICAL LIST OF PORTRAITS

ABERCROMBIE, LIEUT. CECIL HALLIDAY, R.N.	18
ALEXANDER, SEC.-LIEUT. HARRY, 1st Batt. Grenadier Guards	20
BAIN, CAPTAIN DAVID M'LAREN, 3rd Batt. (att. 2nd Batt.) Gordon Highlanders	22
BAIRD, PRIVATE JAMES ALEXANDER STANSON, N.Z.	24
BEDELL-SIVRIGHT, SURGEON DAVID REVELL, R.N.	26
BERRY, CORPORAL HENRY, Gloucester Regiment	28
BLACK, CORPORAL ROBERT STANLEY, Canterbury Battalion, N.Z.	30
BLAIR, SEC.-LIEUT. PATRICK CHARLES BENTLEY, Rifle Brigade	32
BRETT, SEC.-LIEUT. JASPER THOMAS, Royal Dublin Fusiliers.	34
BURGESS, CAPTAIN ROBERT BALDERSTON, R.E.	36
CAMPBELL, LIEUT. JOHN ARGENTINE, Inniskilling Dragoons	38
CHURCH, CAPTAIN WILLIAM CAMPBELL, 1/8th Scottish Rifles (T.)	40
DEANE, CAPTAIN ERNEST COTTON, M.C., R.A.M.C.	40
DEWAR, SERGEANT HENRY, Wellington Mounted Rifles, N.Z.	42
DICKSON, LIEUT. WALTER MICHAEL, 11th Batt. Argyll and Sutherland Highlanders	42
DINGLE, CAPTAIN ARTHUR JAMES, 6th East Yorkshire Regiment	44
DOBBS, LIEUT.-COLONEL GEORGE ERIC BURROUGHS, R.E.	44
DOWNING, SERGEANT ALBERT, Wellington Battalion, N.Z.	46
EDWARDS, CAPTAIN WILLIAM VICTOR, Royal Irish Fusiliers.	48
FORREST, MAJOR WALTER TORRIE, M.C., King's Own Scottish Borderers	50
FRASER, CAPTAIN ROWLAND, 1st Batt. Rifle Brigade	52
GALLAHER, SERGEANT DAVID, Auckland Battalion, N.Z.	54
GEEN, SEC.-LIEUT. WILLIAM PURDON, 9th Batt. King's Royal Rifle Corps	60
GORDON, MAJOR ROLAND ELPHINSTONE, R.A.	62
HAIGH, CADET-OFFICER LEONARD, O.T.C., A.S.C. Mech. Transport	64
HANDS, CAPTAIN REGINALD HARRY MYBURGH, South African Artillery	64
HARRISON, LIEUT.-COMMANDER ARTHUR LEYLAND, V.C., R.N.	66
HENDERSON, LIEUT. JAMES YOUNG MILNE, 11th Batt. Highland Light Infantry	68

LIST OF PORTRAITS

HODGES, CAPTAIN HAROLD AUGUSTUS, 3rd Monmouths (att. 11th South Lancashire Regiment)	70
HOWIE, SEC.-LIEUT. DAVID DUCHIE, R.F.A.	72
HUGGAN, LIEUT. JAMES LAIDLAW, R.A.M.C.	74
INGLIS, REV. RUPERT EDWARD, C.F., att. 16th Infantry Brigade	76
KENDALL, LIEUT. PERCY DALE, 10th Batt. King's Liverpool Regiment (Liverpool Scottish)	78
KING, LANCE-CORPORAL JOHN ABBOTT, 10th Batt. Liverpool Regiment	82
LAGDEN, CAPTAIN RONALD OWEN, 4th Batt. King's Royal Rifle Corps	88
LAMBERT, LIEUT. DOUGLAS, 6th Batt. the Buffs	90
LEDGER, SERGEANT SEPTIMUS HEYNS, 2nd Batt. South African Infantry	94
LEWIS, MAJOR BRINLEY RICHARD, R.F.A.	96
MACLEAR, CAPTAIN BASIL, Royal Dublin Fusiliers	98
M'NAMARA, SEC.-LIEUT. VINCENT, R.E.	102
M'NEECE, PRIVATE JAMES, N.Z.	106
MAYNARD, LIEUT. ALFRED FREDERICK, R.N.V.R.	108
MILROY, LIEUT. ERIC, 8th Batt. Black Watch	110
MOBBS, LIEUT.-COLONEL EDGAR ROBERTS, D.S.O., 7th Batt. Northants Regiment	114
MOLL, SEC.-LIEUT. T. M., Leicestershire Regiment	120
MORKEL, TROOPER JAN WILLEM HUNTER, 1st Mounted Brigade Scout Corps, S.A.	122
NANSON, SERGEANT WILLIAM MOORE BELL, 1/10 Manchester Regiment	124
NELSON, CAPTAIN THOMAS ARTHUR, 1st Lothians and Border Horse	126
OAKELEY, LIEUT. FRANCIS ECKLEY, R.N.	128
PALMER, LIEUT. RONALD WILLIAM POULTON, Royal Berkshire Regiment	136
PEARSON, PRIVATE JAMES, 9th Royal Scots	144
PHILLIPS, SERGEANT LOUIS AUGUSTUS, Royal Fusiliers	146
PILLMAN, CAPTAIN ROBERT LAWRENCE, 10th Batt. Royal West Kent Regiment	148
PRITCHARD, CAPTAIN CHARLES MEYRICK, 12th Batt. South Wales Borderers	152
RAPHAEL, LIEUT. JOHN EDWARD, Duke of Wellington's West Riding Regiment	155
ROBERTSON, CAPTAIN LEWIS, Cameron Highlanders	160

LIST OF PORTRAITS

ROSS, SERGEANT ANDREW, 29th Canadians 166
ROSS, PRIVATE JAMES, London Scottish Regiment 170
SCHWARZ, MAJOR REGINALD OSCAR, King's Royal Rifle Corps . 172
SELLARS, PRIVATE GEORGE MAURICE VICTOR, Auckland Battalion, N.Z. 172
SIMSON, LIEUT. RONALD FRANCIS, R.F.A. 174
SLOCOCK, SEC.-LIEUT. LANCELOT ANDREW NOEL, 10th Batt. Liverpool Regiment 176
SMYTH, MAJOR ROBERTSON, R.A.M.C. 180
STEWART, MAJOR ALBERT LEWIS, D.S.O., Royal Irish Rifles (att. Machine Gun Corps) 182
STEYN, LIEUT. STEPHEN SEBASTIAN LOMBARD, R.F.A. . . 184
SUTHERLAND, SEC.-LIEUT. WALTER RIDDELL, 8th Batt. Seaforth Highlanders 186
TARR, LIEUT. FRANCIS NATHANIEL, 1/4th Leicestershire Regiment 192
TAYLOR, CAPTAIN ALFRED SQUIRE, R.A.M.C. (att. Highland Light Infantry) 198
TAYLOR, ENG.-CAPTAIN CHARLES GERALD, R.N. 200
TAYLOR, CORPORAL REGINALD, N.Z. 202
THOMAS, SEC.-LIEUT. HORACE WYNDHAM, Rifle Brigade . . 204
THOMAS, COMPANY SERGEANT-MAJOR RICHARD, 16th Batt. Royal Welsh Regiment 206
TODD, CAPTAIN ALEXANDER FINDLATER, 1/3rd Norfolk Regiment 210
TURNER, LIEUT. FREDERICK HARDING, Liverpool Scottish . 212
WADE, LIEUT. ALBERT LUVIAN, Middlesex Regiment (att. 6th Trench Mortar Battery) 216
WALLACE, LIEUT. WILLIAM MIDDLETON, 5th Rifle Brigade (att. Flying Corps) 220
WALLER, SEC.-LIEUT. PHILLIP DUDLEY, S.A. Heavy Artillery . 222
WATSON, TEMP. SURGEON JAMES HENRY DIGBY, R.N. . . 224
WESTACOTT, PRIVATE DAVID, 2/6th Gloucester Regiment . 226
WILL, LIEUT. JOHN GEORGE, Leinster Regiment 228
WILLIAMS, CAPTAIN JOHN LEWIS, 16th Batt. Welsh Regiment . 230
WILLIAMS, LIEUT.-COLONEL RICHARD DAVIES GARNONS, 12th Batt. Royal Fusiliers 230
WILSON, CAPTAIN CHARLES EDWARD, Queen's Royal West Surrey Regiment 232
WILSON, LIEUT. FRANK R., Auckland Battalion, N.Z. . . . 234
WILSON, LIEUT.-COMMANDER JOHN SKINNER, R.N. . . . 236
YOUNG, CAPTAIN ERIC TEMPLETON, 8th Scottish Rifles . . 236

AUTHOR'S FOREWORD

> "Sound, sound the clarion, fill the fife,
>   To all the sensual world proclaim
> One crowded hour of glorious life
>   Is worth an age without a name!"

THIS is no time for tears. Those whose memory we attempt to honour in the sad but proud Record which follows, would not, I feel sure, wish it otherwise. Theirs has been a man's end; shall we begrudge them that, or, regretting them, as all of us do, give rein to emotions which our Game teaches us from the day of our first puny effort in a match to keep under control? Rather might we shed tears of envy than of grief. For there is not one among us who does not envy them their glorious deaths for King, for Empire, and for the Right. Their splendid loyal example will live as long as the British race. It will never be forgotten how Rugby Football, instantly patriotic, went to War almost as one man directly the Call came. Their reply to that Call was like the rush of forwards at the moment of kick-off; and, writing as I do at a time when there is not a vestige of a sign of Peace, nothing is more certain than that Rugby Football will stay in the fighting line; will, if necessary, fight to get there right up to "No-side." The Game teaches this, too. Nothing like the answer of the Rugby Football world to the Call has ever before been seen in British history.

War was declared on Germany at midnight of August 4-5, 1914. The first move in the Rugby Football world occurred on August 5, 1914, when the Birkenhead Park Club handed over its ground to the military; and one of the prime movers in this instant patriotic act—its former captain and moving spirit, the late Lieutenant P. D. Kendall, killed in action—went into military training on August 6, 1914.

Only seven days after the declaration of War the Scottish Football Union circularized its clubs, informing them of a contribution by the Union of £500 to the National Relief Fund; of its resolve to offer the Inverleith ground to the military; suggesting that, where possible, their clubs should do likewise; and ending by cordially asking all the members of their clubs " to do something for which the training in discipline and self-control given by our Game has fitted them." The S.F.U., though the War was only seven days old, were nearly too late! In a very short time most Scottish Rugby clubs had disappeared off the earth, the last member handing in the books of his club to one of the Union's committee men, and going off to prepare himself for the War, just as though that was his daily business.

In England it is less easy to call the Rugby Union Committee together, or to get in touch with them, especially during the holiday month of August, than it is in Scotland; but August had not run its course before the Rugby Union also circularized its clubs for the purpose of raising Rugby Football battalions. Of course they were too late, though it was no fault of theirs; and their proposal actually fell through for lack of men! All had already joined up, or had made arrangements to do so.

One company of Rugby men in particular was recruited by the energy and personal attraction of a Rugby Union committee man, the late Lieutenant-Colonel E. R. Mobbs, D.S.O., who, so early as September 14, 1914, marched away from the Northampton Barracks at the head of the company he had raised, to entrain for a military camp.

In Ireland a meeting was called by the Irish Rugby Union, and the Irish Rugby Union Volunteer Corps became a *fait accompli* before the Expeditionary Force had landed in France. For this movement the late F. H. Browning, the beloved President of the I.R.U., who was destined to be foully murdered later on by Germany's allies, the Sinn Fein, was responsible. Within a month two hundred men from this Volunteer Corps had enlisted in the Royal Dublin Fusiliers.

Almost without exception, the Rugby Football nations were in khaki as quickly as that material was procurable. This volume tends, however inadequately, to record the fate of those among this ardent body of Patriots who had won International honours at our Game. I am only too well aware of its shortcomings, but, inasmuch as no man could do these men justice, these may be, I hope, pardoned and overlooked. It has to be borne in mind—and what Rugby Unionist will ever forget it?—that these splendid fellows were the cream of the Game in which they had gained their International Caps. What must be the dimensions of the Roll of Honour of the rank and file of the Rugby game, those equally fine Patriots who failed to win the highest earthly honours, to win an even higher? We may be sure they are worthy of these, their leaders, the men they envied and honoured in life, and with whom they are now one glorious team on the other side, beckoning to us to play the Game, and to keep the Game the great national asset it is in case the Motherland calls again.

Ay! if she calls again, and whenever she calls again, Rugby Football will be the first to line out; bending forward eager for the moment the fight begins, and ready to " stick it," come what may.

The letters I have been privileged to read during the task of compiling this volume have borne in upon me the fact, if indeed I had never thought of it before, that the Rugby Football player makes the best fighting man, be he sailor or soldier. There is ample evidence of that.

Lying smashed by Turkish bullets, in hospital, a New Zealand officer assured me that one of his chief troubles on Gallipoli was to keep back the Rugby players! " Out of every twenty 'first into' the Turkish trench, eighteen were Rugby men," said he.

In his stirring appreciation of Jack King, my friend R. F. Oakes, the old Durham and England forward, and the warm-hearted secretary of Yorkshire County R.U., includes the remark of a commanding officer, which provides further evidence as to this fact, if any is needed.

In the course of watching even an ordinary everyday kind of match the thought often offers itself: " This is the game that breeds men." William Webb Ellis little knew what he was doing for his race on that day at Rugby School when he "first took the ball in his arm and ran with it, thus originating the distinctive feature of the Rugby game, 1823 A.D.," according to the inscription on the tablet on the wall at Rugby. Many dates in our history are much less deservedly famous than the year 1823, but should be so no longer, for then was born the game which made the Men Who Did at the most critical period in our history —this War.

When considering the question of claims to be included in this Roll of Honour it was decided, while erring, if at all, on the side of inclusion, to include only those killed in action, died of wounds, or died of illness due in any way to active service. I have bowed to the decision of the relatives of J. H. Dods, the Scottish International, who lost his life in the blowing up of H.M.S. *Natal*, and have not included him, as he was a civilian in mufti at the time, and not on duty of any kind. On the other hand, L. Haigh, who died in England from the results of exposure incurred while undergoing military training to go to the Front, has been included, and, as I think all will agree, rightly so.

Owing to difficulties—such as the wide distances separating our far-flung battle lines; the sinking of mails which were bringing material for this book from New Zealand or South Africa; and from other causes, among which may be named the non-publication of casualties by the French Government—I have not been able to make all the biographies so complete as I wished to do. For results as they are, I have to thank heartily, and with the greatest reverence of which I am capable, all those parents, or nearest relatives, of the fallen who have responded so readily to my request for information and for the photo which they would prefer to appear in this *Livre d'Or* of Rugby Football. It merits such a title by the mere publication of the list of names of our Grand Dead.

In my request for these things I wrote, thanks to the kind suggestion of Professor E. B. Poulton, as follows :—

"I fully understand and sympathize with the feelings of those who shrink from publicity of any kind; but I venture to suggest that the part taken by the players of this noble game is such that it becomes our duty to permit their lives to stand forth for the benefit of future generations, when, in the period of reconstruction, the nation will surely need all the strength that high example can bring. It is only by such means as are here contemplated that the lives of our noblest and bravest can speak to their younger brethren and help them to achieve the best that is in them."

The response to my appeal was so ready, that within two months I had obtained over fifty photographs and the details concerning practically every one of the English, Scottish, Irish, and Welsh Internationalists who have fallen; with many kind expressions of sympathy with the work I was doing, and the most undeserved compliments concerning my share in it. Under such circumstances the burden of a very sad task has been much lightened; and how sad it has been few who have not perused the correspondence I have been honoured to see, or who have not had the personal acquaintance of many of those who have fallen, or who have not for several years watched their rise to football fame and progress in its exacting paths, can realize.

In this I have, too, to acknowledge, as I most cordially do, the ready assistance given me from time to time by Professor E. B. Poulton; by Mr. J. Aikman Smith, Scottish Football Union; by Lieutenant-Colonel W. S. D. Craven, R.H.A., D.S.O.; by Major J. Rainsford-Hannay, D.S.O.; by Lieutenant-Colonel J. E. C. Partridge, Welsh Regiment; by Captain W. A. Millar, Coldstream Guards (Captain of the South African team, 1912–13); by Messrs. J. Fulton (the famous Irish full-back); J. G. Hirsch; H. W. Carolin (South African team, 1906–7); E. Wray Palliser, C.M.G.; G. H. Dixon, New Zealand Rugby Union; Lieutenant E. E. Booth, New Zealand Team of 1905; Captain C. J. B. Marriott, Secretary Rugby Union; C. F. Ruxton, Secretary of the Irish Rugby Union; R. L. Aston (Tonbridge, Cambridge, and England); T. H. E. Baillie and L. Speakman (Old Haileyburians); C. S. Arthur, Secretary of the Cardiff Club; E. G. Loudon-Shand (Dulwich, Oxford, and

Scotland); Prob.-Surgeon R. Hall, R.N.V.R.; T. S. Hamilton; F. H. Dauncey, and many others too numerous to mention here, and by all those who have so very kindly written an "appreciation" of the old friend or acquaintance they have lost. All have assisted with the instant readiness of the true Rugby Unionist, and the chief honour for the production of this Record remains theirs.

I have specially to thank Mr. D. M'Kenzie, of Wellington, New Zealand, for the very thorough way he responded to my request, conveyed to him through Mr. G. H. Dixon, the manager of the New Zealand Rugby team of 1905 in the United Kingdom, for details and photographs of New Zealand Internationals. These reached me just as I was despairing of including anything more than the bare names of New Zealand's International players. As though to accentuate their sacrifice the registered packet arrived, *via* Vancouver, just as the "Take Cover" warning had rung out for an air raid, and I read of their manly deaths seated in a kind of temporary dug-out, surroundings which lent an air of sharing, even if only in a very safe kind of way, some of the perils they had undergone. When we pause to consider that the total number of New Zealand "reps," as they call their Internationals, is only 211, the first New Zealand Representative XV. being dated 1884, and that "of that number fully one half is ineligible, because of age, for military service; many have died; and several have boys of their own in the fighting line, while others are married men with prospective 'reps' in their families," to quote Mr. M'Kenzie, New Zealand's Roll of Honour, numbering nine as it does, is well worthy of this great home of the Game. We on this side certainly salute their dead with reverence, and are as proud as they are in that grand country to include them in this deathless scroll.

I have thought it well to draw up in easily read tabular form what I have named a Record of Patriotism. This shows at a glance the month and year in which each International joined his Majesty's Forces, and the month and year in which each went to the Front. Of the fifty-eight United Kingdom Internationals not previously in the Army or Navy (the similar dates of the dozen Colonial Internationals have not all been obtainable, hence

AUTHOR'S FOREWORD

the only reason for their exclusion from this fine Record) who have fallen, twenty-eight "joined up" in August 1914, most of these in the first dozen days of war. Including those who joined in September, the number rises to thirty-nine. This means that over 67 per cent. were in the Service for active war purposes within two months of the declaration of war. Of the remaining nineteen, or 33 per cent., when war was declared, five were so far overseas as India, Egypt, South Africa, the Arctic Circle, and the States. The case of Andrew Ross of Scotland was a notable one. He was in the Arctic Circle when war broke out, but was drilling in the first fortnight of November 1914. P. C. B. Blair (Fettes and Scotland), H. W. Thomas (Monmouth and Wales), L. A. N. Slocock (Marlborough and England), all threw up lucrative appointments abroad in answer to the Call. It was due only to this that their respective dates are not August 1914.

And above all soars the fact that not a Rugby player, certainly not one whose biography appears in this book, waited for conscription.

The working-man sections of the Rugby game in the United Kingdom played the game equally with their Public School and University brothers, just as they had been used to do on the field, and as nobody ever had a doubt they would when the Call came. The names of H. Berry, D. Westacott, W. M. B. Nanson, and E. J. R. Thomas are honoured equally with any of the others. That fewer of them are numbered on this Roll of Honour is solely due to the fact that their numbers are fewer than those of Public School men in Rugby Football. Following is the Record of Patriotism, and in it the names appear in the chronological order in which their owners were taken from us; where two fell on the same date, the first whose name appeared in the casualties is written first here.

All figures given and dates quoted in this book are those in the family records of the individual concerned and in the official list of Internationals published with the authority of the Rugby Unions. Regarding the dates of International matches it has to be said that the official dates given in the Rugby Union Handbook are misleading. Thus the South Africans of the 1912-13 tour did not play Scotland in 1913, as stated against the names of the Scottish players in the Rugby Union Handbook, but on November 23, 1912, as stated elsewhere in the same publication. While notice of errors of omission and commission in regard to dates in this volume will be welcomed by the Author, all possible care has been taken to verify and check all the dates, and it is believed that they are correct. Only Rugby Union, and not Northern Union, *bona fide* Internationals were qualified for inclusion.

Du reste, the time has come to bid *Adieu* to our splendid Dead. It is with feelings of gratitude to them and of a fierce pride in the deathless fame they, by their glorious sacrifice, have given to the record of Rugby Football in this War, that I do so. To one who has seen almost every one of them at his very best, full of life and vigour and grace and manliness on the field of play, their deaths have been like the wrench of parting with friend after friend. In this I am very far from being alone. Thousands knew them as I did, admired and loved them as I did. They will agree with me that these men have raised an imperishable memorial of high example that Time cannot change. Other of our race of Games-men may have vied with them, but none have equalled the peerless performance of players of Rugby Football in this the greatest struggle our race has ever had to endure. To the end of Time these men will live.

> " England ! if thy will be yet
> By their great example set,
> Here beside thine arms to-night
> Pray that God defend the Right.
>
> " So shalt thou when morning comes
> Rise to conquer or to fall,
> Joyful hear the rolling drums,
> Joyful hear the trumpets call.
> Then let Memory tell thy heart :
> ' England ! what thou wert, thou art ! '
> Gird thee with thine ancient might.
> Forth ! and God defend the Right ! "
>
> HENRY NEWBOLT.

E. H. D. S.

LONDON, *January* 31, 1918.

Record

	NAME	Nationality	School
1.	R. F. SIMSON	Scottish	Edinburgh Academy
2.	J. L. HUGGAN	Scottish	Watson's College and Darlington
3.	C. E. WILSON	English	Dover College
4.	J. H. D. WATSON	English	King's, Canterbury
5.	J. ROSS	Scottish	Fettes
6.	L. ROBERTSON	Scottish	Fettes
7.	F. E. OAKELEY	English	Osborne and Dartmouth
8.	F. H. TURNER	Scottish	Sedbergh
9.	C. G. TAYLOR	Welsh	Royal Naval College
10.	P. D. KENDALL	English	Tonbridge
11.	R. O. LAGDEN	English	Marlborough
12.	A. F. TODD	English	Mill Hill
13.	R. W. POULTON PALMER	English	Rugby
14.	H. BERRY	English	St. Mark's, Gloucester
15.	J. PEARSON	Scottish	Watson's
16.	B. MACLEAR	Irish	Bedford
17.	D. M'L. BAIN	Scottish	Edinburgh Academy
18.	W. M. B. NANSON	English	Lowther Street School, Carlisle
19.	W. C. CHURCH	Scottish	Glasgow Academy
20.	E. T. YOUNG	Scottish	Fettes
21.	P. C. B. BLAIR *	Scottish	Fettes
22.	F. N. TARR	English	Uppingham
23.	W. P. GEEN	Welsh	Haileybury
24.	W. M. WALLACE	Scottish	Edinburgh Academy
25.	A. J. DINGLE	English	Durham
26.	D. R. BEDELL-SIVRIGHT	Scottish	Fettes
27.	E. C. DEANE	Irish	Corrig, Kingstown
28.	R. D. GARNONS WILLIAMS	Welsh	Magdalen College School
29.	D. LAMBERT	English	St. Edward's, Oxford, and Eastbourne
30.	H. ALEXANDER	English	Uppingham
31.	W. M. DICKSON †	Scottish	South African College
32.	V. M'NAMARA ‡	Irish	University, Cork
33.	R. B. BURGESS	Irish	Portora High School
34.	D. D. HOWIE	Scottish	Kirkcaldy High School
35.	L. A. PHILLIPS	Welsh	Monmouth Grammar Sch.
36.	R. S. SMYTH	Irish	Dungannon Royal School
37.	A. ROSS §	Scottish	Royal High, Edinburgh
38.	C. H. ABERCROMBIE	Scottish	Berkhamsted

* Was in Egyptian Civil Service, August 1914 to January 1915.
† In South Africa when war broke out.

atriotism

Date of joining Service	Date of going to Front	Date of Death	
Regulars	August 1914	September 14, 1914	1.
August 1914	August 1914	September 16, 1914	2.
Regulars	August 1914	September 17, 1914	3.
August 1914	August 1914	October 15, 1914	4.
August 29, 1914	September 15, 1914	October 31, 1914	5.
Regulars	August 1914	November 3, 1914	6.
Royal Navy	August 1914	December 1, 1914	7.
August 1914	November 1, 1914	January 10, 1915	8.
Royal Navy	August 1914	January 24, 1915	9.
August 6, 1914	November 1, 1914	January 25, 1915	10.
August 1914	February 1915	March 1, 1915	11.
August 1914	October 1914	April 20, 1915	12.
August 1914	March 1915	May 5, 1915	13.
August 1914	August 1914	May 9, 1915	14.
August 1914	February 1915	May 22, 1915	15.
Regulars	March 1915	May 24, 1915	16.
August 1914	December 1914	June 3, 1915	17.
Reservist	February 1915	June 4, 1915	18.
August 1914	May 1915	June 28, 1915	19.
August 1914	May 1915	June 28, 1915	20.
January 1915	June 1915	July 6, 1915	21.
August 1914	February 1915	July 18, 1915	22.
August 1914	May 1915	July 31, 1915	23.
August 1914	August 1914	August 22, 1915	24.
August 1914	—	August 22, 1915	25.
January 1915	April 1915	September 5, 1915	26.
Regulars	September 1914	September 25, 1915	27.
September 1914	September 1915	September 27, 1915	28.
August 1914	June 1915	October 13, 1915	29.
July 1915	October 1915	October 17, 1915	30.
—	October 1915	October 1915	31.
December 1914	June 1915	November 29, 1915	32.
November 1914	January 1915	December 9, 1915	33.
September 1914	August 1915	January 19, 1916	34.
September 1914	November 1915	March 14, 1916	35.
Regulars	September 1914	April 5, 1916	36.
November 1914	September 1915	April 6, 1916	37.
Royal Navy	August 1914	May 31, 1916	38.

Delayed in joining by examinations.
Was in the Arctic Circle when war was declared.

Record o

	NAME	Nationality	School	Age
39.	J. S. WILSON	Scottish	Royal College, Trinidad	32
40.	R. FRASER	Scottish	Merchiston	26
41.	E. J. R. THOMAS *	Welsh	Ferndale Board School	35
42.	R. L. PILLMAN	English	Rugby	23
43.	J. L. WILLIAMS	Welsh	Cowbridge Grammar Sch.	34
44.	E. MILROY	Scottish	Watson's	28
45.	L. HAIGH	English	Sandringham House School, Southport	35
46.	L. A. N. SLOCOCK †	English	Marlborough	29
47.	J. KING	English	Giggleswick	33
48.	C. M. PRITCHARD	Welsh	Newport Intermediate	33
49.	H. W. THOMAS ‡	Welsh	Monmouth Grammar	25
50.	R. E. INGLIS	English	Rugby	52
51.	A. F. MAYNARD	English	Durham	22
52.	J. T. BRETT	Irish	Royal School, Armagh	21
53.	J. G. WILL	Scottish	Merchant Taylors'	24
54.	B. R. LEWIS	Welsh	Swansea Grammar School	26
55.	T. A. NELSON	Scottish	Edinburgh Academy	40
56.	W. T. FORREST	Scottish	Kelso High School	37
57.	A. L. WADE	Scottish	Dulwich	35
58.	J. E. RAPHAEL	English	Merchant Taylors'	35
59.	G. E. B. DOBBS	English	Shrewsbury	33
60.	E. R. MOBBS	English	Bedford Modern School	34
61.	A. S. TAYLOR	Irish	Campbell College, Belfast	28
62.	J. Y. M. HENDERSON	Scottish	Watson's	26
63.	D. WESTACOTT	Welsh	Grange National School, Cardiff	30
64.	A. L. STEWART	Irish	Royal Belfast Academical Institution	28
65.	S. S. L. STEYN	Scottish	Diocesan College, Rondebosch, S.A.	26
66.	P. D. WALLER	Welsh	Glasgow, Islay & Llanelly	28
67.	W. V. EDWARDS	Irish	Campbell College, Belfast	30
68.	J. A. CAMPBELL	Scottish	Fettes	4
69.	G. A. W. LAMOND	Scottish	Kelvinside Academy	3
70.	W. R. HUTCHISON	Scottish	Glasgow High School	2
71.	H. A. HODGES	English	Sedbergh	3
72.	R. H. M. HANDS	English	Diocesan Col., Rondebosch	
73.	A. L. HARRISON	English	Dover College	3
74.	R. E. GORDON	Scottish	King's, Canterbury	2
75.	W. R. SUTHERLAND	Scottish	Teviot Grove Academy	2
76.	R. O. SCHWARZ	English	St. Paul's School	4

* Delayed by duty in Glamorgan Police Force.
† Delayed by business in the States.
‡ Delayed by business in Calcutta.

Patriotism—Continued

International Caps	Date of joining Service	Date of going to Front	Date of Death	
2	Royal Navy	August 1914	May 31, 1916	39.
4	August 1914	January 1915	July 1, 1916	40.
4	January 1915	December 1915	July 7, 1916	41.
1	September 1914	May 1916	July 9, 1916	42.
17	September 1914	December 1915	July 12, 1916	43.
12	September 1914	October 1915	July 18, 1916	44.
7	July 1916	Died in England	August 6, 1916	45.
8	September 1915	January 1916	August 9, 1916	46.
12	August 1914	April 1915	August 9, 1916	47.
14	1915	June 1916	August 14, 1916	48.
2	January 1916	May 1916	September 3, 1916	49.
3	1915	July 1915	September 18, 1916	50.
3	September 1914	October 1914	November 13, 1916	51.
1	September 1914	April 1915	February 4, 1917	52.
7	August 1914	September 1914	March 25, 1917	53.
2	September 1914	March 1915	April 2, 1917	54.
1	August 1914	September 1915	April 9, 1917	55.
8	August 1914	1915	April 19, 1917	56.
1	August 1914	September 1915	April 28, 1917	57.
9	August 1914	May 1916	June 11, 1917	58.
2	Regulars	August 1914	June 17, 1917	59.
7	September 1914	May 1915	July 29, 1917	60.
4	October 1914	1914	July 31, 1917	61.
1	1915	1915	July 31, 1917	62.
1	November 1914	February 1915	August 28, 1917	63.
3	August 1914	October 1915	October 4, 1917	64.
2	—	—	December 1917	65.
6	August 1915	February 1916	December 14, 1917	66.
2	September 1914	February 1916	December 29, 1917	67.
1	1915	1916	December 1917	68.
3	August 1914	1917	February 25, 1918	69.
1	September 1914	—	March 22, 1918	70.
2	August 1914	February 1915	March 24, 1918	71.
2	August 1914	—	—	72.
2	Royal Navy	August 1914	April 23, 1918	73.
3	Royal Artillery	August 1914	August 30, 1918	74.
13	September 1914	May 1916	October 4, 1918	75.
3	August 1914	August 1914	December 1918	76.

The Roll of Honour

SHOWING THE NAMES ACCORDING TO FOOTBALL NATIONALITY

Note.—Throughout this list the years given after each name refer to the era during which each played in International matches.

ENGLAND

1. Capt. C. E. WILSON	Queen's Regiment	1898
2. Surg. J. H. D. WATSON	Royal Navy	1914
3. Lieut. F. E. OAKELEY	Royal Navy	1913-14
4. Lieut. P. D. KENDALL	Liverpool Scottish	1901-3
5. Lieut. R. O. LAGDEN	King's Royal Rifle Corps	1911
6. Capt. A. F. TODD	Norfolk Regiment	1900
7. Lieut. R. W. POULTON PALMER	Royal Berks Regiment	1909-14
8. Corpl. H. BERRY	Gloucester Regiment	1910
9. Sergt. W. M. B. NANSON	Manchester Regiment	1907
10. Lieut. F. N. TARR	Leicester Regiment	1909-13
11. Lieut. A. J. DINGLE	East Yorkshire Regiment	1913-14
12. Lieut. D. LAMBERT	The Buffs	1908-11
13. Lieut. H. ALEXANDER	Grenadier Guards	1900-2
14. Capt. R. L. PILLMAN	Royal West Kent Regiment	1914
15. Pte. L. HAIGH	A.S.C.	1910-11
16. Lieut. L. A. N. SLOCOCK	King's Liverpool Regiment	1907-8
17. Lce.-Corp. J. KING	Liverpool Scottish	1911-13
18. Rev. R. E. INGLIS	Chaplain to the Forces	1886
19. Lieut. A. F. MAYNARD	Royal Naval Division	1914
20. Lieut. J. E. RAPHAEL	West Riding Regiment	1902-6
21. Lieut.-Col. G. E. B. DOBBS	Royal Engineers	1906
22. Lieut.-Col. E. R. MOBBS	Northants Regiment	1909-10
23. Capt. H. A. HODGES	Monmouth Regiment	1906
24. Capt. R. H. M. HANDS	S. African Heavy Artillery	1910
25. Lieut-Com. A. L. HARRISON	Royal Navy	1914
26. Major R. O. SCHWARZ	King's Royal Rifle Corps	1899-01

SCOTLAND

1. Lieut. R. F. SIMSON	R.F.A.	1911
2. Lieut. J. L. HUGGAN	R.A.M.C.	1914
3. Pte. J. ROSS	London Scottish	1901-3
4. Capt. L. ROBERTSON	Cameron Highlanders	1908-13

The Roll of Honour—Continued

5. Lieut. F. H. TURNER	Liverpool Scottish	1911–14
6. Pte. J. PEARSON	Royal Scots	1909–13
7. Capt. D. M'L. BAIN	Gordon Highlanders	1911–14
8. Capt. W. C. CHURCH	Scottish Rifles	1906
9. Capt. E. T. YOUNG	Cameronians	1914
10. Lieut. P. C. B. BLAIR	Rifle Brigade	1913
11. Lieut. W. M. WALLACE	Rifle Brigade, att. R.F.C.	1913–14
12. Surg. D. R. BEDELL-SIVRIGHT	Royal Navy	1900–8
13. Lieut. W. M. DICKSON	A. and S. Highlanders	1912–13
14. Lieut. D. D. HOWIE	Fife and Forfar Yeomanry	1912–13
15. Sergt. A. ROSS	Canadian Scottish	1905–9
16. Lieut. C. H. ABERCROMBIE	Royal Navy	1910–13
17. Lieut. J. S. WILSON	Royal Navy	1908–9
18. Capt. R. FRASER	Rifle Brigade	1911
19. Lieut. E. MILROY	Black Watch	1911–14
20. Lieut. J. G. WILL	Leinster Regt., att. R.F.C.	1912–14
21. Capt. T. A. NELSON	Lothians and Border Horse	1898
22. Major W. T. FORREST	K.O.S.B.	1903–5
23. Lieut. A. L. WADE	Middlesex Regiment	1908
24. Lieut. J. Y. M. HENDERSON	Highland Light Infantry	1911
25. Lieut. S. S. L. STEYN	R.F.A.	1911–12
26. Lieut. J. A. CAMPBELL	Inniskilling Dragoons	1900
27. Lieut.-Col. G. A. W. LAMOND	Royal Engineers	1899–05
28. Capt. W. R. HUTCHISON	Royal Scots Fusiliers	1911
29. Lieut. W. R. SUTHERLAND	Seaforth Highlanders	1910–14
30. Major R. E. GORDON	R.F.A.	1913

WALES

1. Eng.-Capt. C. G. TAYLOR	Royal Navy	1884–87
2. Lieut. W. P. GEEN	Rifle Brigade	1913
3. Lieut.-Col. R. D. GARNONS WILLIAMS	Royal Fusiliers	1881
4. Sergt. L. A. PHILLIPS	Royal Fusiliers	1900–1
5. Sergt. E. J. R. THOMAS	Welsh Regiment	1906–9
6. Capt. J. L. WILLIAMS	Royal Fusiliers	1907–11
7. Capt. C. M. PRITCHARD	South Wales Borderers	1905–10
8. Lieut. H. W. THOMAS	Rifle Brigade	1913
9. Major B. R. LEWIS	R.F.A.	1912–13
10. Pte. D. WESTACOTT	Gloucester Regiment	1906
11. Lieut. P. D. WALLER	S. African Heavy Artillery	1909–10

The Roll of Honour—Continued

IRELAND

1. Capt. B. MACLEAR	Royal Dublin Fusiliers	1905–7
2. Capt. E. C. DEANE	I.M.S.	1909
3. Lieut. V. M'NAMARA	Royal Engineers	1914
4. Capt. R. B. BURGESS	Royal Engineers	1912
5. Major R. S. SMYTH	R.A.M.C.	1903–4
6. Lieut. J. T. BRETT	Royal Dublin Fusiliers	1914
7. Capt. A. S. TAYLOR	R.A.M.C.	1910–12
8. Major A. L. STEWART	Royal Irish Rifles, M.G.C.	1913–14
9. Capt. W. V. EDWARDS	Royal Irish Fusiliers	1912

NEW ZEALAND

1. Sergt. A. DOWNING	5th Reinforcements, Wellington Batt.	1913–14
2. Sergt. H. DEWAR	New Zealand Mounted Rifles	1913
3. Corpl. R. S. BLACK	10th Reinforcements, Otago Mounted	1914
4. Lieut. F. R. WILSON	Auckland Infantry Battalion	1910
5. Pte. J. A. S. BAIRD	—	1913
6. Pte. G. M. V. SELLARS	1st Auckland Infantry Battalion	1913
7. Pte. J. M'NEECE	—	1913–14
8. Corpl. R. TAYLOR	6th Reinforcements	1913
9. Sergt. D. GALLAHER	21st Reinforcements	1903–5

SOUTH AFRICA

1. Pte. J. W. H. MORKEL	South African Horse	1910–12–13
2. Pte. G. THOMPSON	South African Infantry	1910–12–13
3. Lieut. T. M. MOLL	Leicestershire Regiment	1910
4. Sergt. S. H. LEDGER	South African Infantry	1910–12–13

CECIL HALLIDAY ABERCROMBIE

LIEUTENANT CECIL HALLIDAY ABERCROMBIE, Royal Navy, was born at Mozufferpore, India, on September 12, 1886, and fell in action on *Defence* at the Battle of Jutland, on May 31, 1916, aged 29. He was educated at Allan House, Guildford, at Berkhamsted School, and on H.M.S. *Britannia*. He was in the 1st XI. and XV., both at school and of the *Britannia*, and on the training-ship won for his Term the High Jump, Long Jump, Racquets, Fives, and Swimming, thus early his versatility proving the shadow of the coming event. In 1902 he passed out of *Britannia*, and on *Hyacinth* was one of the party which landed for the capture of the Mullah's stronghold at Illig in 1904. He received the general East African medal with clasp for his services in Somaliland. At the outbreak of war he was on the Mediterranean station, and returned early in 1915.

As for his prowess at Rugby football I feel I cannot do better than give verbatim the following appreciation of it from the pen of one who was aware of it first-hand. He wrote:—

"Abercrombie's forward play can best be described as that of a dashing player 'full of beans.' His personality was that of a breezy sailor with an abundant energy, and this was characteristic of his play. He was always doing something. If he was not in the centre of every scrum, he intended to be there. Possessed of splendid physique, great speed and height, and a good pair of hands, he was, needless to say, a fine touch player, but his forte was getting among the opposing backs, as he seldom or ever made a mistake in a hard low tackle. He was a splendid place kick, and could place a very long ball, and is credited with some good performances in this important part of the game. Abercrombie was a typical Rugby player. During the game he put every ounce of energy he had in his composition into play, and gave his opponents as hard a time as possible, taking and giving knocks with entire impartiality. The moment the game was over, be the result a win or a loss, his opponents were sportsmen and friends, for whom he could not do enough. Rugby football is a great and a true sport, and it is men like Abercrombie who maintain its traditions."

A sentiment which will be instantly echoed by every one who understands the game at all, or who knew Abercrombie. We write sometimes as regards cricket of such and such a player as being just the type one would like to take boys to see, the idea being, of course, that the imitative powers in the young may have full scope on the most suitable subject. Well, the same might have been said of Abercrombie in Rugby football. He, and Basil Maclear, Ronny Poulton, Freddy Turner, Lewis Robertson, Oakeley, "Toggie" Kendall, Mobbs, Noel Slocock, Frank Tarr, John Raphael, and Ronny Lagden were all of the same mould, glorious models for all youngsters. No plaster saints any of them, thank Heaven! but straight, clean, and very hard, true Britons. Abercrombie's very vitality alone was worth travel to witness. Some called him a "winger," and when he was not chosen for Scotland, though playing just as well as ever, they used to say: "Oh yes, of course he wings, and Scotland won't play any but solid scrummagers," as though MacEwan, Monteith, and "Darkie" Sivright had always been first down and last up! That Abercrombie possessed no little aplomb, a little incident which it is easy to write now after the event cost Scotland that much debated French match at Colombes, Paris, in 1911, tends to prove. Things were getting rather desperate towards the end of the game, and after a long spell near the French line, Abercrombie at last got over the line with the ball, but in an endeavour to get nearer the posts he ran back again over the goal-line, owing

LIEUT. CECIL HALLIDAY ABERCROMBIE, R.N.
Photo: Swaine, London

to the presence of opponents in in-goal, and was there tackled and downed, another scrum close to the line being the net result of his ill-chosen manœuvre. He thereupon claimed a try where he had crossed the goal-line! But A. O. Jones had recollections of a law of the game which requires the player to place his hand on the ball in the opponents' in-goal or on the goal-line, and the game proceeded. To Abercrombie's temporary disgust, but if anybody knew he was on a bad case, he did. He was in all respects a delightful player to watch, and must have been a most charming man in whose company to play. A fine free cricketer of the sort which plays the game in the spirit in which its laws were meant to be read and interpreted, he was invaluable to Hampshire, and might have played, had he had the opportunity, for England one day. The last time I saw him was, I think, in 1914 choosing a bat in Philip Need's room at Lord's, and he knew what he wanted and meant to have.

Naval officers who were familiar with him have penned the following words in letters, these extracts from which I have been greatly privileged in being allowed to use. No man could wish for a more graceful tribute than that of the fellow-officer who wrote that he felt quite sure the last gun-firing on *Defence* was Abercrombie's. Men do not invent such feelings, and when they express them we know they are writing the straight truth. Of the glorious action of *Defence* writes one who witnessed it from a battleship:—

" They drew the fire of several enemy ships upon themselves, which should have been concentrated on the Battle Fleet, and undoubtedly their sacrifice enabled our ships to return the fire unmolested and saved many lives that might otherwise have been lost. Their death was such a gallant one, that nobody could wish for anything different or more glorious, and their action was witnessed by the whole Fleet with intense admiration and sympathy, as they could not possibly stand such a hell of fire, and yet they were still firing away themselves right up to the very last. In those few full minutes there was sufficient heroic duty to fill an ordinary lifetime, and I feel certain he would not have wished otherwise. He was such a good friend and such a delightful shipmate that his loss will, indeed, be mourned throughout the Service, where he was particularly well known and appreciated."

One of his late Captains wrote : " You and I are in a position to realize to the full the loss that the country has sustained by the death of your husband. I feel perfectly sure that it was his gun that was being fought when the ship gave her final plunge— directly I heard of it, I felt it."

Another wrote : " It will comfort you to know that the spirit displayed by those gallant fellows in *Defence*, added materially to the confusion of the Germans. The Fleet is very proud of them, and nothing I have ever read in history can surpass their deliberate and magnificent sacrifice."

And yet another : " I can honestly say that I should have been more content being killed beside him than anywhere else."

A brother officer wrote : " From the first day I met him he always inspired me with the profoundest respect, and I felt instinctively he was a man above the average, and the finest type that England produces. 'He was a man, take him for all in all, we shall not look upon his like again.'"

A friend who had often played cricket against him wrote: " The action, indeed, is itself typical of him, for many is the time on the cricket field, when odds looked black for his side, I have seen him come in and go baldheaded for the bowling, his sole idea being his side first, himself last, get the runs or get out. He was not only a fine officer, but a great example of a British gentleman, and a sportsman through and through, no matter what the penalty was. Nothing could have made him miss that fight. We, in the other service, are so full of the gallant action, that our feelings are those of pride that we belong to the same race as Abercrombie and the others who went with him. My only wish

SEC.-LIEUT. HARRY ALEXANDER
1st Batt. Grenadier Guards

being that he could have come through it safely to realize the name that squadron has made for itself."

Even in the stress of such moments as those during which these plain tributes were penned, men do not write like this except about a man worth writing about. Abercrombie will always be remembered with gratitude, and mourned with sincerity, by every true lover of the Rugby game who ever had the good luck to see him playing it.

Abercrombie played for Scotland against England and Ireland in 1910; and against Wales and France in 1911 and in 1913, six times in all.

HARRY ALEXANDER

SECOND-LIEUTENANT HARRY ALEXANDER, 1st Battalion Grenadier Guards, was killed in action at Hulluch, France, on October 17, 1915, aged 36. Born at Oxton, Cheshire, on January 6, 1879, Alexander was educated at Bromborough (1888–91), at Uppingham (1891–97), and at Corpus Christi College, Oxford (1897–1900). He was in the Uppingham XV.'s of 1895 and 1896 as a forward, in the Cricket XI. 1897, the Hockey XI. 1897, and the Fives VI. in 1897. He played for Oxford v. Cambridge at Queen's Club in 1897 and 1898, Oxford winning the first by 2 tries to nil, and losing the second by 1 goal and 2 tries to nil. Between 1900 and 1902 he won seven English International Caps—namely, v. Scotland, 1900–1; v. Ireland, 1900–1–2; and v. Wales 1901–2. In addition to these honours Alexander played for Middlesex, for Cheshire, for the North, for Birkenhead Park, and for Richmond, ending his football career as Captain of Richmond in 1905–6. He was always a very strenuous forward; the harder the work the better he liked it. His shock head of auburn hair was never seen very far away from the ball, and he will be also remembered as one of the most painstaking, almost punctilious, place-kickers of modern, or any, times. The results generally justified the minute care he took in making the " place " and in aiming the ball. Possessed of a beautiful baritone voice, Alexander was a professional singer when war broke out, and he soon set about obtaining a commission, which he did on July 23, 1915, going into training in London and at Marlow, and thence to the Front on October 4, 1915. He was killed outright by a shell during a bombing attack. In addition to his athletic achievements above referred to, Harry Alexander had played in inter-county Hockey matches; was a well-known skater and bandy player at Davos Platz and St. Moritz; and having latterly taken up golf had soon played his way to a scratch handicap. He was a great believer in : " Whatso'er thy hand findeth to do, do it with all thy might."

DAVID M'LAREN BAIN

CAPTAIN DAVID M'LAREN BAIN, 3rd Battalion Gordon Highlanders, attached 2nd Battalion Gordon Highlanders, was killed in action near Festubert on June 3, 1915, aged 23.

Born at Edinburgh on September 10, 1891, Bain was educated at Edinburgh Academy Preparatory School from 1897–1900, at Edinburgh Academy from 1900–10, and at Trinity College, Oxford, from 1910–14. He was a forward in the Academy 1st XV. from 1907–10, and Captain of the XV. in the season of 1909–10. He was in the XI. 1909–10, and Vice-Captain of it in 1910. He was in the Fives team 1909–10 and Captain of it in 1910, and in the Shooting VIII. in the same two years. Bain played for Oxford against Cambridge in 1910, 1911, 1912, 1913; was Secretary of the Oxford University Rugby Union Club in 1912–13, and Captain in 1913–14. He played for Trinity at Rugby football, cricket, and golf. Bain had the rare honour of being chosen reserve for Scotland against England at Inverleith in 1910, while still at Edinburgh Academy. A few boys, notably

CAPTAIN DAVID M'LAREN BAIN
3rd Batt. (att. 2nd Batt.) Gordon Highlanders

the Neilsons of Merchiston and J. G. Milton of Bedford, have played in International football while still at school, and K. G. Macleod also would have achieved this rare feat if the Fettes authorities had given their permission. In March 1911 Bain made the first of eleven appearances for Scotland in the Calcutta Cup match at Twickenham. He played in every match for Scotland of the two years 1912 and 1913 against England, Wales, and France; against the South Africans in 1912; against Ireland in 1913 and 1914; and against Wales in 1914. Bain captained the Scots against Ireland in 1914, and only those who wanted somebody else to captain the side said he did not do it well. Then he was deposed, and another Oxonian, the late F. H. Turner, captained Scotland in the next match; that, too, like the Irish one, was lost. The fact was Scotland had not at the time a better team than either the Irish or English ones; no captaincy could have won either of these games. But a trifle like that does not trouble those who had prophesied a Scottish victory. These have to hang somebody, so, after the Irish 2 tries to nil at Dublin in 1914, they hung Bain, and said it would never have happened had Freddy Turner been in command. When, with Turner in command, at Inverleith shortly afterwards, and Bain not playing, Scotland again lost, they said it was the referee! Such things have to pass for fair and "expert" criticism. Bain was, in fact, a jolly good captain, both by example and precept. In some respects he was better than Turner, who spoke hardly enough, though more when in charge of a Club than an International side. Bain was one of those forwards one saw not very much of in the loose, which is generally a good sign, tending to mean that if he is any good at all he is very good. He was certainly a sure tackler, good at the line-out, and with an excellent knowledge of the game. Off the Rugby field at Oxford, he was a member of Vincents in 1910, and President of it in 1913–14. On going up he was chosen Senior Commoner of his year. He was also a member of the Claret Club and Triflers of Trinity College. When war came he was about to go in for the examination for the Egyptian Civil Service. Both the Headmaster of the Academy and the Head of his College wrote most warmly to his mother of his fine example and great influence for good. Bain, who had been in the Academy from its beginning, joined the Army early in August 1914, and went into training at Aberdeen, where he was in charge of musketry, and also assistant-adjutant. He went to the Front in France in December 1914, and was wounded at Neuve Chapelle in March 1915. Promoted Captain early in May, he returned to France on May 20, to meet a soldier's death less than a fortnight later. He was killed by the shell which wrecked his dug-out. His Commanding Officer wrote of him that "he was beloved by all ranks, and his tall commanding figure, riding at the head of his men, will long be missed," and that he had himself lost a dear friend. Many of his fellow-officers wrote in similarly appreciative strain. David Bain was in every respect a popular man, and his kindly face, lit up by peculiarly pale bluey gray eyes, will long be remembered and mourned.

JAMES ALEXANDER STANSON BAIRD

PRIVATE JAMES ALEXANDER STANSON BAIRD died of wounds received in action in the field in France on June 7, 1917, aged 23. His injuries consisted of gunshot wounds in the hands and abdomen. Baird was born in Caversham (Dunedin), and was educated at Caversham School. He took a keen interest in all sports, especially football, and interested himself greatly in the Cadet Corps at the school. He was of a cheery nature, and quick to see the bright side of things—a general favourite with everybody. He was an orphan and an only child.

Jimmy Baird started his football career with the Zingari-Richmond Football Club, Dunedin, in the year 1911, when he played in the third-grade team (flag winners). In 1912 he was

PRIVATE JAMES ALEXANDER STANSON BAIRD, N.Z.

promoted to the 1st XV.—runners-up for the Senior flag. In 1913 he had a successful year. ❡He played in the Zingari-Richmond Seniors, and they won the Otago Rugby Union's Championship. He represented Otago in the inter-provincial matches, and finished the season by being selected to play for New Zealand against Australia on the Carisbrook Ground, Dunedin—a splendid record for so young a player. This season, however, practically finished his football, for at its conclusion a serious illness overtook him (pleurisy and pneumonia), which prevented him from playing in 1914.

DAVID REVELL BEDELL-SIVRIGHT

SURGEON DAVID REVELL BEDELL-SIVRIGHT, Royal Navy, died of blood poisoning on Gallipoli on September 5, 1915, aged 34. Born at North Cliff, North Queensferry, on December 8, 1880, Bedell-Sivright was educated at Fettes College, Edinburgh, and at Cambridge University. He was in the XV. at Fettes, and for four years, 1899–1902, at Cambridge, being Captain of it in 1901 and 1902. From 1905–9 he played for Edinburgh University, and as he was Captain of the XV. for two seasons, enjoyed the rare distinction of having been Captain of two University fifteens. One of the most remarkable forwards in the history of Rugby football, D. R. Bedell-Sivright played in twenty-two International matches for Scotland, and captained the National Fifteen against the New Zealand team of 1905. If a plebiscite was taken on the question: " Who was the hardest forward who ever played International football? " Bedell-Sivright would get most votes if the voting was confined to players, and probably so in any event. M. C. MacEwan, the Ryans, L. Robertson, and some others would all be in the running, but this Fettesian would win. It has been placed on record that only once in his football career was " Darkie " Sivright ever even hurt! That was when he made the slip, a remarkable one for so experienced a player, of attempting to tackle Basil Maclear "high." It was a wiser, though not a very much chastened, "Darkie" who, a few minutes later, jog-trotted back to rejoin the game from his temporary bed of straw outside the touch-line at Inverleith in February 1907. I can see him now, with his well-known gait, his elbows sticking out, and head hanging forward a trifle, as he fairly plunged into the back of the scrum, almost viciously, as though burning to redeem his character for invulnerability. Of him one who knew him well in Edinburgh has sent the following appreciation :—

"My earliest recollections of 'Darkie' Sivright are, when I was a small boy at school in Edinburgh, seeing him tearing down the football field, the terror of all School sides, and the admiration of the young Fettes boys. Going straight from Fettes up to Cambridge, he very quickly made his mark in the first-class Rugger world, gaining his Blue the first season. He was always a very, very hard player, and took an absolute delight in the game. To the uninitiated onlooker 'Darkie' appeared to be a rough player, but this was not so ; it was only his great strength that made him a danger to the other side. I have only once seen, or heard of, him being laid out on a football field, and that was at an International match between Scotland and Ireland, when he and Basil Maclear collided ; it was a case of one giant coming up against another, and 'Darkie,' probably being in a disadvantageous position, went under. A friend of 'Darkie's' once charged him with being an 'over-zealous' player, but he replied, 'When I go on to that field I only see the ball, and wherever it goes, I go too, and should some one be in the road, that is his own lookout.' He played four seasons for Cambridge, and captained the team two consecutive seasons. Of course, during this time he gained innumerable Caps for Scotland, and was for a long time one of the best forwards who ever donned a jersey. He

SURGEON DAVID REVELL BEDELL-SIVRIGHT, R.N.

Photo: Stearn, Cambridge

became a player of repute, not only in this country, but also in the Colonies, touring through South Africa, Australia, and New Zealand, and gaining new laurels every day. After going to Cambridge, a rumour went round Edinburgh that 'Darkie' intended taking up the study of medicine. At the time this was treated as a huge joke, no one thinking that it was seriously meant; but in due course he 'arrived,' and immediately set at rest any doubt as to his seriousness in studying medicine, for he forthwith commenced to settle down, and to work like the most studious bookworm. Nothing could seduce him away from his books, and at the end of the first term he passed through the class examinations with first-class honours. His work, however, could not prevent him from being just as keen as ever on Rugby football. He played for Edinburgh University, where he was always a tower of strength, and helped to keep that team one of the foremost in the country. He eventually became Captain of Edinburgh University—surely a unique record for any man to have been Captain of Cambridge and Edinburgh Universities. He finished his medical course with first-class honours, and took up some responsible hospital appointments.

"When the war broke out, 'Darkie,' like all other Rugby football players, joined up, and took a commission as Surgeon, R.N. I shall never forget the last meeting I had with him. I met him in Southsea one day; he was at that time Surgeon at Haslar Hospital, and arranged a little dinner-party at Eastney Barracks. There were present on that occasion, 'Darkie'; Cartwright, the old English captain; Maurice Dickson, the old Marlborough, Oxonian, and Scottish football player; Paddy Murray and Russell-Cargill, old Edinburgh Academicals; 'Ronnie' Fox, the old Free Forester wicket-keeper; and many other men well known in Rugby, cricket, and hockey circles. 'Darkie' was strangely silent this evening, and seemed quite preoccupied, and not like his old self. Shortly afterwards he went out to ill-fated Gallipoli, where he contracted blood-poisoning, and died very rapidly. I have seen a man who was with him nearly to the last. He tells me that 'Darkie' had returned from a long spell in the trenches at an advanced dressing-station, and came down properly fagged out. He got bitten by some sort of insect, and, being in a weak condition, poisoning set in, and he died two days after in a hospital ship, before it had weighed anchor. 'Darkie' died fighting; and thus passed away one of the finest men who ever left that famous nursery of Rugby football, Fettes College.

" 'Darkie' also made a name for himself at boxing, and on several occasions entered for the Scottish Heavy Weight Championship, which he won one season, not by particularly scientific boxing but by hard punching. I remember Dr. Coghlan, who met him on one occasion and beat him, telling me that when he saw 'Darkie' come into the ring, he at once made up his mind that, whatever else happened, 'Darkie' must not hit him, or it would be 'good-bye' to his chances of gaining that coveted honour. 'Darkie' was a man who, whilst very reserved and shy in himself, had a host of friends.

" 'Tis sad to think of such a man being cut off in the prime of life. He died, as he had lived, a fighter to the end, and one may truly say of his life, ' 'Tis done, 'tis well done.' "

Bedell-Sivright joined the Royal Navy on January 25, 1915; trained at Royal Naval Hospital, Haslar, and at Royal Naval Division camp at Blandford, before proceeding with the Royal Naval Division to the Dardanelles in April 1915. He died there of acute septicæmia.

" Darkie " Sivright was one of the best read and most travelled men playing first-class football. When at the 'Varsity it was understood that the Law was his goal; but he took a different view of life as the result of tours abroad with Mark Morrison's team to South Africa, and the United Kingdom team, which he captained himself in New Zealand, and it was the experiences on this

CORPORAL HENRY BERRY
Gloucester Regiment

Photo: Jones, Gloucester

last tour that decided him to settle in Australia in the business of stock-rearing. But, as he said to an intimate afterwards, " at the end of a year's jackerooing I took stock. What was I, with an average amount of brains and rather more of money, doing ? Simply prostituting the one in order to increase the other ; it wasn't good enough, and so I chucked it, and with reluctance came home to medicine." From the same source we learn that " Darkie " had a larger library than any undergraduate his friend ever knew, and that most of his books were underlined with enlightening annotations. When he won the Scottish Heavy Weight Boxing Championship he was reading a solid twelve hours a day. An incident after Bedell-Sivright had won this championship on a foul reveals the open and fine character of the man. His opponent was a miner from Musselburgh. On the way back to Edinburgh Bedell-Sivright sought out the vanquished, and, taking him into his first-class carriage, apologized to him for the decision, which, he said, had spoiled a good fight. From the Front he wrote to this friend : " It makes me swear that I am a medico. I'd be ten times more useful with a parcel of jam-tin bombs and a few Turks in front of me, than as a sort of qualified vet." Any one who ever saw him in spate with those of the rest of a Scottish pack who could keep pace with him would never wish to change places with a Turk, or any one else, if the " Darkie " had been a combatant instead of a medical officer.

D. R. Bedell-Sivright's first International match was Scotland v. Wales in February 1900. He did not play again until February 1901 against Wales, but then he played in every match of the seasons 1901, 1902, 1904, 1906, and 1907. In 1903 he played against Wales and Ireland only ; in 1905 he played only against New Zealand ; in 1908, only against Wales and Ireland—a total of twenty-two Caps. Downright sheer hard play in all phases of the forward game was his forte. He was not out to excel in specialities, and did not hope or attempt to shine at hooking, or heeling, or dribbling, or tackling, or handling, or at the line-out.

He just played this game for all it and he were worth, utterly heedless of all else during the forty minutes each way. A grand forward to have on your side, and beyond dispute one of the eight best of his time. Certainly one who will be remembered and spoken of so long as the Rugby game is played.

HENRY BERRY

CORPORAL HENRY BERRY, Gloucester Regiment, was killed in action on May 9, 1915, at Festubert, France, at the age of 33. He was educated at St. Mark's School, Gloucester, and joined the Army in 1899. He served in the South African War, for which he had the medal, and at St. Helena and in India. He had fifteen years' service, but until just before his death he had always refused promotion. He left a widow and two children. He fell in such a place as to render it impossible to recover his body. Berry was Captain of D Company football team for five seasons, during which period they held the Regimental Shield and were unbeaten. For his Company he proved his versatility by playing for them at Hockey and Association Football. Concerning his football career an old friend of his has written :—

"Berry had retired from first-class football when recalled to the Colours, but he was in his day a splendid forward. He joined the Gloucester City team on returning from service in India, and was originally tried in the three-quarter line, in which position he had always played for his Regiment. His physique, however, fitted him admirably to be a forward, and his introduction to the pack proved a great success. Fast and clever, he shone especially in the loose footwork and at the line-out. In a few weeks he had made his place in a strong City team secure. County honours followed, and in 1910 Berry achieved his highest ambition on being selected to play for England v. Wales at Twickenham. It was in this match that England broke the long series of defeats

CORPORAL ROBERT STANLEY BLACK
Canterbury Battalion, N.Z.

sustained from Wales, winning by 11 points to 6. That Berry fully deserved his honour was shown when he retained his place in the English team for all the matches of that season. The Irish match was a pointless draw, but England beat France, 11 to 3, and Scotland, 14 to 5, Berry scoring a try in both these games. A return of malaria affected his health after this, and though he played for some time longer he never regained his best form, and no more football honours came his way. Berry was in the Army Reserve when war broke out and was soon in the thick of the fight."

I remember Berry well as a fast and dashing forward, who was extremely useful to his side once the ball had become loose. This is not to say that he shirked the heavy work, a most unfair imputation often undeservedly thrown at the forward who is seen to be busy in a passing advance. Berry was no shirker, whether at football or in his profession. Of that one may be sure, without having had the honour of his personal acquaintance. He was on all counts a very fine specimen of his type of player, and when these are good they are usually very good indeed. Rugby football will always remember Berry of Gloucester as one such, and not without gratitude. For their example is all to the good of our most manly game.

ROBERT STANLEY BLACK

CORPORAL ROBERT STANLEY BLACK was attached to a reconnoitring party in the Battle of the Somme, which went out on the evening of September 15, 1916, and was reported " missing " on the 21st of the same month. On April 27, 1917, he was reported " killed in action." He left New Zealand as a corporal, attached to the Tenth Reinforcements, Otago Mounteds, and remained in Egypt for a short period; but being anxious to reach the firing-line, obtained a transfer to the Pioneer Corps. He was subsequently transferred to the 2nd Battalion, Canterbury Infantry Battalion, to which he was attached at the time of his death.

Robert Stanley Black was born at Arrowtown, Central Otago, on August 23, 1893. He was educated at the local school, and in 1907 entered the Otago Boys' High School, where he remained until 1911, being a resident pupil for four years. He matriculated in 1910, and early in 1911 joined the staff of the Bank of New South Wales, Dunedin, where he remained until the date of his enlistment. His father was manager of the Bank of New Zealand at Arrowtown. Black joined the Pirates Football Club, Dunedin, in 1911, being then eighteen years of age, and having just finished a brilliant football career at the Otago Boys' High School. For the first two matches of the season he played in the 2nd XV.; but his play was such that he was raised to senior rank, and the same year was chosen for Otago in several representative matches. He continued playing with the Pirates until 1915, when, in consequence of the depletion of the ranks of the playing members through enlistments, the Club was unable to put a senior team in the field. The Club, however, put in a junior team, but the Rugby Union would not allow Black to play in any grade except senior. He joined Otago University Football Club in 1915, and played for them that year. During his membership with the Pirates he played for the South Island against the North in 1912 and 1914, and was also a member of the New Zealand team which visited Australia in 1914 and won the whole of the ten matches in which it engaged. In the inter-island match in 1912, which was played in Napier, he had the bad luck to meet with an accident, which kept him out of the game altogether for the remainder of the season.

Black was one of the dashing type of five-eighths now so seldom found in the game. When he was selected for the 1914 New Zealand team, a fellow-scribe wrote that " he was the fastest thing on two legs in the team." His great asset was his speed off

SEC.-LIEUT. PATRICK CHARLES BENTLEY BLAIR
Rifle Brigade

the mark, and the pace at which he could do the first 15 yards was amazing. Though nimble and fast, he did not use his speed only, but had a keen eye for an opening, which he would seize immediately, and would then work into his supporting backs again. Altogether he was a dashing, straight-running and clever five-eighth, and was generally accepted as the best produced in Otago during the last ten or fifteen years. The Sports Master of the Otago Boys' High School wrote of him :—

" Black was one of the most brilliant five-eighths we have had during my long connection with the School, and gave promise of doing great things in the football world after he left School, a promise that was amply fulfilled, as was shown by his brilliant career in the Otago and New Zealand representative teams."

Though a famous footballer, his greatest popularity was won off the field. Of a quiet, kind, unassuming nature, with a subtle sense of humour, Bobby Black was the idol of his very large circle of friends, and his everlasting good humour and kindly nature endeared him to all with whom he came in contact. His retiring disposition kept him out of positions in clubs for which he would have been eminently suited, but anything in the nature of self-advertisement was absolutely unknown to him. It was with the greatest regret the news of his death was received in Dunedin, for a brilliant footballer, an adept lawn-tennis player, a proficient oarsman, and last, but not least, a gentleman in the truest acceptation of the term, was lost to the community.

PATRICK CHARLES BENTLEY BLAIR

SECOND-LIEUTENANT PATRICK CHARLES BENTLEY BLAIR, the Rifle Brigade, fell in action at Ypres on July 6, 1915, aged 23. Born at Wanlockhead, Dumfriesshire, on July 18, 1891, Blair was educated at Fettes College, Edinburgh (1903–10) and at King's

College, Cambridge (1910–14). He was a member of the Fettes XV. for three years, and played four times against Oxford in the packs of 1910–13, thus taking part in the last four Inter-'Varsity matches played. His five International matches were: v. South Africa, November 1912; and v. Wales, Ireland, England, and France in 1913. Blair was a truly magnificent specimen of young manhood, standing six feet, and weighing fully thirteen stones, and splendidly proportioned. He was one of the hardworking type, very good in the tight scrum and at the line-out; but, owing to lack of pace, never very conspicuous in the open. In that branch of the game only did he fall short at all of the exacting requirements of the modern forward game. He was able to bring a very lively intelligence to bear on all he did, and I am informed that he is the only International who ever took 1st Class Honours at any University. Passing into the Egyptian Civil Service (Finance Department), he had only just taken up his appointment out there, full of the richest promise for a most brilliant future. All this he gave up and came back in January 1915, after a bare four months' service, to take his place in the fight. Truly an outstanding example for future generations of patriotism in its very highest sense. He trained at Cambridge; was commissioned in March 1915; left for the Front in the first week in June of that year to meet the noblest of deaths—killed by a shell as he was scaling the German parapet leading his men.

> "Till the roll's called in heaven, lad,
> You may well take your rest."

JASPER THOMAS BRETT

SECOND-LIEUTENANT JASPER THOMAS BRETT, 7th Battalion Royal Dublin Fusiliers, died in Ireland through illness contracted on active service, on February 4, 1917, aged 21. Born at Kingstown, Co. Dublin, Ireland, on August 8, 1895, Brett was educated

SEC.-LIEUT. JASPER THOMAS BRETT
Royal Dublin Fusiliers

Photo: Caswall Smith, London

JASPER THOMAS BRETT

at Monkstown Park School, Kingstown, and at the Royal School, Armagh (1909-12). He was well known as an athlete during schoolboy days. He broke all school records at Monkstown Park School, with 19 feet 4 inches for the Long Jump, while still under fifteen years of age, also winning the High Jump the same year. He held the School Cup for Athletics at Monkstown Park for three years. Later, at Royal School, Armagh, he also gained cups for athletics, and he captained the Rugby team as well as the XI. there.

His play in the centre for Monkstown in 1912-13-14 won for him his Irish Cap, as a wing against Wales in March 1914, his only appearance in International football, though he was present when Ireland played France in Paris as a reserve.

It was during September 1914 that Brett enlisted in the " Pals " Battalion of the Royal Dublin Fusiliers, training at the Curragh and Basingstoke. He went to the Front in April 1915, and took part in the landing at Suvla Bay and also in the Battle of Chocolate Hill. After a very arduous time in Gallipoli he took part from Salonika in the Balkan expedition. He was in the last line of retreat there, and in October 1915 he accepted a commission, which had indeed been offered to him on a previous occasion. Having been in hospital twice in Alexandria and Salonika, and having suffered from dysentery and trench fever, he was invalided home on account of ill-health, finally relinquishing his commission for the same reason.

Though he saw so much service in so short a time Brett was never wounded; but under the strain of campaigning and the unhealthy conditions, especially at Salonika, his health gave way completely.

He was a good correspondent, writing home many interesting and graphic descriptions of his experiences, especially of those at Suvla Bay, where so many of his friends fell beside him. His former headmaster, Mr. C. V. Stoney, J.P., D.L., M.A. (Cantab), wrote in high praise of his conduct at school, on leaving which

Brett obtained first place in the examination for solicitors' apprentices or articled clerks, prior to his apprenticeship to his father, Mr. Wm. Jasper Brett. Had this young soldier lived, he would have gone in for his final for the solicitor's profession in October 1917. His was another very young life cut short all too early, terminated by this futile War, a tragedy regretted by all who knew him, and especially by the Irish Rugby world which knew him best.

As a Rugby player Brett was sound; he had good defence as well as attack, and the fact that Ireland played him, though a centre, on the wing points to his possession of pace. He had won a cup at golf, and there is no doubt that by his death Ireland lost one of her most promising young all-round athletes.

ROBERT BALDERSTON BURGESS

CAPTAIN ROBERT BALDERSTON BURGESS, Royal Engineers, was killed at Armentières on December 9, 1915, aged 24. Born on December 25, 1890, when war came he gave up a growing and lucrative practice at the Irish Bar, for which he had been educated at Portora High School and Trinity College, Dublin. He was the best forward in the invincible Portora team, in whose ranks was the great drop-kicker and punt, R. A. Lloyd. At Dublin Burgess was Honorary Secretary of the T. C. D. Rugby Football Club, and while there played in all the inter-province matches of 1913–14. A fine fast forward and good tackler, he was one of those who was sacrificed by the Irish selectors after the South Africans, of November 1912, had made hares of the whole Irish fifteen, the backs of which were more to blame than the forwards—if any blame attaches to the members of an outclassed and outplayed fifteen—for the 4 goals and 6 tries to nil defeat; which constitutes the "record" defeat in International football in the United Kingdom, since England scored 13 tries against Wales at

CAPTAIN ROBERT BALDERSTON BURGESS, R.E.

Blackheath in 1881, and excluding matches with France. That was Burgess's single appearance in the Irish XV. He was, apart from Rugby football, a fine rider to hounds, a good shot, and an expert salmon fisher. On the outbreak of war Burgess did special work in Ireland and France for the French Government, was gazetted Second-Lieutenant in the Army Service Corps in November 1914, and was promoted Captain of Royal Engineers in January 1915. That he was an extremely popular man goes unsaid. His Commanding Officer wrote of him :—

"The late Captain Burgess was an excellent officer, always ready for his duty day and night, and was the most popular officer in his section."

He was the fourth Irish International to fall—Maclear, Deane, and M'Namara predeceasing him; and although reports published at the time said he had died of wounds, the facts above are as given to me by his father.

JOHN ARGENTINE CAMPBELL

LIEUTENANT JOHN ARGENTINE CAMPBELL, Inniskilling Dragoons, was born in the Argentine Republic, October 20, 1877, and was reported missing in France on December 1, 1917. The first news of him came from a trooper in his regiment, who was a prisoner in Germany, and who wrote saying that he had carried him, severely wounded, to a German dressing-station, and asking for information about him. Later, in January 1918, a card came from a wounded officer in Germany, stating that Lieutenant Campbell had died of wounds in a German hospital. So died one of Scotland's best and bravest sons, whose name will ever be honoured by all who knew him.

He was at Fettes for ten years, from May 1887 to July 1897, and few have left a greater mark on the School life. He played forward in the Rugby team from 1893 to 1897, and was Captain in his last year, and his cricket record is exactly similar. He was also in the hockey eleven, and represented the School at fives. Going up to Trinity, Cambridge, in the autumn of 1897, he at once received his Rugby Blue, and played thrice against Oxford at Queen's Club, being captain in his last year. He secured his Athletic Blue in 1898 for putting the weight. In 1900 he obtained his Scottish Cap, appearing against Ireland. He was a typical Scottish forward, of the sort that has won so many games for Scotland, playing desperately hard from start to finish—a sound tackler, and a firm believer in the value of vigorous forward play.

He was in the Argentine when war broke out, and in 1915 he returned home to join the colours. After a training period in England, he went out to France in the spring of 1916 with the 17th Lancers, being transferred later to the Inniskilling Dragoons. His friends do not need to be assured that he did his duty well, or that his loss was deeply regretted in his regiment.

"Alike at Fettes, at Cambridge, and in the Argentine, his manliness, his straightness, and his modesty won the love and respect of all who came in contact with him, and the letters received from the regiment testify to the fact that it was the same at the front. One officer in his letter said that from the general to the last-joined recruit every one admired, respected, and loved him, and the colonel said that he was the most magnificent specimen of mankind he had ever come across."

The foregoing paragraph is from the pen of one who knew him intimately from early boyhood, and as a tribute leaves little to be added by those who admired him as a great Rugby forward and splendid all-round athlete. Of him it could with truth be said that he always "played the game."

LIEUT. JOHN ARGENTINE CAMPBELL
Inniskilling Dragoons
Photo: Vandyk, London

WILLIAM CAMPBELL CHURCH

CAPTAIN WILLIAM CAMPBELL CHURCH, 1/8 Scottish Rifles (T.), was killed in action on Gallipoli on June 28, 1915, aged 31. He was born in Glasgow, and was educated at Glasgow Academy, a school in Switzerland, and at Glasgow University. He was at the Academy from 1893–1901, in Switzerland in 1902, and at the University from 1904. He was wing three-quarter in the Academy XV. in 1900 and 1901, and was a very expert member of the Academy's Gymnastic Team. For the Glasgow Academicals he played regularly in 1904–7, and in 1904–5 their XV. were Scottish Club Champions. Captain Church played several times in the famous Inter-City for Glasgow v. Edinburgh, and in Scottish Football Union Trials, until he got his Cap and played in a disastrous match for Scotland at Cardiff in 1906, when the Scots forwards lost their heads, and the match, by trying to pick up in the loose, though they were undoubtedly the better eight. Wales won by three tries to a penalty goal, and the whole Scottish three-quarter line played below form, an unnerved game. Captain Church was gazetted Second-Lieutenant in the Territorial Force on May 5, 1913, Lieutenant on December 23 of the same year, Captain on July 7, 1914, and Staff-Captain on August 5, 1914. All this time he was greatly interested in the Boys' Brigade, and did much to promote swimming among the boys in Glasgow. The manner in which Captain Church met his death was typical of a wing three-quarter. He had sprinted on ahead of a charge, and was within ten yards of the Turkish trenches when he was killed by a machine-gun bullet.

" Billy Church might be summed up," writes an old friend of his, Commander J. A. Henry, R.N., " as a thorough good fellow, who always played the game. He was a good man to play with or against; and his many games on the wing for Glasgow Academicals, for Glasgow in the Inter-City, and for Scotland v. Wales, brought him many friends. I saw the match at Cardiff, and Billy failed to do himself justice that day. He was a quiet, unassuming man, who did a lot of good work on the Scottish Rugby Football Union, for he always had the good of the game at heart."

ERNEST COTTON DEANE

CAPTAIN ERNEST COTTON DEANE, R.A.M.C., M.C., was killed in action north of Neuve Chapelle on September 25, 1915, aged 28. Born at Limerick on May 4, 1887, Deane was educated at Corrig, Kingstown (1901-4), and at the College of Surgeons, into which he passed with honours (1904-9). He was Captain of the Corrig XV., and also of the Adelaide Hospital XV. and Monkstown XV. At his School Athletic Sports he carried off most of the events. His career as an International centre three-quarter was cut short by an accident when, playing against Oxford University, he sustained a broken leg in the same season, 1909, in which he had just played against England at Dublin, when Ireland were beaten by 1 goal and 2 tries to 1 goal. This was his only appearance in the Irish team. As an all-rounder in the realm of outdoor pursuits Deane was well in the first flight, as, in addition to being a good centre three-quarter, he was a fine rider to hounds, a good shot, held his own at lawn tennis, was a keen fisherman, and good golfer. He had a most lovable disposition and was as modest as he was plucky. Entering the R.A.M.C. in July 1911, first of the Irish candidates trained at Millbank and Aldershot, he went to India in 1913, and to the Front in France with the First Indian Expeditionary Force in September 1914, landing at Marseilles on the 26th of that month. Deane was twice " mentioned " and was awarded the Military Cross. The details of his manly end are as follows :—

" We had a big battle on the 25th," wrote his Colonel, " and your son went to try to help some wounded in, and was killed,

CAPTAIN WILLIAM CAMPBELL CHURCH
1/8th Scottish Rifles (T.)

CAPTAIN ERNEST COTTON DEANE, M.C., R.A.M.C.
Photo: Chidley Studios, Liverpool

his death being instantaneous. . . . Every one knew Deane as one of the bravest of the brave, and it was only the other day that he got one of the best deserved and gallantly won honours when he was awarded the Military Cross. I cannot tell you how sorry I am about your son, and how much I sympathize with you and yours in your loss. He was the most gallant fellow I have ever met, and we all loved him in the Regiment, both officers and men. He was just a part of us, and the few of us left mourn his loss very deeply."

" A better or a pluckier officer it would be hard to find," wrote another Colonel under whose orders Deane had served.

" He went out in the face of almost certain death to help the wounded," wrote another officer, while the Chaplain summed him up as " straight, fearless, indefatigable."

A true son of Erin and of Rugby football, which teaches its votaries, those of them who study and excel at it, these things.

HENRY DEWAR

SERGEANT HENRY DEWAR, who left New Zealand as a member of the Main Body of the New Zealand Reinforcements, was a Wellington, Taranaki, and New Zealand representative Rugby player. He was killed in action at Anzac Cove, Gallipoli, on August 9, 1915, aged 33.

" Norkey " Dewar was born in Wellington, and attended the Berhampore School, where he started his football career as a Public School representative player. He played afterwards for the St. James' Juniors, and then the Melrose Senior XV. Dewar first played as a Wellington representative against Canterbury in 1907, and was also a member of the team that played against the British side that toured New Zealand in 1908, under the captaincy of A. F. Harding. Altogether, Henry Dewar wore the Wellington representative jersey on eleven occasions during the 1907 and

1908 seasons. Later he went to Taranaki, where he kept up his form. His best year was in 1913, his play in the match against Auckland going a long way towards winning the Ranfurly Shield for Taranaki.

There were higher places still left for him on the Rugby Scroll of Honour, and in 1913 he played for the North Island against the South. The New Zealand Rugby Union sent its representative team to California that year, and Dewar showed fine form among the forwards in that victorious side. He was a front-ranker, although he could play equally well in any other part of the scrummage.

"Norkey" was a splendid man in every sense of the word—straight and strong, and one who commanded respect from all who knew him. He enlisted from Stratford in the main body, joining the Wellington Mounted Rifles as a Private, but was promoted to Sergeant while in camp at Awapuni, near Palmerston North. He captained the Wellington Mounted Rifle team in Egypt, which played with success against other New Zealand and Australian teams. He was an engineer by profession.

WALTER MICHAEL DICKSON

LIEUTENANT WALTER MICHAEL DICKSON, 11th Battalion Argyll and Sutherland Highlanders, fell in action in October 1915. Dickson was educated at South African College, South Africa, and at University College, Oxford, where he went as a Rhodes Scholar. His ability as a full-back with the Blackheath XV. carried him into the Scottish National team in the Welsh match of 1912, and he gained seven Caps in all—namely, v. Wales 1912–13, v. France 1912–13, v. England 1912, v. South Africa 1912, and v. Ireland 1913. Dickson was a fine field and accurate left-footed punt, thus possessing the chief requirements for the position in modern Rugby; but his tackling, owing to his slowness,

SERGEANT HENRY DEWAR
Wellington Mounted Rifles, N.Z.

LIEUT. WALTER MICHAEL DICKSON
11th Batt. Argyll and Sutherland Highlanders

Photo: Ayton, Edinburgh

was not up to the standard of his handling and kicking. He was in addition very deaf, and it says a great deal for his fielding and kicking powers, and knowledge of the game generally, that he rose to the position in the Rugby world he did.

Concerning his deafness a good story has reached me. Dickson took part in the French match on the Parc des Princes, Paris, when there was something very like a riot after the game, and when the referee, A. Baxter, had to thank that great French wing three-quarter, Failliot, for getting him safely away from the ground in his car. My most vivid recollection of that game is seeing the mounted cuirassiers falling-in in in-goal and galloping across the pitch to intercept the crowd, which was running from the far side in a mood which meant that their intention was likely to develop into something more serious than a mere vocal demonstration. Dickson, quite oblivious of the noise, turned to a brother Scot as the team was making its way to the pavilion, and remarked cheerfully : " It's awfully sporting of them to take their licking like this, isn't it ? " He was soon disillusioned.

A most reticent man, almost shy, due entirely to his deafness, he was not perhaps very well known up at Oxford—not so well, for example, as the late S. S. L. Steyn of his time, and also a South African Scot, who was as jovial and bursting with merriment as " Mike " Dickson was self-effacing. But E. G. Loudon-Shand (Dulwich, Oxford, and Scotland), who had rooms next to Dickson, once told me " Mike " was one of the kindest and best of fellows imaginable. Dickson was about 26 years of age when he went up to Oxford in 1912, and was a very good cricketer; but he gave up the game when he came to England, and interested himself much in the breeding of bull-dogs and in motor racing. He used to drive occasionally at Brooklands. He went to the Front with the Argyll and Sutherland Highlanders about October 1915, as he was in South Africa when war broke out.

ARTHUR JAMES DINGLE

CAPTAIN ARTHUR JAMES DINGLE, 6th East Yorkshire Regiment, fell in action at Suvla Bay on August 22, 1915, aged 23. He was born at Hetton-le-Hole, Co. Durham, and was educated at Bow, Durham, at Durham School, and at Keble College, Oxford. He played centre three-quarter for Oxford against Cambridge in 1911, and after returning to his old School as a Junior Master, he played regularly for the Richmond Club, Surrey, and for Durham County, until he got his English Cap in 1913 against Ireland, and in 1914 against Scotland and France. He played also for the North and in the Rugby Union's Trial Matches. A sturdy centre, he wanted a lot of stopping once on the move, but was always rather apt to drop passes. Like the majority of old Public School boys and Rugby men, he joined the Service in the first month of the War. He went through all the hard fighting after the landing on Gallipoli untouched, until, while holding a trench which his men had captured the previous day, he was shot at dawn through the temple. Captain Dingle's memory will always be cherished as that of a good all-round sportsman—at School he was distinguished at football, cricket, rowing, and gymnastics —and a most unassuming and modest man.

The following lines from *The Ballad of Suvla Bay* were written with direct reference to this gallant Oxonian:—

"Broad and simple and great of heart,
   Strenuous soul in a stalwart frame,
Whatever the work he took his part,
With energy strung from the very start
   To learn the rules and play the game.

"He'd played for an English side before,
   And all unspoiled by the crowd's applause,
He took for his side their greeting roars.
And so, in the greater game of war,
   He gave his life for his country's cause."

J. S.

CAPTAIN ARTHUR JAMES DINGLE
6th East Yorkshire Regiment

Photo: Ball, Stockton

LIEUT.-COLONEL GEORGE ERIC BURROUGHS DOBBS,
R.E.

GEORGE ERIC BURROUGHS DOBBS

LIEUTENANT-COLONEL GEORGE ERIC BURROUGHS DOBBS, Royal Engineers, Légion d'Honneur, died of wounds on June 17, 1917, at Poperinghe. His wounds were sustained the same morning, and were inflicted by what is known as a " dud " shell, while he was inspecting a new front-line cable trench. He was buried at Poperinghe.

Thus ended one of the heaviest forwards who ever played for England. Like a few other Rugby Internationals Dobbs was educated at an Association football playing school, in this case the famous one of Shrewsbury. There he played for his House as goalkeeper for three years. In the second of these years his House won the Challenge Cup, and in the third year he was Captain of the XI. He rowed in the School 2nd VIII., and twice for his House, besides winning the Junior Challenge Oars for House second boats. Captain of the winning Tug-of-War team, he won also the Putting the Weight Competition, a feat he repeated later for Woolwich against Sandhurst. His Preparatory School was St. Stephen's Green, Dublin. Gazetted to the Royal Engineers from Woolwich in 1904, he served in England, Singapore, and Limerick. He went to France at the outbreak of war, and was awarded the Legion of Honour after the retirement from Mons, later on being thrice mentioned in dispatches.

Lieutenant-Colonel Dobbs' Rugby football honours included Woolwich, 1902–4; Devon, 1905–7; Plymouth Albion, 1905–6; Llanelly, 1906–7; R.E., 1907–8; culminating with England v. Wales and v. Ireland in 1906.

Born on July 21, 1884, he was in his 33rd year. I have been permitted to give the following extracts from the letters of his brother officers: "He was admired and beloved both in work and play," wrote one.—"He lived for only three or four hours after he was hit," wrote another; "but his behaviour was a perfect sample of that of a real soldier."—" The whole Headquarters Staff" (he was at the time of his death at the H.Q. XVIII. Corps) "mourn the loss of a brave man and a universal favourite," wrote a third.—" I served with him through the retreat and the advance," wrote an intimate of his. "During that period we had very strenuous days, often twenty-two hours of hard work and marching, but he never altered a jot from his cheery self. You will like to know in what high esteem he was held and how he was loved by the N.C.O.'s and men who served under him." No officer desires a finer epitaph than is in the last few words of this extract.

ALBERT DOWNING

SERGEANT ALBERT DOWNING was born in Napier on July 12, 1886. He was educated at the Marist Brothers' School there, which he left in 1904, and was employed as a clerk successively by the Excelsior Dairy Co., Ltd., Barry Bros., Ltd., and Ellison and Duncan, Ltd., merchants. He enlisted on February 2, 1915, and left New Zealand with the Fifth Reinforcements (Wellington Battalion) on June 13, 1915. He was killed in the landing at Suvla Bay on August 8, 1915, aged 29. Downing, who was the eldest son of Mr. J. Downing, of Napier, was a fine specimen of New Zealand manhood, being 6 feet in height, and of splendid physique. He was one of Nature's gentlemen, and was remarkably popular with all who knew him.

"Many writers—myself among the number," writes Mr. D. M'Kenzie, "have argued that there are many New Zealand representative players outside the four centres—Auckland, Wellington, Christchurch, and Dunedin—but who, through lack of opportunity, are not given a fair chance of selection when International teams are being gathered together. Yielding to persuasion from the country unions, the New Zealand Rugby Union

SERGEANT ALBERT DOWNING
Wellington Battalion, N.Z.

decided in 1911 and 1912 to send two teams representative of the country unions on tour through the Dominion to play against the bigger unions. It was because of this that Downing got his chance, for he showed such outstanding form as a forward, that all the critics agreed that he was certain of a place when next a Dominion representative team was selected; and it came to pass. Downing was widely known in the New Zealand Rugby world, and he was one of the best-natured players who ever donned a jersey; always playing the game in the best acceptation of the term. He was ' on the ball ' from start to finish, and took the hardest knocks with a smile. He disdained to ' get one back ' on a vicious opponent; rather would he pause to help a fallen ' enemy.' He was noted for his studied loyalty to the Rugby game, having more than once disdainfully rejected overtures to desert to the professional code. His Rugby record was as follows : Played for Marist Brothers Old Boys, Napier, 1909-10-11; Hawke's Bay representative, 1909-10; North Island Country representative, 1911-12; New Zealand representative—California, 1913; Australia, 1914; Marist Brothers, Auckland, 1913-14; Auckland representative, 1913-14."

"Doolan," as he was affectionately and familiarly known, was deeply mourned by all his old Rugby friends.

WILLIAM VICTOR EDWARDS

CAPTAIN WILLIAM VICTOR EDWARDS, Royal Irish Fusiliers, fell in action near Jerusalem on December 29, 1917, aged 30. A son of Mr. Alfred Edwards, The Laurels, Strandtown (born there October 16, 1887), this Irish International was an Accountant by profession, at the time of the outbreak of war. But he was, too, a keen soldier, as he served in the 6th Battalion East Belfast Regiment of the Ulster Volunteer Force, from which Corps he joined the Army, and saw a great deal of service with the Irish

Division, being both wounded in the head and gassed. A splendid specimen of a man, Edwards was a member of the Malone Club XV. when he played for Ireland in 1912 against England and against France. Also an International at water polo. Captain Edwards was the first man to swim Belfast Lough.

Captain Edwards belonged to the School teams both at Coleraine and Campbell College, and was afterwards a member of the Malone Football Club, and then of the Knock Rugby Club, Belfast, which side he captained in the years 1911–12. He played for Ulster v. Leinster, January 29, 1910; v. Stade Français, March 3, 1910; v. Munster, January 14, 1911; v. Leinster, January 21, 1911; v. South Africa, 1912; v. Leinster, 1912; and v. Munster, 1912; and was also Captain of the Malone Club in 1911–12. Captain Edwards was a forward, and got his Cap against England and France in 1912 for Ireland.

His war record was a fine one. He got his commission as Second-Lieutenant on September 22, 1914, and proceeded to Tipperary, Co. Tipperary, Ireland, to join the Service Battalion (7th Royal Irish Fusiliers). In December 1914 he was promoted to Lieutenant, and in June 1915 to Captain in the same battalion. The training course completed at the Royal Staff College, at Camberley, Pirbright Camp, near Woking, and Bordon Camp, Hants, in February 1916 the Irish Division proceeded to France. Edwards saw a good deal of heavy fighting in France with this Division in 1916, and was twice in the casualty lists, suffering from gas poisoning on the first occasion, and again from a wound in the head received at the capture of Ginchy. In recognition of distinguished services he was transferred to the Regulars with the permanent rank of Captain, his new regiment being the Royal Dublin Fusiliers.

Captain Edwards was by profession a Chartered Accountant, and received his final certificate on May 28, 1914. He was a man of splendid physique, occupying a prominent position in athletic circles in the North of Ireland. He was a magnificent swimmer

CAPTAIN WILLIAM VICTOR EDWARDS
Royal Irish Fusiliers

Photo : Lafayette, Dublin

and a general all-round sportsman. He held the 220 Yards Irish Swimming Championship, and his most notable feat was to swim Belfast Lough, from Whitehead to Bangor, which he accomplished on August 16, 1913. He entered the water at Whitehead, Co. Antrim side, at 3.10 p.m., and at 7.10 the same evening landed at Clifton, Bangor, Co. Down side, to the accompaniment of the loud cheers of a very large crowd that had flocked to view the closing stages. He also represented Ireland on several occasions in Water Polo Internationals.

While in Tipperary, Captain Edwards assisted in the foundation of Active Service Masonic Lodge, No. 415 Tipperary, of which he remained a member up to the time of his death.

Schools.—Thanet College, Margate; Coleraine Academical Institution at Coleraine, Co. Derry, Ireland; and Campbell College, Belmont, Belfast.

WALTER TORRIE FORREST

MAJOR WALTER TORRIE FORREST, M.C., King's Own Scottish Borderers, was first reported missing, and then, the statutory period having elapsed, he was presumed to have been killed on April 19, 1917, in the second attack on Gaza, in Palestine, aged 37.

Born on November 14, 1880, at Kelso, Forrest was educated at Kelso High School, where he soon made his mark at the School games. It was with the "Teris" of Hawick that he became first famous in the first-class Rugby field, and he was a particularly good player in the Seven-a-Side Tournament, at which the Hawick Seven were often such terrors, the tournament being a great annual feature in the Border country after the Rugby season is over at the end of March. It was while Forrest was a Hawick player that he got his Cap for Scotland against Wales in 1903. He worked his way up by a good game for the South against the Anglo-Scots on the Greenyards, almost in the shadow of Melrose Abbey, and thence into the Rest v. Cities match. His rival in that game was R. T. Neilson, who had already played six times for Scotland, though not since 1900; but I believe the vote must have been almost unanimous for the Borderer after this game. Anyway, Forrest played in every International match for Scotland of the seasons 1903–4, and again in 1905 against Wales and Ireland, and it has to be recorded that in 1903 and 1904 Scotland was International Champion, in spite of a hammering at Swansea by 4 goals (1 penalty) and 1 try to 1 try. He would, of course, have played in the Calcutta Cup match of 1905 but for breaking his collar bone when playing for Hawick against Galashiels two days before the Scots were due at Richmond. The accident ended Forrest's International career; but when the bone had knit he used to play three-quarter in club games for the Kelso Club, which had now been raised to first-class status, and did much to help his native town team. He was also in the winning Kelso Seven at the Seven-a-Side held that year at the Jed Forest Games. Forrest's versatility was great, as he was able to take his part in the Kelso Soccer eleven, and was useful at cricket, golf, and fishing, as was only to be expected of a son of a famous tackle-maker. Ambidextrous, Forrest batted right and bowled left; while, as a full-back, he did most of his punting and all his place-kicking with the left foot. He was partial to drop-kicking, and as a tackler one of the best of full-backs. Great dash and energy, almost too much some said, were the outstanding features of his play, some of which was of the helter-skelter type, which caused somebody to remark that "Forrest gets into these 'hats' for the sake of getting out of 'em!" Except that he was a much better kick than the South African, Forrest's play was rather like that of A. W. F. Marsburg of a couple of seasons later. He took risks cheerfully, and got out of them by his very daring and vivacious style of play.

Major Forrest was a Territorial officer before the war, and took a keen interest in the affairs of the Church, being a deacon in

MAJOR WALTER TORRIE FORREST, M.C.
King's Own Scottish Borderers

Photo: Crowe and Rodgers, Stirling

Trinity United Free Church, and also for a while a member of the choir. He was through the Gallipoli campaign, and present on the memorable 12th of July 1915. Mentioned in dispatches, he also won the Military Cross.

ROWLAND FRASER

CAPTAIN ROWLAND FRASER, 1st Battalion The Rifle Brigade, was killed in action on the Somme on July 1, 1916, aged 26. Born at Perth on January 10, 1890, Fraser was educated at Merchiston Preparatory (1900–3), Merchiston Castle (1903–8), and at Pembroke College, Cambridge (1908–11). He was in the Merchiston XV. from 1905–8; in the XI. for the same years, Captain of it in 1908; and in the School Gymnastic VIII. from 1905–7. He won the Weight Putting in 1907 and 1908. Fraser played for Cambridge against Oxford in 1908–10, and was Captain in 1910. He was never on the winning side, though the match of 1908 was drawn, one goal each. Nor was he any luckier when playing in the Scottish National XV., as he did four times in 1911, and every time on the losing side, this being the only year France won an International match. It must be rare, indeed, for a University Blue and International to play in seven 'Varsity and International games, and never have the good fortune to be on the winning side. Had Fraser played in his fourth year at Cambridge he would not have broken this unfortunate sequence of defeats. He was, naturally, in no way to blame for this extraordinary record; and was, in fact, a really good forward of the very sound and hard-working, honest type, a good dribbler, and a magnificent tackler.

Captain Fraser received his commission in the Rifle Brigade on August 15, 1914, and went into training with the 6th Battalion at Sheerness. He crossed to France on January 4, 1915, was promoted Lieutenant in August 1915, and Captain in November of that year. He was machine-gun officer from July 1915 to November 1915, and trained with the machine gun at St. Omer, whence he went to meet a plucky death terribly wounded. Of his wounding and very brave end, the following details have been sent to me :—

" He was leading his company in an attack when he was shot in the side by a machine-gun bullet, within a few yards of the German trenches. His orderly got him into a shell-hole and dressed his wound, but he was again hit in the side by shrapnel. He only lived for six hours, his orderly staying with him till the end." In a letter to his own people the orderly said : " Captain Fraser was one of the bravest men that has ever lived, and he died like the officer and gentleman that he was." In a letter from a brother officer, I read : " Roley died as he had lived, thinking never of himself, but only of others and his Company. The Battalion mourn a very gallant officer, to whom they owe more than I can say. I cannot speak too highly of his gallantry and devotion to duty, and no company commander was ever more loved by his men. He was the whitest man I ever knew."

Reverting to his career as a player, Fraser was asked to captain the Cambridge XV. again in 1911, but was unable to go back a fourth year. In the close match with Oxford in 1910 (4 goals and 1 try to 3 goals and 1 try) Fraser's captaincy only just failed to turn the scale, though Cambridge were expected to be much the weaker side. He was chosen to lead the Scots pack against Wales and Ireland, probably in consequence of this 'Varsity match display. After going down he played for Edinburgh University, and at cricket for the Grange Club and for Perthshire County. In his Division in France there were twenty-seven Rugby Internationals he had played with or against. In April 1915 he played in a game out there for the 4th Division against a freshly arrived South Midlands Division, the new arrivals natu-

CAPTAIN ROWLAND FRASER
1st Batt. Rifle Brigade

Photo: Langfier, London

rally winning. The most pathetic part of his brave death has to be recorded. He came home in June 1916, on four days' leave, to be married on June 20 to Miss May Dorothy Ross of Invinidi, U.S.A., and returned to France next day. He fell ten days later. The heart of the entire Rugby football world bows in respectful sympathy before such sorrow, especially as it concerns one of the most popular of her sons.

DAVID GALLAHER

DAVID GALLAHER, who was killed in action in France early in October 1917, was probably one of the best known Rugby footballers the world over. He captained the famous " All Blacks " team from New Zealand in its tour of Great Britain and Ireland. Gallaher was born in Belfast about forty-six years ago, and went to New Zealand, as a child, with the Vesey Stewart immigrants. For some time he lived with his parents at Tauranga, but later went to Auckland. From his boyhood he was recognized as a capable athlete, his prowess being exhibited chiefly at Rugby football.

He first entered big Rugby in 1896, when he gained a place, as a member of the Ponsonby Club, in the Auckland representative team. He won similar distinction the following year, also in 1899, 1900, 1903, and 1904; and in 1905 was chosen one of the team to tour the British Isles. Prior to the big tour he had represented the North Island in 1903, and New Zealand in 1903 against New South Wales and Queensland, and in 1904 against D. R. Bedell-Sivright's British team.

When the New Zealand team of 1905 was selected, the New Zealand Rugby Union appointed Gallaher Captain of that combination, the governing body deciding that he was the strongest man amongst those selected. That he justified their confidence is a matter of history.

Gallaher played a big part in helping on the fortunes of Rugby football, more particularly in Auckland. For many years he coached the boys of the Auckland Grammar School in the ethics and practice of the game; was sole selector of Auckland representative teams; and assisted in the selection of North Island and New Zealand representative teams. He was through the South African War, returning as Regimental Sergeant-Major. After the return of the " All Blacks " he settled down, and married a sister of A. H. Francis, a capable Auckland and New Zealand representative forward. On the outbreak of the present War he was eager to join the forces, but was for some time detained on account of his family ties. When the news came through that a younger brother had been killed in action, he could not be held back. He enlisted the same day, and left New Zealand as a Sergeant in the Twenty-second Reinforcements.

To the football public of the United Kingdom he was known as the Captain and wing forward of the famous New Zealand team which toured in these islands in 1905. That season he was the most discussed man among the sporting sections of the community, mainly by reason of the alleged iniquities he perpetrated as wing forward, both as regards putting the ball unfairly into the scrum and by playing a scientifically obstructionist game while his forwards were heeling. Some of his traducers, and it was noticeable that scarcely any one of any consequence was among them, did not stick at saying he was an unfair player, no matter which set of forwards had the ball. Long before the need for the present volume had arisen I stated in print my opinion that Gallaher was a fair player. It was my lot to see more matches of that much discussed tour than any man living now—and only one man not of their team saw more of their games than I did—and I state unhesitatingly that I never saw Gallaher put the ball into the scrum unfairly, certainly never with spin on it, as was freely alleged against him, though, so far as I am aware, only in Wales. The exigencies of an unfair position on the field,

SERGEANT DAVID GALLAHER
Auckland Battalion, N.Z.

as we understand Rugby football, doubtless often made Gallaher appear to the untrained eye as something of an *agent provocateur*; but I cannot think of a player who would have gone through such a long tour in that position with such serenity, and at the same time have made so many friends among his keenest opponents. This is not the place for a discussion upon the wing-forward position as played in New Zealand. We do not like the position, and it will never be part of the game in the four Home Unions. Gallaher was so enamoured of it that in the excellent book on the game, to which he and W. J. Stead (Vice-Captain of the team of 1905) put their names, published soon after the tour was over, the joint-authors expressed their unhesitating belief that if they ever played again in England they would find the wing-forward everywhere. Never did experts make such a blunder. I don't suppose either of them was under any delusion that the success of the tour was due to the wing-forward. In any formation on the field that New Zealand team would have won just as many matches against the same opponents, including the one against Wales. This was lost mainly because the referee wouldn't have the wing-forward at any valuation; and the general blotting out that player received that day was speedily reflected in the play of the rest of the team, which, short of full strength before kick-off, owing to the absence of G. W. Smith, played a long way below its real form, quite irrespective of the trite and true adage that a team plays as well as its opponents permit it to play. That was the only game in which I saw the urbanity of Gallaher in the least disturbed. Doubtless, his Army training through the South African War stood him in very good stead in his difficult position on this tour—a position calling for exceptional powers of tact and discipline both on and off the field. In his way a bit of a martinet, the New Zealand Captain would stand no nonsense from any one; and as for communicativeness, he and his team manager, G. H. Dixon, positively vied with each other as to which could be dumber than any oyster at the slightest suspicion of any chiel who seemed likely to be takin' notes. On such occasions the weather and the excellent play of their opponents of three matches ago were never-failing topics for them to refer to.

Although I was often in the company of this team at places so separated as Camborne, Bedford, Glasgow, and Limerick, I don't suppose I spoke twenty words all told to Gallaher. If so, I cannot remember more than half a dozen or so in return. He had a great admiration for Basil Maclear and for Gwyn Nicholls, also E. T. Morgan, but verbosity was not his. As a captain, Gallaher was the personification of silence, a veritable Sphinx. I never saw him lose his temper during a game, or after one for that matter. Some one had written something with an air of authority about Gallaher's delinquencies, making him out several degrees blacker than any raven—a fit subject for comparison with some of the undesirable characters of history. Another expert tried to draw the New Zealander as to his opinion on the accusations. "Has —— ever played in a Rugby match?" was the terse reply of a man who obviously knew at once whether a critic knew his subject, and heeded only the sayings and writings of men who equally obviously came under that heading. Take him all in all, this hard-bitten Colonial, as tough as a bit of leather, the sort of player one never saw winded or in the least bit hurt during a match, was one of the characters of Rugby football. As such it was not surprising that, although he had done his share in the South African War, he was not long in throwing up a lucrative and responsible post in New Zealand to be with his fellow Rugby men in the firing-line once more. Even his greatest enemies of that tour will have heard with a genuine sense of regret of his death. To his admirers, among whose numbers I am proud to be, it came as a great shock; though, once we knew he was in France, as no surprise. I have been fortunate enough to obtain the following tribute to a fine man from one of the members of his great team of 1905. I append it in full :—

DAVID GALLAHER

"Skipper 'Dave' Gallaher.

" The news of the sad and sudden death of my old skipper 'Dave' has distressed me beyond measure. Ever since his arrival at Sling Camp with the New Zealand Reinforcements, and during his all too brief sojourn here in France, I have been in constant communication with him. In fact his last letter came almost simultaneously with the notification of his end.

" In this letter he states, with his usual philosophy (and he was ' some philosopher '), ' Here I am in good health and spirits amongst the boys; it's like old times again. So far I have a whole skin, though *life here, on the whole, is a matter of chance.* So long, "Old Horse." Heaps of luck and good wishes from your old pal, Dave Gallaher.'

" In the face of what has happened, his words were tragic and almost prophetic. Dave had a great love for Britain and its people, and simply revelled in a long talk over '.the old bygone days.' Every letter he asks for the address of first this and then that one, friends made in 1905-6.

" Dave was a man of sterling worth, slow to promise, but always sure to fulfil. Girded by great determination and self-control, he was a valuable friend, and could be, I think, a remorseless foe. He would reason everything out his own way, even if it took him two pipe fills of tobacco—and he loved his pipe. Thus he was a great theorist in other matters as well as football, and his opinion was always worth having. Never thrusting himself forward, he always liked to ' get the strength of the other chap first.'

" As an opponent in play he was simply merciless, wanted everything and all; but I honestly think he ever meant to be nothing but legitimate and fair. To us ' All Blacks ' his words would often be, ' Give nothing away; take no chances.' As a skipper he was somewhat of a disciplinarian, doubtless imbibed from his previous military experiences in South Africa. Still he treated us all as men, not kids, who were out 'to play the game' for good old New Zealand. We responded accordingly, and never even broke a pane of glass on the whole tour.

"As a travelling companion he was ever fit, keen, and ready for anything. As our manager, George Dixon, used to say with his Yorkshire dialect, 'Our Dave's a keen blade.' His greatest regret on that tour was the lateness of the Welsh fixtures. He foresaw the likelihood of staleness.

"In one match Gillett took his place as wing forward, and seated in the grand stand he could overhear such remarks as, 'Look at that terrible man Gallaher, off side as usual,' and loud cries of 'Off side, Gallaher!'

"'By Crikey! I didn't know that I was so popular,' says Dave to me.

"Just before a certain International match, when the ground was frozen hard and our reception almost as chilling, I caught Dave sitting down in despair almost, looking at the two footballs given to us to play with in a few minutes. He was vexed. 'Look, "General,"' he said. 'A frozen ground like flint to play on, and these balls blown up as hard as the hobs of hell (on purpose I suppose); they'll bounce to glory and spoil our passing.' I took the balls and soused them well in water, thereby slackening them. He was pleased.

"Since his return to New Zealand after the tour he has always helped the old game along, acting as Selector for the Auckland Rugby Union and coaching Junior teams.

"In the huge list of fallen International Rugbyites in this gigantic match of 'Right v. Might,' the name of 'Dave' Gallaher stands out pre-eminently clear for all time.

"Ernest E. Booth.
"B.A.P.O.I., France."

WILLIAM PURDON GEEN

SECOND-LIEUTENANT WILLIAM PURDON GEEN, 9th Battalion King's Royal Rifle Corps, was killed in action at Hooge, Belgium, on July 31, 1915, aged 25. He was born at Newport, Monmouthshire, and educated at Northam Place, Potter's Bar, Haileybury College, and Oxford. At Haileybury he kept wicket for the XI., and was a splendid centre three-quarter in the XV., of which he was Captain in 1910, one of the best centres Haileybury ever possessed. On going to Oxford he was played out of his place as a wing three-quarter, for which he never had the real pace requisite for the highest class football. He played against Cambridge at Queen's Club in 1910-11-12-13, when Oxford won the first two and lost the last two matches. At Newport the Welshmen rightly judged and generally played him as a centre; but he played for Wales as a wing against South Africa in 1912, and England and Ireland in 1913, these three being his only International Caps.

Geen joined the 60th in August 1914, like most Rugby men, there being no waiting upon the order of his going. He was in training at Petworth in Sussex for some time, and went to the Front in May 1915. The 9th were with the 14th Light Division in the Second Battle of Ypres in that month. After nearly six weeks continuous fighting, the Battalion was withdrawn for a short spell of rest, but, two days later, were ordered back to reinforce the 41st Brigade. Of Geen's death Major John Hope wrote :—

" Geen fought gloriously, and was last seen alive leading his platoon in a charge after being for hours subjected to liquid fire and every device the Germans could bring to bear to break through. Seventeen officers and 333 other ranks of this battalion were killed in this engagement, in which officers and men showed themselves worthy of the best traditions of their Regiment."

Here, again, we see the Rugby game played on a more serious field. Geen " fought gloriously," he was last seen " leading his platoon in a charge." Alter the words ever so slightly and we are almost watching a Haileybury *v.* Bedford or an inter-'Varsity, or Wales *v.* England match, over again, with the natty and trim figure of Billy Geen easily distinguishable in the thick of everything, on account of his curly fair hair. He was always one of the neatest looking of three-quarters, with a three-quarter's legs and gait. A fine power of drop-kicking was his, and his play in the centre reminded one very much, on account of his dodging style, of the play of a class centre in the old three three-quarter days. As a cricketer Geen " kept " respectably and played for Monmouthshire in the Minor Counties Championship, but Rugby football was his game, and in that his capacity for doing odd things, while it may have sometimes caused a flutter in the dovecots of the grave and reverend selectors of teams, succeeded not only in disturbing them, but also the opponents of his fifteen. Of course he played for the Oxford University Authentics at cricket, and also for Blackheath and for the Barbarians at the Rugby game.

An Old Haileyburian, who knew Geen well, has penned the following tribute :—

" An individual player of singular capabilities was lost to International football when Billy Geen gave his life. He was as swiftly into the Army on the declaration of war as he used to zig-zag through most defences before that event. He was essentially a player of moods, and rarely shone behind a beaten pack, though there were notable exceptions. He had an astounding power of quick side-stepping in a confined space, that was bewildering in the extreme to his opponents. Difficult to combine with, perhaps Poulton more than any one else was the man who came nearest a complete understanding with him : their individualism was of a similar type. On his day he was so truly

SEC.-LIEUT. WILLIAM PURDON GEEN
9th Batt. King's Royal Rifle Corps

Photo: Williams, Newport

brilliant that one thought instinctively ' only Geen could have done that.' His playing career was interrupted more than once by accidents (he was chosen, but did not play, for Wales in the first match of the 1914 season, and probably lost four Welsh Caps in consequence.—E. H. D. S.); but he triumphed over them, and would certainly have gone far in normal times. He was also a fine cricketer, but footer was his enthusiasm. In mid-July, after perhaps knocking up 50 or so, and keeping wicket with genius and certainty, he would plunge with relief and gusto into a long chat on footer ' shop.' He is a heavy loss to Rugger and his many friends. T. H. E. B."

ROLAND ELPHINSTONE GORDON

MAJOR ROLAND ELPHINSTONE GORDON, Royal Artillery, was born at Selangor, Straits Settlements, on January 22, 1893, and died of wounds in England on August 30, 1918, aged 25.

He was educated at King's School, Canterbury, whence he passed into Woolwich in 1911, and speedily made his mark as a centre three-quarter of much above average merit. He was soon playing in "the Shop" XV., and directly he appeared in more public matches than, unfortunately, are those of the Woolwich and Sandhurst teams, it was seen that Scotland had a treasure added to their back division for the asking. I saw all three of Gordon's International games, those against France, Wales, and Ireland in 1913, and it is positively true, that though new to the type of match and also to his partners on the three-quarter line, one at least of whom was a bizarre performer at best, the youngster never put a foot wrong right through the whole two "forties." The Frenchmen could simply make nothing of him in his first International, which was played at the Parc des Princes, Paris, early in January. It was an easy occasion upon which a " colt " might have been upset, as the huge crowd was somewhat vociferous in its objection to the referee's reading of the rules of the game; but, like all great players, Gordon played each match on its merits, heeding nothing of the behaviour of the onlookers, or of opponents, whatever its nature. I cannot recall, more than six years later, if he actually scored a try, but try-getting was never part of his game. His was a splendid example of true centre-three-quarter play, and since H. H. Vassall's Oxford days no player has appeared who, in action, was a better model for budding aspirants to centre-three honours than R. E. Gordon.

His next experience of the biggest football was a most depressing one, as the Welshmen did not play the game at Inverleith, literally humbugging the referee right through the piece, and winning by 1 goal and 1 try to nil; and one of the Scottish wings (not the late W. R. Sutherland, almost needless to add) cost Scotland the game by two blunders, due to an ignorance of the game that seemed abysmal. In his third and last game before sailing for India, and being robbed by those marching orders of the most coveted honour in the Rugby football world—namely, participation in an England v. Scotland match—Gordon revealed himself almost as a master by beating the Irishmen off his own bat, and sending W. A. Stewart in with four of the seemingly "softest" tries ever seen in International Rugby since back-play became so scientific. If the Frenchmen could make nothing of him in January, the Irishmen made very much less of him in February. The times they collared him after he had made an opening and had passed the ball were legion. Except Gwyn Nicholls and H. H. Vassall no such superb "bluffer" as Gordon has adorned an International three-quarter line in this century. We were all looking forward to seeing him in opposition to the late R. W. Poulton Palmer, and either the late J. H. D. Watson, or the late F. N. Tarr—Tarr rightly got the place—in the English match, when we heard he was sailing for India. As England won by only a try to nil at Twickenham, it is a football certainty

MAJOR ROLAND ELPHINSTONE GORDON, R.A.
Photo: Denney, Teignmouth

that business abroad once more cost Scottish Rugby an International match.

At Poona Gordon was well in the forefront, of course, and in the few matches he played in proved to be probably the finest back ever seen in Rugby football in India. And then this vile War. He went to Mesopotamia with his battery in November 1914, and was very severely wounded during our summer of 1915, to be invalided home to Devon the following year. Recovering, he became the moving spirit at the R.F.A. Cadet School at Exeter, and had such a good convalescence, thanks to a fine constitution, that he was able to play fairly regularly for the Cadets XV. during the winter of 1916–17. Before returning to the fight he played in one more big game, that at the Rectory Field, Blackheath, in March 1917, against the Army Service Corps XV., then undefeated. It was mainly due to his great performance in the centre that they were beaten, his winning try in the last minute of the match once more revealing masterly ability at the centre-three game. That was the last time I saw him play, and the memory of it will never fade.

Gordon was a strongly built man of about six feet high, and possessed the very deceptive speed which means so much on the football field. Like all the greatest players, he was always moving fast, and towards the goal-line, while he was bluffing with hands and head. So many players attempt the bluffing, but forget to run fast during the attempt, so that when they are felled their side has not progressed much in the desired direction. Gordon was a natural player of great gifts, who, had he not been in the Army, would have been world famous at the game, as his effortless play always bore the unmistakable hall-mark of class. He had the faculty of playing well whoever were his partners, or the opposition. I never saw him on a wet day, but his style of running, which was of the firmest, gave one no fears on this important point. He was, indeed, one to be envied—his happy disposition, his peerless ability at our great game, and his glorious death.

LEONARD HAIGH

CADET OFFICER LEONARD HAIGH, who died of double pneumonia, incurred in training in England, on August 6, 1916, was born on October 19, 1880, at Prestwick. Educated at Sandringham House School, Southport, he was a member of both the Association football and cricket elevens there; on leaving School he played hockey for some time, but eventually began to play Rugby with the Manchester Rugby Football Club. By steady but regular stages he played for Manchester, for Lancashire, for the North v. South, for Rest v. England, and for England v. South before he gained the first of his seven English Caps—namely, v. Scotland, Ireland, and Wales in 1910 and 1911, and v. France in 1911. His football career was thus a most remarkable one, as he did not get his Cap until he was thirty years of age, a time when most International players have retired from that class of football. Moreover, Haigh was very well worth his Cap at that advanced football age. But he was a good all-rounder, so was always physically fit, being a good fisherman and shot and useful at golf. He was keen on motoring, from the mechanical view point; and it was due to this knowledge that he was in the O.T.C. of the Army Service Corps Mechanical Transport. Next to that of the late Lieutenant-Colonel E. R. Mobbs, Haigh's was perhaps the most remarkable instance of rapid rise to International class in the Rugby game.

REGINALD HARRY MYBURGH HANDS

CAPTAIN REGINALD HARRY MYBURGH HANDS, South African Artillery, died of wounds received in action. He was educated at Diocesan College, Rondebosch, South Africa, from 1898–1907, whence he went as a Rhodes Scholar to University College, Oxford, in 1907.

CADET-OFFICER LEONARD HAIGH
O.T.C., A.S.C. Mech. Transport

CAPTAIN REGINALD HARRY MYBURGH HANDS
South African Artillery

For the following facts and appreciation I am indebted to one who knew him well :—

"He got his Rugby Blue in both 1908 and 1909, and played for England against Scotland and France in 1910. Why he did not play afterwards I do not know, as he was at his very best after that. I believe he returned to South Africa in 1911 or 1912. He played a lot for Blackheath and was thought a lot of there, and all the South Africans used to swear by him as a tip-top forward. We saw a good deal of him on Barbarian tours, and I always considered myself very lucky whenever he accepted an invitation, as in my opinion he was a very fine player and readily adapted himself to any style, which just suited our mixed packs. The bigger the game, and the better the company, the better he played; in fact, I consider that during his Oxford career, and more especially just after, he was good enough for any side. He was a Barbarian member from 1908 to 1911, and was on tour at Easter 1911. Being without a fixed home in England he, like all South Africans, was glad to come; and we were very glad to have them, for nicer fellows one could not wish to meet. And Reggie Hands was one of the best of them. He was quiet, unassuming, and modest, and would not willingly hurt a soul, but all the same was very determined, and had views on most things above his age.

"He joined the South African Heavies and came to England with H. C. Harrison's Heavy Brigade, which went through the South-West African campaign. Reggie and his brother both had commissions in this when they arrived in England, and he did very well in France. As a Rugger player, a companion, and a man, he was the very best—a perfectly true sportsman, who would never take the slightest mean advantage in any game, and he had not the least use for the ultra-clever brigade, who only thought of winning anyhow. Bluffing the referee or anything of that sort did not appeal to him, and he was a very great asset in every way to any touring side."

ARTHUR LEYLAND HARRISON

LIEUTENANT-COMMANDER ARTHUR LEYLAND HARRISON, V.C., Royal Navy, was born at Torquay on February 3, 1886, and fell during the ever glorious feat of *Vindictive* at Zeebrugge, on April 23, 1918, aged 32. He was educated at Dover College as his Preparatory School. He became a Naval Cadet in September 1902, a Lieutenant October 1908, and Lieutenant-Commander October 1916. He was present at the Battles of Heligoland, 1914, Dogger Bank and Jutland, 1916. His ship was *Lion*, from which he was sent to *Vindictive* for the deathless raid. His Club football career was with the United Services and Hampshire, before he played for the Navy *v.* Army in 1914. That was his best season, and in it he played for England *v.* Ireland and *v.* France. Lieutenant-Commander A. L. Harrison, who was a very sturdy and tireless forward, was mentioned in dispatches after the Battle of Jutland. The manner in which he met his death was typical. He was second in command of the storming party from *Vindictive* on the Mole at Zeebrugge. Wounded before landing, he was killed on the Mole while leading the attack on a machine gun.

During the war football season of 1916–17 Lieutenant-Commander A. L. Harrison was very much to the fore in the scratch games played at the Old Deer Park, Richmond, and it goes without saying that though past the age at which men receive their first 'National Cap, he was so fit that he would have played many more times for England but for the War. His game was the sturdy, bustling type, and he was quite a good place-kicker. In March 1914 he had the honour of being presented to His Majesty before the Navy *v.* Army match at Queen's.

To the general delight of all his friends and of Rugby men in general, it was announced in March 1919 that the supreme honour of a posthumous V.C. had been accorded this gallant sailor. I cannot do better than quote the *London Gazette* of March 17, 1919, from which it will be apparent that never was

**LIEUT.-COMMANDER ARTHUR LEYLAND HARRISON,
V.C., R.N.**

the Cross " For Valour " more bravely won or more fittingly bestowed :—

" LIEUTENANT-COMMANDER ARTHUR LEYLAND HARRISON, R.N.

" For most conspicuous gallantry at Zeebrugge on the night of April 22-23, 1918.

" This officer was in immediate command of the naval storming-parties embarked in *Vindictive*.

" Immediately before coming alongside the Mole Lieutenant-Commander Harrison was struck on the head by a fragment of a shell which broke his jaw and knocked him senseless. Recovering consciousness, he proceeded on to the Mole and took over command of his party, who were attacking the seaward end of the Mole. The silencing of the guns on the Mole head was of the first importance, and though in a position fully exposed to the enemy's machine-gun fire, Lieutenant-Commander Harrison gathered his men together and led them to the attack. He was killed at the head of his men, all of whom were either killed or wounded.

" Lieutenant-Commander Harrison, though already severely wounded and undoubtedly in great pain, displayed indomitable resolution and courage of the highest order in pressing his attacks, knowing as he did that any delay in silencing the guns might jeopardise the main object of the expedition—that is, the blocking of the Zeebrugge-Bruges Canal."

JAMES YOUNG MILNE HENDERSON

LIEUTENANT JAMES YOUNG MILNE HENDERSON, 11th Battalion Highland Light Infantry, was killed in action on July 31, 1917, at the Battle of Flanders, aged 26. Born in Edinburgh on March 9, 1891, Henderson was educated at George Watson's College, where, when thirteen years old, he was already in the 2nd XV., getting his 1st XV. cap when only fifteen. It is said of him that he was the best stand-off half ever produced by Watson's College. He was a very versatile gamesman, and did great things for the Watsonians' XV., besides being good at cricket, hockey, swimming, badminton, and billiards. He was certainly the next best to P. Munro I have ever seen in Scotland's National XV. He was fated to play but once therein, and that was in the first Calcutta Cup match played at Twickenham, when he played a game that augured very well indeed for his and Scotland's future. For a first appearance it was wonderful, betraying an absence of nerves and a presence of the " big-match temperament " that was most marked. I am perfectly certain that had not " J. Y.," as he was known, gone to take up a business appointment in Travancore, South India, in 1911, his name would have been writ large in Scotland's International song and story. In India he played for Madras *v.* Bombay and *v.* Calcutta in the tournament at Bombay. Later he became works manager to Messrs. M'Vittie and Price, Willesden, London, and when war came was very soon in the Army, being mentioned in dispatches, and present at Loos in September 1915 and several other actions. As a tribute to his memory, his fellow employees at Willesden had his portrait painted and hung in the Board room of the firm. When " J. Y." fell in the forefront of battle a splendid young Scot was taken from us, and the game of Rugby football was robbed of an ornament. Perhaps no man who has played in but one International game will be so well and so long remembered as he was, and in that fact rests a great tribute to the man himself apart from his personal prowess on the football field. The following extract from his last letter home, dated July 26, 1917, is eloquent of him, and will long be quoted with pride by all who knew him. It is : " If I have to go, I will be quite happy, as I will go out doing my duty." Brave words these, straight from the heart of a brave young Scot.

LIEUT. JAMES YOUNG MILNE HENDERSON
11th Batt. Highland Light Infantry

Photo: Bacon, Edinburgh

HAROLD AUGUSTUS HODGES

CAPTAIN HAROLD AUGUSTUS HODGES, 3rd Monmouths, attached 11th South Lancashire Regiment, was born at the Priory, Mansfield Woodhouse, on January 22, 1886, and fell in action near Mons on March 24, 1918, aged 32. He was educated at Roclareston House, Nottingham, from 1895-99; at Sedbergh from 1899-1904; and at Trinity College, Oxford, from 1905-9. He was in both the XI. and XV. at Sedbergh, and Captain of both for his last two years there. He got his Blue in his first year, and was Captain in 1908, playing in the meantime twice for England in 1906 against Wales and Ireland. Hodges was a very fine forward, and Captain of one of the strongest Fifteens Oxford ever placed in the field. His game was that of Sedbergh all through, his fault being the usual one among forwards from an essentially forwards breeding school—of a tendency to regard the back division in the light of interlopers in the game of Rugby football. But he was a good Captain, and the backs of the Oxford XV. of 1908 were such as to prevail over any such idiosyncrasies on the part of their team leader. Hodges got his commission on August 27, 1914, and went to France in February 1915. He was a Master at Tonbridge School when war broke out, and it is comment worthy that Tonbridge had two years later the record pack of forwards in the history of Public Schools Rugby football. After leaving Oxford Hodges spent some months in Paris, studying and attending lectures at the Sorbonne. Captain Hodges met his death in the following manner: On the night of 24th to 25th March he was sent out to find the exact whereabouts of the battalion on the right of his own. He walked into a building, believed to be held by our men, but which was actually in the possession of the enemy. Doubtless, he was shot at once, though for some months hopes were entertained that he had been taken prisoner.

DAVID DUCHIE HOWIE

SECOND-LIEUTENANT DAVID DUCHIE HOWIE, R.F.A., died of pneumonia at Cairo on January 19, 1916, aged 27. He was born at Rosebery Temple, Midlothian, and was educated at Kirkcaldy High School, where he was a forward in the School XV. for three years, and where he won the Nairn Cup, which is given to the champion athlete of the school, in 1903. The war very soon called this fine young Scotsman, for it was on September 8, 1914, that he enlisted as a trooper in the Fife and Forfar Yeomanry. Until April 1915 he trained in England, receiving a commission in the 1st Highland Brigade, R.F.A., before sailing for Gallipoli in August 1915. It was during the evacuation of Anzac that he caught the fatal chill, to die on active service for King and Empire as truly as any of his fellows who earned the proud distinction "fallen in action."

D. D. Howie was a useful forward, who won his way by sheer merit into the national pack of Scotland against Wales, Ireland, England, France, and South Africa in 1912, and against Wales and France in 1913, seven Caps in all. Scots selection committees seldom err in regard to forwards, and they certainly did not do so in his case. On all counts Howie was a fine player of Rugby football, and a most popular man.

JAMES LAIDLAW HUGGAN

LIEUTENANT JAMES LAIDLAW HUGGAN, R.A.M.C., 3rd Battalion Coldstream Guards, was killed in action on the Aisne on September 16, 1914, aged 25. Born at Jedburgh, Roxburghshire, on October 11, 1888, Huggan was educated first at Watson's College, Edinburgh; and afterwards at Queen Elizabeth's Grammar School, Darlington, and at Edinburgh University. He learned the Rugby game with the Jed Forest team—the club of

CAPTAIN HAROLD AUGUSTUS HODGES
3rd Monmouths (att. 11th South Lancashire Regiment)
Photo: Hadley, Nottingham

his native town—with whom he played wing three-quarter for several seasons. At Darlington he was Captain of the School cricket and football clubs in 1905 and 1906, and was Victor Ludorum there in 1903-5. He played wing three-quarter for Edinburgh University, where he was also in the Association Football XI., a rare achievement, and an Athletic Blue as well. After playing a while with London Scottish he was twice chosen, and played for, the Army v. Navy, and it was his splendid play in one of these games which at last decided the Scottish selectors to play him for Scotland v. England in 1914. He scored one of the Scottish tries in that memorable match, and was, as his southern admirers knew he was certain to be, one of the best three-quarters in the game. Huggan's forte was an all-out dash and energy, hard for the line, as hard as he could go. This lent to his game a character for sheer " bullocking," which, I believe, told against him, but which was unmerited. His tackling was sturdy and good, his kicking fair; but it was in carrying out the chief duty of a wing, which is to score tries, that Huggan shone. A most popular and likable man, he was always warmly appreciative of merit in others, and liked, above all things, to play wing to the late R. E. Gordon, R.A., a preference in which he was not singular.

The following fuller details concerning him have been very kindly supplied by a committee-man of the Scottish Football Union:—

"Dr. Huggan," he writes, " was a son of the late Mr. Robert Huggan, engineer, Allerley, Jedburgh, and of Mrs. Huggan, Mayfield Road, Edinburgh; and his uncle is ex-Provost James Laidlaw, J.P., of Allan, Jedburgh, to whom he was warmly attached. Colonel J. A. G. Drummond Hay, writing to a Jedburgh lady (Miss Eugenie Rose-Innes), from the Regimental Headquarters of the Coldstream Guards, Buckingham Gate, on October 5, 1914, said: 'Yesterday I saw Lieutenant Soames, Coldstream Guards, who has just returned to this country wounded. He was on the Staff of the 4th Brigade, to which the 3rd Battalion of this regiment belongs. He is going to write to the Laidlaws (Jedburgh) about Dr. Huggan, as he knows all about him. He told me Dr. Huggan was extraordinarily gallant, and two days before he was killed he was recommended for the Victoria Cross for organizing and heading a party of volunteers to remove a number of wounded from a barn that had been set on fire by the German shell-fire. The work was carried out under a very heavy shell-fire, and all the wounded were saved.'"

Dr. Huggan was three years at Watson's College, and five years at Darlington Grammar School. He passed high in examination for admission to R.A.M.C., and was about to leave for India when war broke out. After graduating, he became house surgeon to Mr. Alexander Miles, surgeon to the Edinburgh Royal Infirmary, who describes him as one of the finest young men he ever met (extract from *British Medical Journal*, October 28, 1916). First-class honours in surgery.

At the presentation of the memorial portrait of Dr. Huggan, at Riverside, Mr. W. Wells Mabon, J.P., vice-president of the Jed Forest Football Club, and a member of the committee of the S.F.U., presided, and in handing over the portrait on behalf of ex-Provost Laidlaw, spoke of Dr. Huggan as " an attractive personality—sunny-hearted and sympathetic, and splendidly courageous. Those high qualities of mind and body which the Rugby game, when properly played, is calculated to encourage, and of which readiness to merge one's own personal interests with those of others is one of the finest, were prominently displayed in the brief but brilliant career of Dr. Huggan. . . . We are proud that our club has had such a hero in its ranks, and I am sure our gallant friends of the Black Watch " (a company of the Black Watch, under Major Murray-Stewart, were at the time stationed at Jedburgh) " will appreciate the opportunity of being associated with us on this interesting occasion. . . . The presence of the portrait on the walls of our pavilion will remind us, and those who

SEC.-LIEUT. DAVID DUCHIE HOWIE, R.F.A.
Photo : Rettie, Kirkcaldy

come after us, of a popular and distinguished Jed Forest player, and a brave gentleman."

In a letter in a London newspaper, Sir Robert Corbet, Bart., of the Coldstream Guards, wrote :—

" Lieutenant Huggan was medical officer to my battalion at the Front. His duty was always to be with them, and, when in action, to give first aid to the wounded. This in nearly every case meant working under fire. I myself have seen Lieutenant Huggan binding up wounded men when the battalion were retiring during a rearguard action, and apparently left to the mercy of the enemy. He was, however, picked up by a passing ambulance, but it was only just luck. I think this may go to show that the duties of the R.A.M.C. officer are those calling for both bravery and coolness. I deeply regret to see Lieutenant Huggan's death reported ; he was one of the many gallant fellows who gave their lives to save others, and in so doing earned undying glory."

To Lieutenant J. L. Huggan's brother, Lieutenant-Colonel G. Fielding, Commanding 3rd Battalion Coldstream Guards, wrote a letter containing the following details of his heroic end :—

" If ever I met a brave man, he was. At Landrecies, when under a heavy fire for some hours during the night, he remained up in the front all night, helping and dressing the wounded as coolly as if he was in a hospital in time of peace. At Villers Cotterets he was conspicuous for his bravery. This was a rearguard action, and the line was being gradually pushed back ; but he was always in the rear, and sometimes even nearer to the enemy, dressing the wounded and helping them back. At the Aisne he was most conspicuous everywhere. On the day on which he was killed he again did a very brave action. There were in a barn about sixty wounded Germans—they were all cases that could not move without help. The Germans shelled this barn and set it on fire. Your brother, in spite of shot and shell raining about him, called for volunteers to help him to save these wounded men from the burning building, and I am glad to say that it was greatly in consequence of his bravery that they were all saved. After he had run this great danger successfully, he moved many of his wounded men to a quarry in rear, when a big shell came into it and killed him and many others. He was buried near where he fell, in the garden of La Cour de Soupir Farm. The whole battalion regretted his loss, as we had all got very fond of him, and admired him as a really brave man, always ready to sacrifice himself for the good of those who should happen to come under him for treatment."

Huggan was the second Rugby International to fall in this War.

WILLIAM RAMSAY HUTCHISON

CAPTAIN WILLIAM RAMSAY HUTCHISON, 6/7th Royal Scots Fusiliers, was killed in France on March 22, 1918. He was born in Glasgow on January 16, 1889, and was therefore in his thirtieth year. He was educated at the famous Glasgow High School, and before leaving in 1905 he captained the School Rugby Team. After his school days were over he played for his old boys' team from 1905 to 1911, being Captain in the season of 1908-9. In his earlier days he was a half-back, but in 1909 he began to play as a forward, with such success that in 1911 he not only represented Glasgow in the Inter-City Match with Edinburgh, but was given his Scottish Cap against England in the same season. This was the only International game in which he took part, but no doubt others would have come his way had he not left Scotland for Canada. He was a hard-working forward, whose long experience of play outside the scrummage was invaluable to him in big matches; and though he was on the losing side in his only International game, the defeat could not be laid to his charge.

LIEUT. JAMES LAIDLAW HUGGAN, R.A.M.C.
Photo: Davis, Edinburgh

When war broke out Hutchison was home on holiday from Montreal, and he joined the 17th H.L.I. in September 1914. After some training he was given a Commission in the Royal Scots Fusiliers, and underwent further instruction at Salisbury, Bristol, and Chelsea. His first active service was in France, whence he was sent to Salonika. He was invalided home after being wounded, and on recovery returned to France, and was stationed at Arras. He was killed in action on the second day of the big German offensive of March 1918. A brother officer writes: " He was my company commander, and the two of us were together during the first two days of the great German push. A critical moment had been reached on the afternoon of the second day. With one half of the company I started to dig a line of defence, while Captain Hutchison, with the other half, went forward on my right to form a strong post. Machine-gun fire was intense, and he was hit when he had gone forward about a quarter of an hour."

Captain Hutchison was a first-class golfer, and while in Canada figured with success in Amateur Championship competitions. Like most good all-round games-men, his was a very popular personality, and he will long be remembered in Scottish and Glasgow Rugby circles.

" *Multis ille bonis flebilis occidit.*"

RUPERT EDWARD INGLIS

REV. RUPERT EDWARD INGLIS, Temporary Chaplain to the Forces, attached 16th Infantry Brigade, 6th Division (consisting of 1st Buffs, 1st King's Shropshire Light Infantry, 2nd Yorks and Lancs Regiment, and 8th Bedfords), was killed while helping to bring in wounded near Ginchy, France, at the Battle of the

Somme on September 18, 1916, aged 53. Mr. Inglis was born on May 17, 1863, the youngest son of the late Sir John Inglis, Defender of Lucknow, and of the late Hon. Lady Inglis. He was educated at Rugby School from 1877–81, and at University College, Oxford, 1882–85. He played for Rugby School XV. in 1879 and 1880, and for the XI. in 1881. He played for Oxford *v.* Cambridge in 1883 and 1884, Oxford winning both matches at Blackheath by 3 goals and 4 tries to 1 goal, and by 3 goals and 1 try to 1 try respectively. Continuing his Rugby football education in the Blackheath pack of nine forwards, R. E. Inglis played for Middlesex, and for South *v.* North at Bradford in 1885. This was followed by his three English International Caps against, in turn, Wales, Ireland, and Scotland in 1886, England winning the first two at Blackheath and Dublin, and drawing the third, no score, at Edinburgh. Mr. Inglis was ordained in 1899 by the Bishop of Beverley, and became Rector of Firthenden, Kent, in that year. I have no record of his football career after 1886, but it is known that he was one of the best forwards playing in the three International games of 1886.

Rev. R. E. Inglis, C.F., volunteered for service, and went to France on July 5, 1915. He went first to No. 23 General Hospital, Etaples; thence to No. 21 Casualty Clearing Station, and in December 1915 joined the 16th Infantry Brigade, 6th Division, remaining with them until his gallant death the following September. Regarding which I have been allowed to quote the following letters from officers of the Brigade :—

Wednesday, September 20, 1916.

"On Monday afternoon, about 3.15, whilst searching for wounded, who had been lying out for several days, he was hit by a shell and killed instantly. . . . Whilst his Brigade (and Division) had been in the big fight he had been acting rather as a free lance—making his quarters back at the transport lines, and going up for longish spells to help with the wounded at the Ad-

REV. RUPERT EDWARD INGLIS, C.F.
Att. 16th Infantry Brigade

Photo : L'Estrange, London

vanced Dressing Stations near the line. One attack,* which his Brigade and others in the Division made last Friday, was unsuccessful, with the result that at nightfall our line was behind the ground over which the troops had to advance. This meant that many wounded had to be left out—some of them, at any rate, until on Monday morning the ground was won by a successful attack. I think that he joined in efforts that were made previous to the successful attack to rescue wounded by night. . . . He had evidently been working rather as a free lance, and had helped in the finding of wounded belonging not only to his own battalion, but to others in the Division. I cannot overstate the sorrow there is to-day in the Brigade. 'They simply loved him,' so said several officers and men in the Shropshires to me to-day."

Colonel Murray, Commanding 1st K.S.L.I., wrote as follows:—

" None knew his worth more than we did, as he had lived with us for so long. One of the bravest men I have ever met, and we see many here, he gave his life to help others. . . . He always was much upset about wounded having to lie out any time, and he had worked day and night to help them. . . ."

And from General C. Ross, Major-General Commanding 6th Division, came this striking tribute:—

" He was killed while bravely attending the wounded under heavy shell-fire. He had already been recommended for the Military Cross for gallantry, and had he lived his name would again have been sent in. His loss is a personal one to all officers and men of the 16th Infantry Brigade, and indeed of the whole

* The attack referred to was against a strong point called The Quadrilateral, and the Field of Honour where he fell, and was buried, is thus described on the map: " Near, but 50 yards north of the junction of the Ginchy-Combles railway with the road running east of Ginchy and west of the trench running north of the junction. The map reference is France, Sheet 57 C. S. W. T. 14 d. 8.9."

Division. He died nobly doing his duty and setting a striking example to others."

Indeed, the mere fact of his volunteering at the age of fifty-one is eloquent of the manner of man this splendid Old Rugbeian was. The last years of his life make of the Rev. R. E. Inglis, C.F., a man to be envied by us all.

PERCY DALE KENDALL

LIEUTENANT PERCY DALE KENDALL, 10th Battalion King's Liverpool Regiment (Liverpool Scottish), was killed in action near Ypres on January 25, 1915, aged 36. Born at Prescot on August 21, 1878, Kendall was educated at Elleray, New Brighton; at Tonbridge School (1890-96); and Trinity Hall, Cambridge. Like a few others he was an International who never got his Blue, though at a university. He was in the Tonbridge XV. of 1895, but at Cambridge actually received no trial! Six seasons later he played half for England v. Scotland, at Blackheath, in 1901; for England v. Wales, at Blackheath, 1902 (Oughtred's match!); and then again against Scotland in 1903, this time as Captain, a rare honour for any one in his third International match, at Richmond. He was not fated to be on the winning side, though this seemed certain at Blackheath in 1902, but an unfortunate mistake, when England were leading by 8 points to 6, with only two or three minutes to go, gave Wales the game by a penalty goal and 2 tries to 1 goal and 1 try, or 9 points to 8. Kendall played for Blackheath and for the Barbarians, but his " football home " was at Birkenhead Park, for which club he played for a great number of years, finishing his playing career as a member of that Club's third XV., in the last season before the War, when that XV. had an unbeaten season and scored over 500 points. Kendall's keen play and sagacious advice while thus " teaching the young idea how to shoot " would have borne fruit but for the War.

LIEUT. PERCY DALE KENDALL
10th Batt. King's Liverpool Regiment (Liverpool Scottish)

Photo: Lankaster, Tunbridge Wells

He was then thirty-five years of age, but could not be surpassed for keenness. In county football "Toggie" Kendall played in forty-five matches for Cheshire, scoring 10 tries for the county. He played for the North in 1900, and again in 1901 and 1903, and it was his form in the first of these three games which won him his International Cap. He was a very good scrum-half without being brilliant, slowness being his fault. On this score I have the opinion of a well-known International, who knew him and his game well. He writes:—

"Kendall was at Tonbridge, and got into the XV. in 1895. He went to Cambridge, but did not receive a trial. He was in the English XV.'s of 1901, 1902, and 1903, and was Captain in 1903. He was very slow; but it was soon seen that he would be a player, so he was told to use the skipping-rope to make himself quicker. This he did, and when I asked him in 1914 whether he still kept up his skipping he said, 'Rather so, and I make my men do so too.' He was always a very plucky and determined player, and was an excellent scrum-half. He never gave up hope and played to the finish. His end was typical of his life."

How typical, perhaps, even my friend did not know, for, when war was declared Birkenhead Park was the first club in the United Kingdom of any game to make the necessary move. *This they did on August* 5, 1914, the club ground and pavilion being offered to the military authorities, and "Toggie" Kendall going off into camp with the Liverpool Scottish, which he rejoined the same day; while J. Baxter (Birkenhead Park and England), Rugby Union Committee-man and Selection Committee-man, went afloat in the R.N.R., and served afloat to the end. For instant patriotism the act of the Birkenhead Park Rugby Union Football Club, through its officials, and chiefly the late Lieutenant P. D. Kendall and Lieutenant J. Baxter, R.N.R., stands out as the most brilliant example on record. They did what they did *within twelve hours of the declaration of war* on Germany.

On October 14, 1914, Kendall received his commission, and went with his regiment to France on November 1, 1914. He was shot in the trenches on the following January 25th, and lies at rest close to the late Lieutenant F. H. Turner, in Kemmel Churchyard, Belgium. Popularity is scarcely the word to be used when writing about such a man as P. D. Kendall. The feeling his fellow-players and men have for such a man is a regard amounting almost to love. One such who could claim his friendship has penned for me the following brief, and as he feels quite inadequate, appreciation. The writer is the well-known Old Haileyburian, T. H. E. Baillie :—

"If it may be said with truth of any man that his friends were legion, that man was P. D. Kendall. At an age when none could have blamed him for remaining at his own responsible work, he at once, like all good Rugger men, chose to be with his friends in the Supreme Task. After serving in the trenches he was gazetted Second-Lieutenant in the same regiment, and within a few days of being commissioned was killed by a chance ricochet. 'Toggie' was one whose whole-hearted, energetic, and unselfish game none who played with him will ever forget. Nor will the younger players, whom, as a veteran, he encouraged by his advice and unfeigned interest, ever forget his unquenchable cheerfulness and delightful companionship. The 'Park' has lost sorely in the War, and those who are left must see that the colours Kendall and others honoured by their standard of play are carried on worthily of their memories."

That this will be done needs no saying. Birkenhead Park has by its deeds on August 5, 1914, created a very proud record to live up to, and the generations of its members to come will show themselves worthy of the splendid man who was one of the chief movers in the making of that record. They cannot do more. It would be unfair to Kendall's memory to even think of doing less.

JOHN ABBOTT KING

LANCE-CORPORAL JOHN ABBOTT KING, 1/10th Liverpool Scottish, was killed in action at Guillemont on August 9, 1916. He was at first reported " missing," but was afterwards " officially presumed " to have been killed. He enlisted on August 6, 1914, as a trooper in the Yorkshire Hussars, and went into training at Hitchin. In April 1915 he went to France, and received rapid promotion to Lance-Corporal and then Corporal, but was transferred at his own request to the Liverpool Scottish as a private. He was soon promoted to Lance-Corporal again.

Born at Leeds on August 21, 1883, King was educated at Giggleswick School, Settle, Yorkshire, from 1897-99. While there he obtained his 2nd XV. colours. He lived in South Africa from 1903-5, playing for the Durbanville and Somerset West Clubs. Returning to England in 1906, he played regularly for Headingley and for Yorkshire, in whose County XV. he was for several seasons the most consistently good forward, and was probably at his best before he was chosen to play for England, which he did in every match from 1910-13, except England v. France at Paris in 1912.

Although I had always the very highest opinion of and admiration for Jack King as a man and a player, I never summed him up so succinctly as did that fine judge of Rugby football, F. J. Sellicks, himself one of Devon's best forwards in his day. His view is: "King was the very best type of amateur—sheer love of the game." As this sturdy Yorkshire patriot was a farmer in a small way upon the slopes of Ben Rhydding, the full value of this kind appreciation will be better understood by Rugby men than by others. The almost indecent haste with which King answered the call was typical of the man and of his race. It was certainly typical of his game, for a feeling of disappointment used to come over spectators if in the thickest of scrums and rough and tumbles of every game in which he played this tough little Yorkshireman was not the central figure. He had trained onlookers to expect this, so that his enlistment within forty-eight hours of our declaration on Germany was the most natural thing for him to do. To him nothing but Duty mattered. So the farm was just handed over to his three sisters, who, with the truest courage, took it over, and have managed it ever since (willing hands among Yorkshire's Rugby football players on leave having helped with the harvest when possible), and Jack King went forth to fight. I well remember how irksome he found the seemingly long spell of training, and that this must have worried him again when in France, as a cavalryman, we see, by his exchange to the infantry " at his own request," giving up rank in order to repeat his habits of the football field and be once more in the thick of it. Every one felt that in trench warfare there was only one thing for Jack King, and that was to be in a front position when the order was given to go over the top.

From one of his intimates comes the following appreciation of Jack King. It is from the pen of the Secretary of the Yorkshire Rugby Union :—

" ' Well played, King—played indeed, Sir ! ! ! '

" How those critical but delightful Twickenham crowds cheered the great little man! And how the breasts of that little but enthusiastic crowd of 'Headingley' and Yorkshire supporters used to swell with a mighty—and a perfectly justifiable—pride, at the great doings of their idolized ' Jack ' King!

" But I wonder how many of those great International crowds of Twickenham, Inverleith, Lansdowne Road, Cardiff, Newport, and Swansea, who were both so astounded and so delighted at the unflinching pluck and great play of this boy, had even the remotest conception of the true greatness of this player ? I don't mean their knowledge of his prowess as a player, but of the greatness of a soulful man ? ' *Mens sana in corpore sano* ' was

LANCE-CORPORAL JOHN ABBOTT KING
10th Batt. Liverpool Regiment

Photo: Bacon, Leeds

never more fitly applied to any man than to Jack King. The 4th August, 1914, is too indelibly inscribed on the tablets of every Briton's memory to be more than casually mentioned here. At that time, and for a few weeks prior to this never-to-be-forgotten day, Jack King had staying with him at his farm at Ben Rhydding, one of his 'Headingley' footer friends, T. D. Lumb—a rare good forward, who, like a great many of the 'Headingley' players, has made the supreme sacrifice. 'Busty' Lumb and Jack were busy haymaking when the former's mobilization papers were handed to him, Lumb being already an enthusiastic Territorial in the Yorkshire Hussars of some years standing. 'Sorry, Jack,' said Lumb, 'but I'll have to chuck now, pack up, and make a bee line for headquarters; we are called up.' Before he left, Jack had just time to make a few inquiries from his friend Lumb as to the mode of procedure *re* joining the Yorkshire Hussars, 'for,' added Jack, 'I intend to come with you.'

"Without fuss or show, and with a few instructions to his sisters as to the management of the farm, Jack King left his home on the morning of Thursday, August 9, 1914, for the headquarters of the Yorkshire Hussars,—never for one moment dreaming, in face of the imperative call of King and Country, that he would have anything but a clean walk, straight in, to this famous Yorkshire Regiment. Jack got his first shock that day: 'Sorry, King,' said the Recruiting Officer, when Jack presented himself, 'but I'm afraid we cannot take you.' 'For why?' inquired King. 'Because,' answered the R.O., 'the Army Regulations state the minimum height to be 5 feet 6 inches—you are only five foot five ! ! !' Jack had reckoned without a thorough knowledge of the King's Regulations !

"For a moment he was completely nonplussed and upset; but quickly recovering himself, he threw out that 45-inch chest of his, and said, 'Well, I've come purposely here to join the same regiment as my friend Lumb, and I'm simply going to stick here until you do take me in !'

"Whether or not Jack managed to grow that extra inch in the three days he waited is not officially stated, but the Military Records show that Jack King became a trooper in his Britannic Majesty's Army on August 12, 1914! This is just one little sidelight of a great many similar instances of love and duty in the life of this famous International.

"Here is another equally true, to which I can personally testify, and one which casts even a greater halo round the memory of this noble-hearted boy. The Yorkshire Hussars, in common with the greater part of the Cavalry in France, at this particular period, were chiefly engaged in patrol and police duty. This by no means appealed to the big heart and active mind of Jack, and after a few months of this kind of work he became very restive, as his frequent letters to me clearly showed, and he began to chafe and fret ' to be more of a soldier ' as he put it ; so he must needs try and get transferred to an infantry regiment. Meeting one day while in France a lot of old Rugby friends, who were members of the 1/10th Liverpool Scottish Regiment—amongst whom was the famous old English forward, L. A. N. Slocock—nothing would satisfy Jack but that he must, somehow or other, join them. Application for his transfer was immediately made. In due course his papers came through, and from that time until the fateful August 9, 1916, he was known in the Army as Lance-Corporal J. A. King, ' X ' Company, 1/10th Liverpool Scottish. Yes, of his own free will, he preferred to share the hard lot of the infantryman in those horrifying, waterlogged, knee-deep mud trenches to the comparatively easier lot and safety of police duty behind the lines. But that was just Jack King. His sense of duty was always such that he steadfastly refused to allow any other considerations to influence him.

"August 9, 1916, was a sad day for the 1/10th Liverpool Scottish. Three times that day did they attempt to take Guillemont, and three times were they repulsed, the flower of this grand Regiment going down before the hellish machine-gun fire of the

Boche. It is a date sacred to every living member of the 'Headingley' Club. Jack King's career as a soldier—just a simple soldier (he refused to listen to any suggestion that he should take up a commission)—was marked by those same traits which had endeared him to all his football friends—brimful of mirth, kind, loving, generous, and absolutely unselfish, ever keen and anxious to do his very utmost in whatever he took in hand; living to do what he died for—duty, nobly done!

"Perhaps if these lines meet the eye of Colonel Davidson, of the 1/10th Liverpool Scottish, he will forgive the liberty I take of quoting a part of an exceedingly kind and sympathetic letter he was good enough to write the Misses King at the time Jack was reported missing:—

"'It is hardly necessary for me to testify to his conduct at such a time—any one who knew your brother would know that he could always be relied upon to play the man. When I saw him, absolutely cool and collected, under a murderous machine-gun fire, with shells falling all round, one thanked God for such a man to set such a priceless example. He was absolutely lion-hearted, and had he come through, I should have promoted him on the field, and recommended him for the D.C.M. It was a sad day for football. We can ill spare men like these; but if another game of football is never played in Britain, the game has done well, for after two years' Command in the Field, I am convinced that the Rugby Footballer makes the finest soldier in the world.'

"What a noble tribute to a noble boy! And can a greater tribute be paid to this fine manly game than that paid to it by this very boy, in a letter written to the writer of this short appreciation just before 'going over the top' for the last time?—a letter which I deeply treasure:—

"'I am absolutely A1 in every way. But one can never tell, and so long as I don't disgrace the old Rugby game, I don't think I mind.'

"Jack King disgrace the Rugby game!! No, never!!!

"A few others may, perhaps, have ascended to higher heights on the football field, but none certainly have ever outshone Jack King in his love for this, the greatest of all games—our beloved Rugger. Perhaps Jack King's greatest charm was his modesty in all things. Not that he was insensible to the wonderful homage paid to him by his many friends and admirers. Far from it, for he had a deep sense of appreciation. But it is equally certain that he never looked for acknowledgement—never imagined himself, or wished others to imagine, that he had done anything more meritorious, either on a football field or when he gave his life for his Country, than the veriest third teamer, or the rawest recruit.

"And, to-day? Not a cheer! Not a flower or a Cross to mark the sacred spot where this hero fell! Jack King would not have it otherwise. But his memory is enshrined in the hearts of all his 'Headingley' and Yorkshire friends. The glorious part he has played is the manifestation of Britain's Soul. He has joined that noble band which has helped to save the world. He now knows the reason of it all.

"Yes, truly, 'Well played, King; played indeed, Sir.'"

> "So you'll live, you'll live, Young Fellow My Lad,
> In the gleam of the evening star,
> In the wood note wild and the laugh of the child,
> In all sweet things that are.
> And you'll never die, my wonderful boy,
> While life is noble and true;
> For all our beauty, and hope and joy,
> We will owe to our lads like you."

"*November* 1917.

"R. F. OAKES."

RONALD OWEN LAGDEN

CAPTAIN RONALD OWEN LAGDEN, 4th Battalion King's Royal Rifle Corps, was killed in action at St. Eloi on March 1, 1915, aged 25. Born at Maseru, Basutoland, South Africa, on November 21, 1889, Lagden was educated at Mr. Pellatt's School, Swanage (1901-3), at Marlborough College (1903-8), and at Oriel College, Oxford (1908-12). When he left Marlborough in 1908 he had, as the *Marlburian* put it, "been in most things for three years, and had captained the Hockey XI. He was Rackets representative for two years, and had also won the Champion Cup. Of course he was in the XI. as a hitter and fast bowler, and he began his Rugby football career as a half-back for his House, whence he was thrust into the school scrum. Up at Oxford he played four years at Lord's, only once on the losing side (and then his brother, R. B., made 61 for Cambridge), and three times, 1909-10-11, at Queen's Club, Oxford winning all three matches—the same three in which Poulton Palmer played for Oxford. Lagden played Hockey for the 'Varsity 1909-12, and represented them at Rackets in 1909. All this time he gazed on life from serious but such straight and kindly eyes, reading Science and taking Honours in Chemistry. Not long after going down he became a Master at Harrow, and was soon Master in charge of the Headmaster's House." Meanwhile, he had played for England *v.* Scotland in the first of the Calcutta Cup matches played at Twickenham, and was one of the best forwards in a game in which there were many good ones. A "knee" stopped his active interest in Rugby football, or he would have had very many International caps, for he was a dashing and strong forward, doing everything with great earnestness. He played this glorious game of ours to the full on the following lines: "So, it is up to every boy at every school which is a nursery for new generations of Internationals to remember that there is in Rugby football something noble that counts for more than winning goals and points." Noble words these—and they were penned by Lagden's father, Sir Godfrey Lagden, K.C.M.G. How well the son gave expression on the field of play to the sentiments so well and truly put by the father some time before the War.

War was in Lagden's blood. He, as a boy, saw some frontier

fighting in the South African War, and was always, perhaps in consequence of that experience, a keen soldier. Thus he served in three O.T.C. contingents, actually giving up several long vacations to undergo military training, so that directly war was declared he joined the 6th Battalion K.R.R.C. at Sheerness, a ready-made soldier. He was very soon a captain, his C.O. early describing him as "a first-rate officer," and he went to France in February 1915, actually leading the night attack in which he fell on the last day of that month.

His was a very brave death. His last efforts for King and Country are described in an official report: "He behaved with the utmost gallantry," wrote his C.O., "and his Company did all that was humanly possible." A survivor, who saw him fall, says he was well away in front, and was the first man to fall: "I went and offered help, but he told me to go with my men; then I saw him get up and struggle forward, but he was again wounded and fell." Speaking of R. O. Lagden and his friend Charles Eyre, the Harrovian, Cambridge, and Yorkshire cricketer, who was killed about the same time, and who was a Master at Harrow with Lagden, the Rev. Lionel Ford, Headmaster of Harrow, said in the course of his sermon at the Memorial Service at Harrow on October 3, 1915: "They are a band of brothers who, from the light of the other world, are beckoning us along. They see! They know! They would sweep us onward to the Light."

Those who knew Ronny Lagden ever so slightly—and I am proud to have had that great privilege—can picture his fighting bravely, in spite of wounds, during those terrible moments on the German parapet when, as I have been told on good authority, the fire was hellish. They see him fall; they see him gather breath and strength for another go at the common enemy. of mankind; they see him rise and try again, spurred on by that indomitable spirit which has made our race what it is, and which, in the persons of men like him, receives its highest form of expression, and then—

CAPTAIN RONALD OWEN LAGDEN
4th Batt. King's Royal Rifle Corps
Photo: Saunders, Harrow

"falling, fling to the host behind—
Play up! play up! and play the game!"

Lagden's must have been a fighting finish, game and true to the last breath, a glorious example to generations of Rugby men and Britons yet to come.

DOUGLAS LAMBERT

LIEUTENANT DOUGLAS LAMBERT, 6th Battalion the Buffs, was killed in action near Loos on October 13, 1915, aged 32. Born on October 4, 1883, at Cranbrook, Kent, Lambert was educated at St. Edward's, Oxford, and at Eastbourne College. He was in the XI. and the XV. at Eastbourne, beginning his football career as a forward in the first game of Rugby football ever played at Eastbourne College, which had just gone over from the Association game. It was soon discovered that the three-quarter line was his proper place; and from that date there he remained, to become one of the fastest wings who ever played Rugby, and certainly one of the most prolific try-getters in Club football ever seen. With John Birkett at left centre to him, the pair became the most famous wing in Club football in the United Kingdom; and though there was sometimes more than a suspicion of Lambert overrunning his centre, and taking the final pass when looking over his right shoulder for it—few referees were fast enough to be up with them!—the number of fair and square tries this pair scored was legion. Of Lambert, his fellow Harlequin, F. M. Stoop, has written to me:—

"As you probably know, he was also a very useful performer at Soccer, golf, and, although he seldom played cricket, yet he was no mean performer as a wicket-keeper, which was perhaps not surprising, as he had a wonderful eye and very safe hands. I don't think I have ever played with any player nearly so good as 'Daniel' at taking a pass anywhere within reach and going at top speed. One season when Birkett was crocked, I played inside to him most of the time, and I can honestly say that he gave me more confidence than any one I have ever played with. One had only to half draw the defence and give him a ghost of an opening and he scored every time. I remember one occasion during this season when he scored 32 points out of 35, and converted all the goals himself. I believe I am right in stating this. I am not sure of the year, but believe we were playing the London Irish."

Another regular member of the Harlequins in their most famous days, Captain W. F. Hill, writes me :—

"Douglas Lambert, affectionately known as 'Daniel' to all his friends, was probably the most discussed player of his day; but whatever his merits as a player, as a man no more popular fellow stepped. He was educated at Eastbourne College, which, at the time he went there, was a Soccer school, but changed to Rugger about half-way through his time at school. The result of his early training was that Lambert was always a useful Soccer player, and once, at least, he played for the Corinthians. He joined the Harlequins in 1903, and for two seasons played in their 'A' team with only occasional appearances for the 1st XV., at that time under the captaincy of the old Oxford and England forward, C. E. L. Hammond. The season 1905–6 saw a great change in the fortunes of the 'Quins; A. D. Stoop, having come down from Oxford, turned out regularly; H. J. H. Sibree developed his abilities as a scrum-half; J. G. G. Birkett joined the team; and Lambert, developing his pace, settled down as wing three-quarter, thus starting his association with Johnnie Birkett as one of the most brilliant of club wings. To some extent Lambert was a player of moods; but, generally speaking, with his long stride, he was one of the fastest players of his time, and a great try-getter. His great pace often took him right away from his own side, and if he had no room to run round a full-back he sometimes hesitated,

LIEUT. DOUGLAS LAMBERT
6th Batt. the Buffs

and got collared while waiting for his own side to come up. This led to what I believe was an unfounded accusation—that he didn't like being collared. While knowing the game thoroughly Lambert trusted almost entirely to his great pace, and had not got the swerve of Jack Raphael, or a hand off like Basil Maclear. His International career was a chequered one, as he was never absolutely certain of his place in the English team, and this undoubtedly affected him. The most tries he scored in one International game was five or six against France; the most in one match, seven for the Harlequins *v.* Marlborough Nomads. He played regularly for Middlesex and skippered them for three seasons, resigning the captaincy owing to the increasing claims of business. In addition to his try-scoring abilities, he was a first-class place-kicker. Harlequin footer was what he loved, and it is probable that as a player he will be remembered chiefly in connection with Birkett as a great club wing. As a man he will be always remembered by those who had the fortune to know him as a most lovable and modest personality."

It is curious, in the light of what this famous old Harlequin forward terms the " unfounded accusation " of hesitation brought against Lambert, that practically the same thing was written about his play at Eastbourne College by a good judge of the game who had seen it *ab initio*, and made the criticism many years ago. Personally, I should say he often hesitated even in his best days; but when a wing gets at all cornered, as in this game is happily inevitable even for the best of them, it is very difficult indeed for a man of Lambert's pace, width of stride and stature, to get out of the difficulty without appearing to hesitate. The small wing, like E. T. Morgan, C. N. Lowe, or F. E. Chapman, can, and does, change step and direction half as quickly again as a Lambert, and yet hesitates equally with the big man. It was a physical impossibility for a player of Lambert's stride and running action to appear other than he did when at all cornered, or when he had outpaced his fellows and was on the horns of the dilemma, whether to punt, to pass, or to run on.

Of the Harlequin team at its best, which Lambert adorned, the following have fallen: R. W. Poulton Palmer, W. B. Grandage, T. Allen, R. O. C. Ward, Æ. Q. Perkins, and D. H. Tripp. Tripp was wounded several times, won the D.S.O., and returned again and again to the fight. H. E. Ward was taken prisoner in 1914. A. D. Stoop was slightly wounded in Mesopotamia. F. M. Stoop was wounded in France; H. J. H. Sibree was wounded in France; K. M. Carnduff was wounded in France; G. Maxwell-Dove was wounded and incurred trench-feet; G. H. Bickley, L. Field, M.C., A. H. Hudson, and G. B. Hudson, who played occasionally, have all fallen; W. F. Hill was wounded in 1915; G. H. Birkett, brother of J. G. G., was wounded; and I. R. B. Bond, who played occasionally, has won the Military Cross. It is a proud record indeed, and the 'Quins, like all other crack Rugby clubs, have proved that to lead in Rugby football connotes leadership in war.

Douglas Lambert leaves a widow and a son, who was born two months after his father's death. That he may become as fine a Rugby player and all-round athlete as his famous father, all who remember that great scoring wing will cordially hope. His is no easy path, though he has a grand example to live up to.

G. A. W. LAMOND

LIEUTENANT-COLONEL G. A. W. LAMOND, Royal Engineers, died at Colombo on February 25, 1918, aged 39. "Geo" Lamond, as he was familiarly known to his friends, was educated at Kelvinside Academy, and was trained as a Civil Engineer in the offices of Messrs. Formans and M'Call, C.E. After serving his apprenticeship he was engaged with the firm of Sir John Aird, Public Works Contractors, both at home and in Egypt, where he was engaged in the construction of the two famous Nile barrages at Esnah, and Assiut and Assuan. In connection with these works, he was decorated with the Orders of the Medjidieh and Osmanieh by the Egyptian and Turkish Governments.

As a lad he was given his place at three-quarter in the Kelvinside Academical XV. in 1895, when only sixteen; and along with Mr. J. T. Tulloch, later President of the Scottish Football Union, had much to do in raising this team to fame in the late nineties. He played centre in the Inter-City and in the Cities team against the Rest of Scotland in 1896, wing in these fixtures in 1897, and again centre for Glasgow in the Inter-City of 1898. In 1899 he won the first of his three International Caps in the Scottish team against Wales, when his partner in the centre was the Rev. H. T. S. Gedge. Characteristics of his play were his skill in drop-kicking with either foot when running at top speed, and his knack of making openings for and feeding his wings. These qualities served him well in his first International, when he dropped the goal which put Scotland ahead of Wales, and had much to do with her victory. He played against England in the same year, but was lost to his country for some time on his profession taking him to Egypt. Returning to England in 1902, when he was employed upon the construction of the King Edward Dock at Avonmouth, he played centre for Bristol City for three years, being Captain of the team, as also of the Gloucester County team. During this period he played against all the leading Welsh clubs; for the Anglo-Scots against the South of Scotland; and for the Cities against the Rest of Scotland, gaining his third International Cap in 1905, when Scotland, after a disastrous season, defeated England at Richmond. Once again his work took him to Egypt, and he retired from Rugby football. During his short vacations at home he proved himself a good tennis player, a more than useful golfer, playing from scratch, and in 1913 taking part in the Amateur Championship of that year at St. Andrews; while some of the lochs and streams, which his brother knows so well, knew his prowess too with the rod among the salmon and sea-trout.

At the outbreak of war he returned home, and after being employed on Government work on Salisbury Plain, he was given a commission in the Royal Engineers, and saw a lot of strenuous service in France, where he was rapidly promoted. In 1917 he was sent to Mesopotamia with the rank of Lieutenant-Colonel, and was on the Staff there in charge of the construction and organization of the new port and works on the twin rivers, being mentioned in Sir Stanley Maude's dispatches. Invalided, after suffering from the fevers prevalent in that country, to Colombo, his resources did not suffice to pull him through an attack of pneumonia. Colonel Lamond was married some six years ago, and is survived by his wife.

SEPTIMUS HEYNS LEDGER

SERGEANT SEPTIMUS HEYNS LEDGER, 2nd Battalion South African Infantry, was reported wounded and missing at the Battle of Arras on April 13, 1917, aged 27. Accepted as dead by O.C. Records, January 30, 1918. Born at Kimberley on April 29, 1889, Ledger was educated at Boys' High School, Kimberley. He played for Griqualand West from 1908-14, in the Currie Cup Tournament; and on tour in the United Kingdom he played for the second South African team, W. A. Millar's, against Scotland, England, Ireland, and France. He was one of the best of the forwards of that team, being quite good enough to make the selectors of the International teams on that tour (W. A. Millar, E. J. Dobbin, and Max Honnet) feel that they had made a mistake when they left him out. This they did only in the game against Wales, Ledger playing in the other three. He was a strapping forward of the big-boned sort; good out of touch and handier in the loose rushes than men of his build sometimes are.

SERGEANT SEPTIMUS HEYNS LEDGER
2nd Batt. South African Infantry

BRINLEY RICHARD LEWIS

I had a chat with him when he was at the Old Deer Park, Richmond, in the winter of 1916, and took that opportunity of taking the accompanying photograph, the last taken of him in football kit. His game seemed as good as ever, and he was always in the vicinity of the ball. On the whole, certainly in the first fifteen forwards of the two lots South Africa sent us in 1906-7, and again six years later, and a thoroughly good fellow to boot.

Ledger joined his regiment in September 1915, and sailed for England the following month. He went to the Front after about a year's training at Borden Camp.

Details of his death have been furnished me direct from his native town. In a letter to a relative there, a N.C.O. of Ledger's regiment stated that he " was wounded and dropped, rose again and went on, but was again wounded. He tried then to crawl into a shell-hole, but was then apparently killed and buried by the same shell." But upon this no official news has been received in South Africa.

BRINLEY RICHARD LEWIS

MAJOR BRINLEY RICHARD LEWIS, R.F.A., was killed in action on the Ypres front on April 2, 1917, aged 26. Born at Pontardawe, Glamorganshire, on January 4, 1891, Lewis was educated at Swansea Grammar School and Trinity Hall, Cambridge. He was Captain of his School Rugby team, and took the maximum number of prizes allowed at his School Sports in both those years. He played for the Swansea XV. when seventeen years old, and appeared in that team regularly during his vacations and after coming down finally from Cambridge. He played for Cambridge against Oxford in 1909-10-11, and would have played in 1912, when he was Secretary of the C.U.R.U.F.C., but for an accident. At various intervals he played for London Welsh and the Barbarians. He got his Welsh Cap against Ireland in 1912 and 1913;

but it was a very serious feature of his football career, and quite unaccountable to Englishmen and especially Cambridge men, that his powers were not appreciated by the Welsh authorities as they ought to have been. Any number of wings played for Wales during the period 1910–13 who were never in Lewis's class in any branch of wing three-quarter play. He had splendid hands, true football pace, pluck, neat kicking ability, without ever approaching greatness in this respect, and he knew the game. He was the best wing of his day in Wales who could boast only a couple of International Caps.

When war broke out Lewis enlisted as a trooper in the Glamorgan Yeomanry, preferring to begin at the beginning; and it is well to know that he met with his reward, as he became a Second-Lieutenant in March 1915, and was promoted on the field for distinguished conduct from subaltern to Major in November 1916, and was mentioned in dispatches in April 1916. He was never a Captain in the Army. He was killed by a shell, and not only Welshmen and Cantabs will long remember the natty little wing whose brisk and clever play was, on nearly every occasion, a feature of the match he was playing in.

The following brief extracts from letters written by his brother officers bear testimony to the esteem in which he was held:—

"He was a very excellent and rising officer," wrote Brigadier-General W. A. M. Thompson, R.A., "and his influence for good was very marked. I knew him well personally, and have always had the highest opinion of him as a soldier, as well as a great respect for his character. He was a very young Battery Commander, and was selected for that responsible position on account of his good work, which he had done at all times."

And again, from Lieutenant-Colonel W. L. E. Rudkin, D.S.O., 122nd Brigade, R.F.A.:—

"He was such a splendid fellow, and he cannot be replaced.

MAJOR BRINLEY RICHARD LEWIS, R.F.A.
Photo: Deaks, Carmarthen

He had done magnificent work since he had been given command of 'B' Battery; he had shown great powers of leadership, and he was beloved by officers and men alike. I had him specially promoted from subaltern to Major, as I knew he would take responsibility. He had great strength of character and was bound to do well always. . . . It is a relief to know that his end must have been absolutely instantaneous—a high velocity shell, which was meant for a battery about 300 yards behind his. He was probably buried in Elverdinghe Cemetery."

BASIL MACLEAR

CAPTAIN BASIL MACLEAR, Royal Dublin Fusiliers, the first Irish International who fell in the War, was born at Portsmouth on April 7, 1881, and was killed in action near Ypres on May 24, 1915, aged 34. Basil, as everybody knew him, was the fifth son of Major H. W. Maclear, "the Buffs," and Mrs. Maclear of Bedford, and grandson of Sir Thomas Maclear, late Astronomer Royal, Observatory, Cape Town. Of the five brothers, three have fallen in the War, the third, Lieutenant-Colonel Percy Maclear, Royal Dublin Fusiliers, Commanding 2nd Battalion Nigeria Regiment, in the Cameroons on August 30, 1914; and the eldest, Lieutenant-Colonel Harry Maclear, D.S.O., near Loos, March 16, 1916. Captain Basil Maclear saw much service. He took part in the South African War in the operations in Cape Colony in November and December 1900; in those in the Orange River Colony, December 1900 to February 1901; as well as in those in the Transvaal from February 1901 to January 1902; and was awarded the Queen's Medal with five clasps. He saw further active service with his regiment in the Hinterland of Aden in 1903. So that it was a man of some experience who, with some of the keen edge of his fleetness of foot blunted—a fleetness that in 1900 won for him the Championship of Bedfordshire over 100 yards in

10 seconds dead on a slightly downhill grass track—came seriously into the reckoning as an International three-quarter back in the season of 1904–5. Few who knew his ability and the fact that he was English born, while his football education—the searching one of Bedford School, than which in his day there was none shrewder or more trying—was wholly English, had any doubt that he would be chosen to play for England. Even the facts that England then had no place-kicker of repute, and one of her selectors watched Maclear in a match at Richmond in which he converted ten tries out of twelve attempts, counted nothing in his favour. He was not even chosen to play in a Rugby Union Trial! Being quartered at Fermoy, Co. Cork, he was eligible to play for Ireland, and the Irish selectors, disregarding entirely the asseverations of their London friends, that no Irishman who when playing in London did not play for the London Irish was ever considered by them, jumped at the chance and played Maclear against England—the irony of it—in their first match of 1905. He scored more than once, had a hand in other scores, and generally speaking led the English team—a rather tired one, it is true—a rare dance from start to finish. I shall never forget the match and the way a " first choice for England " played with the English team! From the first few minutes of that game Basil Maclear was a fixture on the Irish team as long as he was available. And so it proved. Ireland were virtually champions of the season 1905, beating England at Cork by 1 goal and 4 tries to 1 try; Scotland at Edinburgh by rather more than 1 goal and 2 tries to 1 try; to lose in a false-result game at Swansea by 2 goals to 1 try, one of the least deserved victories in the Rugby game I have ever witnessed. The Irish XV. that winter was out by itself in front of those of the other three football " nations," and the most dangerous man in that Irish team, alike in attack, defence, or kicking ability, was Basil Maclear. Again in 1906 and in 1907 he played in every match, but without that fine half, T. H. Robinson, in 1906 the Irish team was not the same side as it had been in 1905;

CAPTAIN BASIL MACLEAR
Royal Dublin Fusiliers
Photo: Rovinson, Camberley

and when Robinson played again in 1907, his partner of 1905, E. D. Caddell, doubtless not fully recovered from the broken ankle sustained in the famous Welsh match of 1906 at Belfast, was not quite the same force. Meanwhile, the Irish selectors had coquetted with formations, playing Basil as a " rover " against England in 1906, at Leicester—I can see him as I write pushing in the scrum!—and generally as a centre, whereas wing was his proper place from the day the astute E. H. Dasent took him out of the School scrum to play three-quarter. There has not been in this century a wing who was more difficult to stop than Basil Maclear—not one. Very heavy, very fast, with a hand-off like the kick of a horse, it was a football fact that the only tackle that could be relied upon to stop him was an overtaking or a sideways tackle while he was partly engaged in getting rid of another adversary, or—as was noted in one memorable International—the " tripping " tackle! That he did not get more tries than he did, and he scored many and sent in many others with tries, was due to the cleverness of oppositions, which, quite satisfied of the hopelessness of their chance once the ball reached Maclear, laid themselves out entirely to preventing it getting to him. How Basil nearly converted what was becoming a crushing defeat from the South African team of 1906-7 at Belfast into almost a win for Ireland by a great individual try, starting from between his own 25 and the half-way line, and following this after the drop-out by another fine run, which nearly produced a score, has often been told; the full details thereof are to be found in my " Book of Football." It was the greatest individual score of the many hundreds I have seen, and surely nobody who saw it will ever forget it. Ireland won five of the nine games against England, Scotland, and Wales that Maclear played in, in 1905-6, and 1907, while the New Zealanders of 1905 beat Ireland 15-0, and the South Africans of 1906 won by the narrow margin of 1 penalty goal and 4 tries to 1 penalty goal and 3 tries. These were Irish Rugby's greatest years in this century, and three of the greatest in her history. Wherever in the future the best players of all are discussed the name of Basil Maclear will be always one of the first mentioned in any company of experienced Rugby men. There were great players in his day, and among them he was one of the greatest.

But while this is so, the public that admired his fine British style of play were not privileged to know Basil Maclear the Man. They knew only the delightful virile three-quarter. As it was at once my privilege and my joy to know the Man I feel I cannot do better than give here the following extracts concerning him. They are published, by permission, from the private letters received by his mother. A General under whom Maclear served wrote:—

"Your son Basil was under my command. What a man he was! The best of examples to young would-be officers—upright; a man among men, leading a noble, blameless life; worshipped by the cadets, and there was no man who could not call him friend unless that man was a cur and a waster. For all time your son's name will be among those of that great band in whose memory the grand words shine out in the Sandhurst Memorial Chapel: '*Dulce et decorum est pro patriâ mori.*'"

"As a man I have always had supreme admiration for Basil," wrote a friend of his, "his amazing modesty in spite of his brilliant abilities appealing to me most strongly. I know what a son he was! Kipling's lines on Lord Roberts seem to fit Basil: 'Clean, simple, valiant, well-beloved, fearless in faith and favour.' As such he will be remembered."

And the following by a stranger, one who had never spoken to Maclear: "He was not only a loss to his family, but to the world. Had he lived there was nothing he could not have accomplished. He was a fine brave soldier, and his influence for good was unbounded."

Probably nobody outside his family knew Maclear better than E. Hastings Dasent, a master at Bedford School. And he wrote in this strain :—

" To all his countless friends it came as a terrible shock to hear that Basil Maclear was dead. It seemed almost impossible to associate the thought of death with that robust, vigorous, and virile personality. Yet, to him, I feel sure that death came as no shock or surprise, and when his time came he was ready for it. Of his career as a great athlete there is no need to speak. Had he been only a great athlete our sorrow would have been less deep, less needed. It is his loss as a man that his friends deplore. For this was no mere trifler with the realities of life, but one who saw life steadily and saw it whole. You would not be long in his company without feeling the earnestness and purpose of the man. His previous services had been great, and of late at the College at Sandhurst, and we know that many, not only of our own Old Boys, but those from other Schools, will look back throughout their lives with gratitude to the help that Basil Maclear gave them to make their lives real. A keen soldier, a great athlete, an honest English gentleman."

Shortly before his death the following report was sent to his General :—

" Captain Basil Maclear, who showed great coolness and knowledge of ground in handling the reserve company of the Battalion, which he was able to bring up almost intact under very heavy fire on April 25, 1915 ; and also for the great power of command which he showed himself to possess, when suddenly called upon to command the Battalion for four days during a trying situation."

For this he was mentioned in dispatches.

Educated at Bedford from 1893-99, and at the Royal Military College, Sandhurst, in 1899 and 1900, Captain Maclear gained the

Sword of Honour on leaving Sandhurst. He was gazetted to the Royal Dublin Fusiliers in August 1900, promoted Lieutenant in 1904. From 1904–8 he served as Adjutant of his Regiment, and got his Company in 1911, being then appointed to the Staff of the R.M.C., Sandhurst, where he remained until he went to the Front in March 1915. While he was at Sandhurst he had an operation, which probably delayed his departure for the fighting line. He fell on the morning of May 24, 1915, toward the end of the Second Battle of Ypres; being killed by shrapnel while leading a bombing party to drive the enemy out of a part of one of our trenches.

And so—

> "In the hot-fit of life, a-tiptoe on the highest point of being
> He passes at a bound on to the other side."

VINCENT M'NAMARA

SECOND-LIEUTENANT VINCENT M'NAMARA, Royal Engineers, 136 Fortress Company, 13th Division, 8th Army Corps, British Mediterranean Expeditionary Force, died on November 29, 1915, aged 24, from the effects of the gas fumes of a mine which he had just exploded under the Turkish lines, the results of which he, with very great bravery, went to investigate. His burial-place is officially described as being at "Lancashire Landing, Line L, No. 9."

The late Lieutenant V. M'Namara was born on April 11, 1891, at Analore, Castle Road, Blackrock, Co. Cork, the residence of his father, Mr. Patrick J. M'Namara. He entered in Hilary Term, 1902, at the Presentation College, Cork, and was there for two years. In the summer term of 1904 he entered the Christian Brothers College, Cork, and remained there seven years, until October 1911, when he went to Cork University as an engineering student, and remained there until December 1914. In June 1913 he passed his first engineering examination, and in June 1914

SEC.-LIEUT. VINCENT M'NAMARA, R.E.

his second, and having studied for his final was awarded the latter in January 1915, just before he left for the Front. It was at his own request that he was attached to the Mining Companies in September 1915, and prior to his gallant death he had had two months of mining and counter-mining in close touch with the enemy. The following letter to a friend from the officer in charge at the time was received by Mr. P. J. M'Namara :—

"Macnamara was in charge of the mining operations on the left section (Fusilier Bluff), where connection had been made with the Turkish workings underground. At one point the enemy were forcing lachrymatory gas through to us, and Macnamara, at great risk, had successfully mined under them and exploded a charge. He was an officer without sense of fear and keenly interested in the work, and, unfortunately, went down to investigate without allowing sufficient time for the gases resulting from our countermine to disperse. He was overcome, and despite the most strenuous efforts made by Lieutenant Bernard, R.E., and several men (all of whom were overcome by the gas in turn) to rescue him, it was impossible to reach him in time to save his life. The loss of this gallant officer was keenly regretted by all the officers and men of the Company, and I would like you to convey my sympathy to his relatives.—Yours very truly,

"(Signed) H. W. LAWS,
"Major, R.E."

A brother officer, Lieutenant Mathews, R.E., wrote of him to his sister :—

"The whole Company here loved him and would have done anything for him, and his whole idea seemed to be to do as much for them as he possibly could. He would even give his clothes away if he saw the men required what he possessed. He lived as a Christian; he acted as a man. . . . His loss will ever be impressed indelibly on my mind. I attended his funeral on the top of a hill here ... throughout the funeral shells were bursting, within a few yards, in our men's dug-outs."

And Rev. Father Legros wrote :—

"Last week I had the honour of blessing the grave of your brave and gallant brother; it was a sad honour, but such sadness is overshadowed by the glory which must of necessity attach itself to the passing away of such a hero. He was too brave to live long under these circumstances."

From the Headquarters of the 8th Army Corps came the following appreciation, which is highly valued in the Irish halfback's home at Blackrock. It is from Brigadier-General J. A. Gibbon, Chief Engineer, 8th A.C., and runs :—

"DEAR MRS. M'NAMARA,—I am writing a line to tell you how deeply we all regret the loss of your gallant son. He died in carrying out a dangerous and difficult duty. His courage and keenness were conspicuous, even in a Mining Company, which is always doing such dangerous and gallant work. Permit me in the name of Lieutenant-General Sir Francis Davies, Commander of the 8th Army Corps, as well as my brother officers, to express our deep sympathy with you in your loss.—Yours sincerely,

"(Signed) J. A. GIBBON,
(Brigadier-General, Chief Engineer,
8th Army Corps)."

From all sides—from personal friends, from strangers, from College and University tutors—the parents of Vincent M'Namara received innumerable letters, all bearing evidence to the great popularity of their son. It is not given to many to have the flag of their late University flown at half-mast on their demise. But instantly, on receipt of the news, the authorities of the University College, Cork, paid this last respect to one of whom, in the words of Professor C. W. L. Alexander, it was written :—

" For your fellow College men, the name of Vincent M'Namara will remain the standard of all that is lovely, honourable, and good in those fields and halls that will know your physical presence no more."

The President of the University College, Cork, wrote to Mr. Patrick M'Namara :—

" No more popular and more highly respected student ever sat on the benches of this College, and it is a real personal grief to me and many others to think we shall not see him again."

Of Vincent M'Namara the best had not been seen in International Rugby. That comes only with experience, and the Irish selectors " found " him only after his magnificent and consistent form at the scrum-foot for, first, the Christian College pack, and then that of University College and of Munster, had forced him before their eyes. He played in 72 matches for his College, only 14 of those being lost, while 49 were won and 9 drawn. M'Namara scaled 11 stone 6 and stood 5 feet 8 in 1912, and was 4 lb. heavier when his football career ended, as it did in 1914, with three Irish International Caps. He was just the type for a scrum-half, and his game was just like himself, proving yet once again how when we watch the play of a man we see his character clearly revealed. That is, M'Namara played as straight as a die, fearlessly, going down to anything, unselfishly and to the last whistle —just as he did in that mine on Gallipoli. But let his partner for twelve years at school and college and for Ireland, the Irish stand-off half, H. W. Jack, tell us something :—

" ' Mackie ' was genuine to the core and noted amongst his fellows for his piety," Jack wrote from the Malay States where, one of a hundred, he had helped to put down the mutiny in 1915, to Mr. Patrick M'Namara. " I cannot possibly forget those memorable days of our friendship, when we shared the ups and downs of a football career, in which he always bore the brunt of attack to make my way easy and to make me conspicuous."

This necessarily brief biography of a plucky young Irishman cannot close better than with that extract from his best chum's letter. Would we not all prefer it thus?

JAMES M'NEECE

PRIVATE JAMES M'NEECE died of wounds received on the Western Front on June 12, 1917, aged 34. He was a son of Mr. and Mrs. James M'Neece, Collingwood, Southland, N.Z. He was a man of exceptional physique, being about 6 ft. 2 in. in height, 14 st. 8 lb. when in form, and, what is rare with an athlete of his proportions, he was remarkably quick of action and alert to grasp an opportunity. Qualities these which combined to make him the great performer he was both on the football and cricket fields. Southland has produced many fine Rugby men, but none to outshine M'Neece, whose manliness as well as his extraordinary athletic powers gained for him general admiration and popularity. He was born in Invercargill, was educated at the Middle School, and was a farmer when he enlisted on May 1, 1916. He commenced his football career with the Waikiwi Club, with whom his play so impressed the Selection Committee of the Southland Rugby Union, that in 1905 he was chosen to play for his Province, and up till 1914 he had so retained his form that each year he was one of Southland's 1st XV. His reputation as a forward spread further afield, and he was selected to play for the South Island against the North Island in 1913; while in the year 1914 he was one of the New Zealand representatives who had a successful tour in New South Wales.

Jim M'Neece was capable of filling any position in the pack, and at times played on the wing as well. He was recognized as

PRIVATE JAMES M'NEECE, N.Z.

one of the most brilliant players in New Zealand. It can be said to his credit that he never used his great strength for any unfair purpose. One of his strong points was his skill at kicking goals, and on more than one occasion he has kicked a goal from half-way. At the line-out he also gained distinction, his height and reach, combined with his weight, rendering him specially formidable in this branch of play.

As a cricketer batting was his forte, and he made many good scores for Southland. He helped Southland to secure the Hawke Cup. Probably his best performance with the bat was against a team of Melbourne Club players, captained by W. W. Armstrong (Victoria and Australia).

Of him, as a soldier, the Commander of his Platoon wrote :—

" During the time James M'Neece had been with the Battery he endeared himself to us all by his unfailing cheerfulness, and his capacity for work was unrivalled. We all feel his loss very deeply. He was in one of the gun teams under my care in the advance at Messines. We reached an objective, and consolidated on the 7th June. There was but little sleep for the next forty-eight hours; but at the end of that time things had cooled down somewhat, and, as I was living in a very deep shell-hole, I sent him (Jim) and another (Lynch) into my hole to have a sleep. They were there for some hours, and then the Boches started shelling very heavily. Jim stood up to see what was doing, when a shell burst near by and a piece of it entered his shoulder close up to the neck. He was quite able to walk, and none of us thought that his wound would be fatal, so it was a big surprise when we received the official advice of his death. You have the satisfaction of knowing that Jim died while doing his ' little bit '—and well he did it, too."

ALFRED FREDERICK MAYNARD

LIEUTENANT ALFRED FREDERICK MAYNARD, R.N.V.R. (acting Captain), fell in action in the attack on Beaumont Hamel on November 13, 1916, aged 22. Born at Anerley, Kent, on March 23, 1894, Maynard was educated at Seaford, at Durham School, and at Emmanuel College, Cambridge (1912-14). He was given his B.A. degree, but, owing to absence on active service, could not attend to receive it. At Durham Maynard was Captain of Rugby Football, of Cricket, of Fives, and of the Gymnasium. For Durham County he made 79 against Lincolnshire and 89 against Northamptonshire. At Cambridge he made 159 against Trinity and 143 against Clare for Emmanuel; but was never in the running for the match at Lord's. On one occasion for Durham City, in a club match, he scored 119 in an hour and a quarter.

Of his cricket prowess in the county match at Sunderland it was written at the time :—

" Maynard, the nineteen-year-old player, was of immense value to the side. He scored 89 in beautifully free fashion. . . . He distinguished himself once more before play ceased for the day. W. H. and J. S. Denton opened the Northamptonshire second innings with hard irresistible hitting, and the total was 125 before they were separated. Then it was that J. S. Denton was magnificently taken in the long field. Maynard was the fielder, and he took a swift, lofty hit on the boundary with his outstretched right hand. The batsman had 84 runs to his credit, and even he showed keen appreciation of the catch."

Maynard played for Cambridge against Oxford at Queen's Club in 1912 and in 1913, scoring a remarkable try in 1913, running close to the touch line from nearly half-way, with the Oxford team the most interested spectators present of his progress, until it was too late to prevent him from scoring. He

LIEUT. ALFRED FREDERICK MAYNARD, R.N.V.R.

played occasionally for the Harlequins, and in 1914 was capped three times for England, though many considered it doubtful policy to play him against Scotland in March of that year at Inverleith, owing to an injury. He was not chosen for the next match against France in Paris. Maynard was a big-boned, heavyweight forward, who required stopping once he had been allowed to get on the move, and was useful in the play at the line-out; but in knowledge of the game during a passing advance by forwards he fell short of the desired standard.

The late Lieutenant A. F. Maynard saw considerable service in this War. Prompt in response to the call, he joined Howe Battalion of the Royal Naval Division in September 1914, and went into training at Blandford, Dorset. He was present at the Defence of Antwerp, the first raid on the Suez Canal, and on Gallipoli, where he was hit in the leg. He held afterwards, during convalescence, two positions on the Staff, and was offered a permanent appointment on the Staff; but the War Office took objection to the appointment on the ground that he was under Admiralty orders and the position was under the War Office. So he rejoined his Battalion at Mudros, where, owing to the great losses sustained by it, and his own promotion, he found himself in acting command for a time. Later, he proceeded to France, and was killed when leading his company in the attack on Beaumont Hamel. From among numerous letters testifying to his great popularity among his College friends, his brother officers, and men, two extracts may be permitted. His Colonel wrote of him as " an officer in whom the utmost confidence could be placed," and of his death while " gallantly leading his men." The Chaplain also wrote referring to the great assistance he had received from Maynard, and by his example while in temporary command of his Battalion at Mudros.

In addition to being an able Rugby player and cricketer, A. F. Maynard was Captain of the Emmanuel Hockey team, and during his convalescence, after being wounded in the leg on the

Gallipoli Peninsula, he was Captain of the Roller Skating Hockey team which won the International Cup at Alexandria.

ERIC MILROY

LIEUTENANT ERIC MILROY, M.A., 8th Battalion Black Watch, was reported missing at Longueval, Delville Wood, on July 18, 1916, aged 28. Born in Edinburgh on December 4, 1887, Milroy was educated at George Watson's College from 1894–1906, and at Edinburgh University, where he took his M.A. degree, from 1906–10. He was in his School XV. in 1905–6 as scrum-half, having as partners T. C. Bowie and J. Pearson. He gained the Watsonian Medal for combined scholarship and athletics. According to the excellent custom in vogue in Scotland, he did not play for his University, but for his School's Former Pupils club—namely, the Watsonians. He was the Watsonians' scrum-half from the season 1906–7 to that of 1913–14, having as partners in turn D. A. Foulis, J. Y. Henderson, and T. C. Bowie. Milroy played twelve times for Scotland, including the "riot" match on the Parc des Princes, Paris, in 1913; and he went with Dr. R. S. Smyth's team to South Africa in 1910, but owing to illness played only thrice. His fine play and qualities fully entitled him to the honour of being Captain of the Scottish XV. in the last International match played before the war, that at Inverleith in March 1914, which was one of the greatest games of the greatest series in Rugby history, and was just won by England. On the outbreak of war Milroy was very soon making his way into the fighting line, as he joined the 9th Royal Scots in September 1914; received his commission in the 11th Black Watch, then in training at Nigg, Ross-shire; went to France on October 1, 1915; and was there drafted to the 8th Black Watch, and promoted Lieutenant in June 1916. Milroy was the best scrum-half Scotland had since poor "Nimmo" E. D. Simson, and one of the very

LIEUT. ERIC MILROY
8th Batt. Black Watch

best, because he recognized to the full the needs of the " open " game, and did not believe Rugby football to be a game for the amusement and exercise of forwards only. Probably his best partner was the late J. Y. Henderson, whose departure for India was a great blow to Scottish Rugby, then badly off for class players behind the scrum.

" My first memory of Eric Milroy," writes an old friend of his, specially for this biography, " goes back fourteen years, when, as a small boy, he acted as scorer for the Cricket XI. of George Watson's College, Edinburgh. It was in the following session that the late Harry Scoular—the Cambridge footballer—returned to his old school as a master, and set about training the XV. in the modern methods of back play. In ' Puss ' (as we called Milroy) he found the pivot on which good three-quarter back play depends—a reliable scrum-half. Little fellow though he was, he learned quickly, under Scoular's careful and assiduous tuition, the mysteries of modern half-back play and the value and necessity of swift and clean service from the scrum. He only played in the School XV. for one season, and the following year found his way into the Former Pupils team, the renowned Watsonians, where his partner at half was D. A. Foulis, now a captain in the Scottish Rifles, with the D.S.O. to his credit. Between them they changed the typical Watsonian game from a hard-scrummaging forward fight to a fast-moving and thrilling three-quarter back game. This development put his side in the very forefront of Scottish Rugby until the war broke out. At different times Milroy had as his partner D. A. Foulis, J. Y. Henderson, and T. C. Bowie, and three-quarters behind like Angus and Pearson, and one wonders if ever again we shall see the great game played as these paladins played it.

" Milroy was not at first thought good enough for International honours, and the innate conservatism of the Scottish Rugby Union kept him in the background, while they experimented with halves who, while they ' represented ' the various teams comprising the Union, signally failed to work out a scientific game when the critical day came. When at length Milroy was chosen, his ability quickly justified the somewhat belated confidence the S.R.U. reposed in him, and this confidence received its seal when he was made Captain of the Scottish team against England in 1914.

" The annual trip of the Watsonians to Wales, and the opportunity of close study of the methods of the famous Welshmen, and particularly those of Owen, had a great influence on his play; there is no doubt that his play more closely approximated to that of the great Welsh masters of the game than did that of any other Scottish half-back. Thus far his athletic career, but that by no means gives the man as we knew him. There is a superficial belief abroad that the athlete may be an adept at his own sport, but that there his gift ends. There was no more striking contradiction of that casual doctrine than Milroy, for he was a very 'brainy' man. At school and university he proved himself a first-rate scholar, with such a special aptitude for mathematics that he took his M.A. degree with Honours in that subject. He was then apprenticed to a firm of Chartered Accountants, passed his examinations with ease, and seemed to have a career of great usefulness opening for him, when the 'Great Call' came, and he joined, with many of his football friends, the 9th (Highlanders) Battalion, the Royal Scots.

" Off the football field he was the most modest and generous of souls, and if one wanted a speedy road to his disfavour, a quotation from the plentiful 'journalese' spent on his achievements on the field made the genial 'Puss' depart from his geniality. That boyish smile, with which he would emerge from the feet of opposing forwards, was an open sesame to a wide circle of friendship, and never could it be said of him that success had in the least turned his head. He was ever sunny, modest, and gentle. Recalling him, one inevitably thinks of 'The Happy Warrior' Wordsworth describes :—

"' Whose powers shed round him in the common strife
Or mild concerns of ordinary life
A constant influence, a peculiar grace;
But who, if he be called upon to face
Some awful moment to which Heaven has joined
Great issues, good or bad, for human kind,
Is happy as a lover; and attired
With sudden brightness, like a man inspired.'

" He vanished from our ken in the inferno of Delville Wood, and while we mourn the tragedy of his death, we treasure the remembrance of his clean, honest, happy nature as a lifelong memory."

EDGAR ROBERTS MOBBS

LIEUTENANT-COLONEL EDGAR ROBERTS MOBBS, D.S.O., 7th Battalion Northants Regiment, fell in action at Zillebeke on July 29, 1917. Born at Northampton on June 29, 1882, he was thus a month short of his 35th birthday when he died. He was educated at the Bedford Modern School from 1892–1900, but though he played for England at Rugby football with very great distinction, and on one occasion for Buckinghamshire in the Minor Counties Cricket Championship, Mobbs' only games honour at School was an undistinguished 2nd XV. jersey! On leaving school he took up hockey with some ardour, playing in an eleven which contained H. C. Boycott, an English International. But he resumed the better game in 1903, playing a few times for the Olney Club, his home being in that village. He played for Northampton for the first time—an event pregnant with import for his future—in 1905, as a half-back. After this he played always as a three-quarter, generally on the wing, his proper place, but later as a centre. It is noteworthy that he got his first International Cap in January 1909, in his fourth season in first-class football. Harking back, he was made Vice-Captain of Northampton in his second season, and Captain in 1907–8, a remarkable tribute to his character and play alike, considering his brief School football career. He remained in the post of Captain honoured—nay, loved—by member and opponent alike, until he retired from the game at the end of the season 1912-13. During his membership of the Northampton XV., from 1905-13, he scored 177 tries, dropped 1 goal, and kicked 2 from tries for the XV., an average of just under 20 tries per season over a period of nine years, in which he never spared himself or picked his matches, but played every week. This achievement alone stamps Mobbs as one of the finest and most loyal players of his time. He played seven times for England, and had the peculiar experience of being one of the two best three-quarters on the field in his first match—that *v.* Australia at Blackheath in January 1909—and of scoring the only English try, and then of being left out of the next chosen England XV.—that against Wales a week later at Cardiff. It was about this time that Welsh expert opinion was to the effect that had they the choosing of the English XV. they would select Mobbs first, and build the back division round him. He actually played against Wales in that game, coming into the team as a reserve! Than his try against the Australians, in conjunction with that most brilliant Uppinghamian, the late Lieutenant F. N. Tarr (Oxford, Leicester, Headingley, and England), I have never seen a better combined score in a very long experience. The movement started at half-way, and it was close to that line that Tarr first gave the ball to Mobbs, who ran outwards, and drawing the nearest opponent, returned the ball to Tarr. The way in which Mobbs kept his position to receive the ball again from Tarr, in spite of most obvious attempts at obstruction, was striking proof that in him England had found a real player of this game. But he was the left wing, and the Selection Committee's seats were on the other side of the ground, and they saw not the fine points that stood out prominently, above all the mediocrity which had preceded it on England's three-quarter line for many seasons, for all to see on that side of

LIEUT.-COLONEL EDGAR ROBERTS MOBBS, D.S.O.
7th Batt. Northants Regiment

the ground. I should not like to be certain about it, but believe that in the course of his successful endeavours to evade the attentions of his obstructionist, Mobbs actually ran outside the touch-line for part of his journey to the line. This is probable, as the clever play occurred at that deceptive bend on the eastern side of the Rectory Field pitch which has cost many a visiting full-back many yards many times. Accustomed to aim according to the position of the crowd, the visitor who has been careless enough not to have a look at his surroundings before kick-off has often been totally deceived as to the angle of his kick. Into the ethics of a player utilizing the ground outside the touch-line in this way I do not propose to enter, except to observe that inasmuch as a player standing in touch-in-goal may score a try, and a player may run up inside touch to put his men on-side, there seems no valid reason why a player may not run inside touch for the purpose of avoiding an opponent whose intent is to play foul. This particular try was impressed on my memory by reason of the fact that it is about the only case in which I have seen the return or in-pass—not the reverse pass, as it is sometimes wrongly termed—produce a score in a match of the first importance, or wherein there was a defence worthy the name. Having got into the English team again, almost as though on sufferance, Mobbs remained in it for every match of the winter of 1909, and was the only player in the East of England who played in every match of that season. He played twice more for England—namely, against Ireland and France, when he was Captain of the English XV. in Paris, 1910; and he scored in every match he played in for England except the scoreless Irish game at Twickenham—a game that was memorable for the dead set two or three Irish forwards made against Mobbs, who was damaged sufficiently to have to retire temporarily during the game, for, I believe, the only time in his career. Even then he came on again, much to the consternation of A. D. Stoop, the English Captain, and would not be repressed. After 1910 he fell out of favour with the selectors for some reason I have never heard, and which doubtless would be very difficult of explanation. For he had many more International matches in him, as on one memorable occasion about 1912 he proved, when Northampton visited Twickenham to play the Harlequins, who were at that moment in great fettle. Northampton happened to be much below par, but how Mobbs rose to the occasion I shall never forget. He seemed to do all the tackling and all the attacking, and I shall be surprised if the Harlequins have forgotten that match. Another memorable game in his career was that in which the Midlands and East Midlands combined defeated the Australians at Leicester in 1909, and were the only English fifteen to beat the tourists. It is not with any intention of attempting to claim a share in that success that I state that I was invited to express an opinion as to the style of game the combined fifteen ought to play. It is, after all, the players who count, not the adviser, when the thing is put to the test of action; but I must say that Mobbs and his men played to my plan as though they had rehearsed it frequently, deeming it senseless to invite counsel and then not follow it. No mention of Edgar Mobbs in the Rugby football field he so adorned is complete without the figures of his truly remarkable, and also "record," achievement in the matter of try-getting. No less than three times did he score six tries himself, twice in inter-county and once in inter-club fray. Here are the figures :—

November 7, 1907.—East Midlands v. Eastern Counties, at Bedford. Three tries in each half. East Midlands won by 1 goal 5 tries to 2 tries, or 20 points to 6.

October 14, 1909.—East Midlands v. Eastern Counties, at Bedford. Two tries in first and 4 in second half. East Midlands won by 5 goals 8 tries to 1 try, or 49 points to 3.

February 6, 1909.—Northampton v. Birkenhead Park, at Northampton. Three in each half. Northampton won by 2 goals 7 tries to 1 penalty goal 1 try, or 31 points to 6.

Thus in these three games, of a total of 100 points to 15, Mobbs scored 54 points unaided by goal-kick points.

Mobbs captained the East Midlands XV. from 1906–13 inclusive, playing in thirty of the thirty-five matches of that period, accident or illness alone being the cause of his absence from five. In addition to Northampton, East Midlands, and England matches he played frequently for the Barbarians, and on tour in France, especially at Toulouse, where he was very well known and naturally very popular. He succeeded that great judge of Rugby football, Mr. E. Hastings Dasent, the East Midlands representative on the Rugby Union Committee, and is the only member of that body who has fallen in action, though Lieutenant-Colonel W. S. D. Craven, R.H.A., D.S.O. (Kent), has been severely wounded, and Captain A. D. Stoop (Central) has been slightly wounded. Those of the remaining fifteen members of the Committee who are not on active service ashore or afloat have been engaged almost from the start of hostilities in work of national importance.

Before dealing with Edgar Mobbs, patriot and soldier, something must be recorded of him as a player. Tall and strongly built, with weight and pace of that far-striding, high-stepping kind, —all knees as the saying goes—Mobbs was admirably adapted from a physical point of view for the position of wing three-quarter. Added to these valuable qualities he had excellent hands for the receipt of passes, a very strong and well-directed hand-off. He would not be noticed by the cognoscenti as remarkably adept at kicking; but for all that he had such a fine control of direction when punting, that I have often seen him from the left wing (when getting the ball after a scrum near the left touch-line) punt across obliquely and over the opposing left wing so accurately that if the ball bounced at all well this punt-pass meant an almost certain try for E. T. Cook, the Northampton right wing. No player I have ever seen could have carried out this particular bit of true football more accurately than Mobbs used to do, so that we may judge him to have been a better kick than on his mere finding of touch—a region of the precincts of a football ground he shunned—we might be inclined to think. In his earliest days Mobbs showed such a disposition to "go high," and, curiously enough, to hesitate in attack, that some of us were deluded into the belief that he might never rise to the highest places; but all of sudden he blossomed into a splendid try-getter, something of a terror to stop because of his knees and his hand-off with good resolute weight behind them, and a defender in his own way second to none, though there was always a "high" tendency in his tackle to the end of his football career. Mobbs had a beautiful disposition for games, being the possessor of a perfect temper, a burning hatred of all things mean and unsporting, and a heart of gold. Generosity had a living incarnation in Edgar Mobbs, from whose lips nobody ever heard a spiteful remark. Full of fun, he was the life and soul of every football team he toured with. Will it ever be forgotten how on a Paddington-Newport non-stop he borrowed the guard's cap and coat, went all along the train collecting tickets here and there with delightful inconsequence, in order to watch the fun when just before the first stop the genuine collection was made? Who but Mobbs could have done this without annoying anybody? Who but he could have fielded in an inter-county cricket match wearing the Cambridge cap and sash, though he had never been in residence at Cambridge, much less a cricket Blue? Much of the happiness in life, such as it is in war time, went out for very many of us Southrons when we heard that this Greatheart had been taken from us. It was one of the saddest days of this terrible war, with its ghastly toll of our best, and generally our youngest, lives.

Of Edgar Mobbs, Rugby football player, the above record may stand. I doubt not it could have been greatly improved upon by others who have played with or against him. Of Edgar Mobbs, patriot and soldier, it has to be written, and it is a proud record, as follows: Applying for a commission in August 1914 he was refused on the score of age! He was then thirty-two. Not long afterwards subalterns of fifty were met on almost every pavement. No refusal ever troubled him when he meant to have a thing. So he at once set about raising a Company in Northampton and the County of Rugby players and athletes generally for a battalion of the Northants Regiment. He had only to raise a beckoning finger in such company. He marched away in mufti at the head of his men on September 14, 1914, and went into training at Shoreham. As his promotions were rapid, even for these times, their dates must be given. Thus he was a Sergeant on September 14, 1914; Temporary-Lieutenant, October 14, 1915; Temporary Captain, July 1, 1915; Temporary Major, September 28, 1915; and Lieutenant-Colonel on April 23, 1916, commanding the battalion in which he had enlisted as a private less than two years previously. He had a lucky escape at Loos, September 1915, when a bullet grazed his nose during an attack; and in 1916 he was severely wounded by shell-burst in the shoulder, necessitating a spell in hospital in England, but he was soon back again with his men.

And then, the end. Directly we read in a daily paper of the heroic act of a Colonel who was also a well-known football player —the censorship making us appear wholly ashamed of our brave men and their deeds!!—we knew instinctively it was Edgar Mobbs. The facts of his grand death are as follows :—

"During the advance on 'Shrewsbury Wood' on July 19, 1917, an enemy 'strong post'—or machine-gun emplacement—was stopping the progress of his line. No messages could be got through. Consequently he went out to ascertain what was the trouble. Finding his men were being badly cut up, he gave an order to one of his captains to take twelve men with bombs to attack the strong post on one side, whilst he, with twelve men, led the attack from another. During the advance he was shot through the neck. Being dangerously wounded and bleeding to death, he crept to a shell-hole, wrote and sent a report to Headquarters and another to the Battery, telling them on what square to train their guns. Having completed his work he died in a few minutes."

His Brigadier-General wrote to his bereaved parents : " He had an extraordinary personal influence over all his men, who would have done anything for him, and he died leading them in one of the most gallant attacks that any battalion has ever made."

Thus, fighting and doing his duty to the last gasp, died Edgar Mobbs, surely one of the finest characters of the many noble ones our race has been robbed of in the course of this insensate rush for world-power on the part of another race which has thoroughly earned the title Unspeakable. Of what avail is it to prate of reparation in view of such losses ? Of none of our most famous games-men can it be more truly written, that we ne'er shall look upon his like again.

T. M. MOLL

SECOND-LIEUTENANT T. M. MOLL, Leicestershire Regiment, died of wounds on July 14, 1916, aged 31. Born on July 20, 1890, at Cape Town, South Africa, Moll was educated at South African College, Cape Colony (1902–8). Captain of the XV. and swimming teams there, he was also a member of the O.T.C. He played for Western Province from 1910–14; but his first experience of big football in South Africa was for Transvaal in 1908, and it was as a Transvaaler that he played for South Africa in 1910 against Dr. T. Smyth's United Kingdom team. He played against them in the third match of that tour at Cape Town on September 5, 1910, when South Africa won by 1 goal and 1 try to nil. Lieutenant Moll also played for and captained the Hamiltons Club, Cape Town.

SEC.-LIEUT. T. M. MOLL
Leicestershire Regiment

On the staff of the Bank of South Africa, Moll was soon in the fighting area, as he served through the South-West African campaign in ridding the country of the pest. He came over to England, and died of wounds sustained the day before on the Western Front. " Toby " Moll was a great favourite in sporting circles at the Cape.

JAN WILLEM HUNTER MORKEL

TROOPER JAN WILLEM HUNTER MORKEL, 1st Mounted Brigade Scout Corps, died of dysentery on active service in East Africa on May 15, 1916. Born at Somerset West, Cape Colony, he learned the game at school in that town and playing for the Somerset West Rugby Club. He played for Western Province from 1911–14, and for South Africa against the British team of 1910 in South Africa, and also in W. A. Millar's tour of 1912–13, in the United Kingdom, in which he played in all four International games. He was a very capable centre three-quarter, especially in attack, neatness being the keynote of his play. He had a very keen sight for the chance of an opening, his cutting-through being a great feature of his game, as was seen in the fourth International match of the 1912–13 tour at Twickenham. A very quiet, unassuming fellow, a man of few words, Jack Morkel made hosts of friends on that tour, during which he was liked as much for the quality of his play as for its purity.

Mr. B. Dods, of Somerset West, who knew Jack Morkel intimately, has written the following interesting appreciation of the best centre of a fine team :—

" War is an infallible test of manhood. In South Africa the present war has proved a powerful test of loyalty and unswerving devotion, of a clear conception of duty, or the opposite. Jack Morkel was a Dutch South African. Employed in an essential industry he could have, had he so elected, remained at home and salved his conscience with the knowledge that he was employed in service necessary to the welfare of the Allies. Animated, however, by a high sense of duty he chose the harder course and joined the South African Horse for service in East Africa. The significance of the Flag was not quite the same to Jack Morkel as to the young man of British birth or extraction. He was a British subject of Dutch descent, and his allegiance and loyalty to the Flag under the protection of which he lived, and for which he gave his young life, were actuated by a clear, cold sense of duty.

"In his manner he was reserved; but, none the less, he was popular with his clubmates and the Rugger fraternity generally. He was a devoted brother and a loyal friend; a true type of South African sportsman, keen and clean. Loyalty to his Club was an outstanding feature of his character. His obligations to his side were always fulfilled, and his obligations in other spheres were observed to an equal degree. In Rugger he excelled; in other forms of sport he could hold his own. He took part in the early operations in British East Africa. He was posted to Van Deventer's Scouts, and preserved a cheerful attitude in spite of the hardships which the Mounted Units in East Africa were called upon to endure. Fever got him early in the campaign. He quickly recovered from the first attack, but was again stricken with dysentery, followed by a second attack of fever which proved fatal.

"Jack Morkel's sacrifice has amply proved his manhood; what more remains to be said?"

Only this, that he will be regretted and remembered just as much by all in the United Kingdom who ever met him as he is in his own home town. He has upheld in the worthiest possible manner the teachings of the Rugby game, which cannot, unfortunately, be written of all British subjects of Dutch descent, and

TROOPER JAN WILLEM HUNTER MORKEL
1st Mounted Brigade Scout Corps, S.A.

Photo: Sport and General, London

his case will stand for all time as a shining example to his countrymen.

WILLIAM MOORE BELL NANSON

SERGEANT WILLIAM MOORE BELL NANSON, 1/10th Manchester Regiment, was killed in action at El Krithia on June 4, 1915, aged 34. Born at Carlisle, he was educated at Lowther Street School, Carlisle, and was thus brought up quite close to the Carlisle Rugby Football Ground, where he came in contact with many past masters of the game in the city and county of Cumberland. There were six boys in the family, all more or less athletes, several now serving with the Imperial Forces in various parts of the Empire. "At school," writes one who knew him well, "he was ever to the fore in all the sports, and was always regarded by his fellow pupils as an outstanding figure, especially in the Rugby games. 'Billy' really began his football career with the Carlisle Junior Team, of which he was a member for five years, the team being at the zenith of its fame from 1895–99, finally becoming amalgamated with the Carlisle Rugby Club. A most enthusiastic Volunteer for many years, Nanson was a member of the 1st Volunteer Battalion the Border Regiment. On the outbreak of the South African War he was one of the first to volunteer for Active Service, being then nineteen years of age. Promoted Lance-Corporal, he took part in all the operations with the line battalion—the famous 1st Battalion Border Regiment—in the Orange Free State and the Transvaal. Always full of energy and a good soldier, he became ill —the result of the heavy marching and sleeping out on the open Veldt—and was invalided down to the coast, whence he was sent home to recoup his health. After convalescence, the old spirit being still there, he volunteered to go out again, did so, and took part in the operations in the Orange Free State. For these services he received the Queen's Medal with three clasps and the King's Medal with two clasps.

"Returning after the war, his love of the old game was still ardent, and he became a member of the Carlisle Rugby Football Club, playing for nine or ten years in all matches as a forward, and was a tower of strength to the club. In County matches he represented the Cumberland County Union, and for two seasons was Captain of the Carlisle Club. He played also for the North, after which he played for England against France and against Wales in 1907. He also played at St. James's Park for Cumberland and Northumberland combined against the South Africans in 1906. He was reserve forward for England *v.* South Africa at the Crystal Palace in 1906, and against Wales at Swansea played three-quarter for a time owing to injury to one of the English backs.

"Nanson joined the ranks of the Northern Union in June 1908, playing with the Oldham team for about four years. He then joined Coventry on the formation of that club, and when it was disbanded he assisted Todmorden, and was still playing for them when he rejoined the Army. He was a member of the Oldham Territorials, known as the 1/10th Manchester Regiment, was called up on August 5, 1914, and went into training at Bury for several weeks. Joining as a Private, he was promoted to the rank of Sergeant the following May. The Regiment embarked for Egypt, thence proceeding to Gallipoli, taking part in the famous landing in April 1915, and he met his end at the Battle of El Krithia, where he was missing (June 4) in front of the Achi Baba line. The last seen of him by his comrades was when he had moved some Turks out of one of the Turkish trenches. He called out, 'Come on, lads! let's shift 'em.' More men followed him, but were called back. Billy turned round, waved his rifle, and went right on into the Turkish lines. The last seen of him was when he was engaged single-handed driving the Turks out of the trench. The casualties were heavy that day, and after the battle the

SERGEANT WILLIAM MOORE BELL NANSON
1/10th Manchester Regiment

Photo: Knott, Oldham

search parties could find no trace of him nor any part of his equipment. Nothing further regarding him having come to light the Army Council came to the conclusion, after thirteen months, that they must presume him as killed, for official purposes. There is no information whatever that he is a prisoner of war.

"The 'Border City' loses in him one of her most illustrious sons in the realm of sport. Nanson always turned out for his Club, and although of a retiring disposition he could always be relied upon—never failing to do his best and to give encouragement to his fellows. His noble example and gentlemanly bearing may well be emulated by the younger generation of the county and city of his birth. There must be many who followed his career, who were members of the Carlisle Club, who are serving on the various fronts in France, Italy, Egypt, Mesopotamia, India, and even Russia, and who are conscious that his memory will live in their hearts, that he died as he played the game for 'Canny Auld Cummerlan.' Nanson has left a widow and two children —a girl and a boy—to mourn his loss."

W. J. M.

THOMAS ARTHUR NELSON

CAPTAIN THOMAS ARTHUR NELSON, 1st Lothians and Border Horse, was killed in action at Arras, France, on April 9, 1917, aged 40. Educated at Edinburgh Academy (1887-95) and at University College, Oxford (1895-99), Nelson was the full-back of the Academy XV.'s of 1893-94, and a centre three-quarter in those of 1894-95. At Oxford he got his Blue in 1897, and played in that and the following year against Cambridge, Oxford winning both matches, at centre three-quarter. It was in 1898 that he won the most honoured distinction in the Rugby game, that of a place in a Calcutta Cup match, as he played centre for Scotland in the drawn game of one goal each, at Edinburgh. A member of the 1st Lothians and Border Horse before the war, Captain Nelson rejoined his regiment at once on the outbreak of hostilities, and went to France in September 1915, where, as Observation Officer for the tanks, he was killed by the bursting of a shell a year and a half later. Of him Colonel John Buchan, a great personal friend of his during and since their Oxford days, wrote in *The Times* :—

"He left Oxford to take his part in the great publishing house which bears his name. He worked hard at the business, and under his hands and those of his colleagues it grew to be perhaps the largest organization of its kind in the world. But his life could not be narrowed to one interest. No employer ever gave more thought to the well-being of his employees, and no master ever enjoyed a more whole-hearted popularity. He had a deep interest in all schemes of social betterment, and, being too modest to preach, he was content to practise. He was a keen Yeomanry officer, a pioneer of afforestation, an ideal West Highland laird. He was the best of sportsmen, not merely because he did everything well and with immense gusto, but because he had in his bones the love of wild life and adventure and contest. But his great endowment was his genius for friendship with all human classes and conditions. His kind, serious eyes looked out on the world with infinite friendliness and understanding. His death makes a bigger hole in the life of Scotland than that of any man of his years."

I have not been able to unearth anything about Captain Nelson's prowess on the Rugby field, as Internationals who have played in only one game are not very well known as such at any time; besides, twenty years ago there was not quite so much written about the game as there is now, so that the records of those days are less fruitful than those of more modern times. There is no doubt that Captain Nelson went up to Oxford with a

CAPTAIN THOMAS ARTHUR NELSON
1st Lothians and Border Horse
From the painting by Laszlo.

great reputation as a three-quarter, and that this he worthily maintained. Off the field or on it, he was a most popular man, and, to judge him only by his many patriotic actions since war broke out, a most public-spirited one as well. How magnificently he fought, the military records clearly prove, as between April 30, 1916, and April 9, 1917, he was mentioned in dispatches on no fewer than three occasions, namely, April 30, 1916; November 13, 1916; and April 9, 1917; the last occasion being for his brave work on the day of his death. He was attached to the Headquarters of the 25th Division, and later as Observation Officer to the Headquarters of the 5th Army Corps. In all respects the late Captain T. A. Nelson ranks very high among Rugby Internationals and patriots who have given their all ungrudgingly, spontaneously, in the cause of Right, of King, and of Empire.

FRANCIS ECKLEY OAKELEY

LIEUTENANT FRANCIS ECKLEY OAKELEY, Royal Navy, was lost at sea on a submarine between November 25 and December 1, 1914, aged 23. Born at Hereford on February 5, 1891, Oakeley was educated at Hereford and at Eastman's before going to the Royal Naval Colleges at Osborne and Dartmouth for the usual courses. He had such a distinguished athletic career that I have no hesitation in dealing with it as fully as, thanks to the great kindness of my informants, I am enabled to. The following extracts from the various College magazines may be allowed to speak for themselves. They give his games, honours won, and refer to his athletic deeds :—

AT OSBORNE—CHRISTMAS TERM, 1904.—*Association :* Shots high and low, and mostly hard, for Oakeley and Law were in shooting form.

EASTER TERM, 1905.—Association colours, as forward. 1st in Consolation Race in Sports.

SUMMER TERM, 1905.—*Assault at Arms:* In sabres the style was generally very good. Jeffreys and Oakeley had a hard tussle in the final—the latter never seemed to quite settle down and do himself justice, possibly through being a bit nervous at his *first public performance.* Final, Oakeley 2nd.

CHRISTMAS TERM, 1905.—" *Association:* With the departure of the Sixth Term to Dartmouth, we are losing many cadets who have been mainly instrumental in setting a high standard of play here, and who, in course of their stay here, have helped us to win many matches. The two who stand out above the rest are Boyd and Oakeley. I believe it would be true to say that neither of them have missed a first-eleven match while they have been here. It will be a long time, probably, before we have such a good centre-half and forward again. They are both fast and clever, and do not know what it is to be beaten."

Association Challenge Cup.—Dormitory Matches: Oakeley played forward for " Duncan," who were beaten in the final round by "Collingwood."

Inter-Dormitory Cup Ties, Rugby.—Oakeley played three-quarter for " Duncan," who won the final by 1 dropped goal and 2 tries to nil. Goal, Fergusson; tries, Oakeley and Tompkins.

Sabre Challenge Cup Competition.—F. E. Oakeley, Challenge Cup and 1st Prize. (He won all his fights.)

AT DARTMOUTH—EASTER TERM, 1906.—*Fencing Notes:* Oakeley won " Drakes " Sabres and Foils after a tie with Laing in Foils. Three cadets will go to London to represent the College against Osborne, and they will be selected from the following: Jeffreys, Babbington, Wellesley, Rivers, and Oakeley.

Sports.—1st in High Jump, under 15 (4 ft. 4½ in.).

Association Notes.—Oakeley has firmly established himself in the team at inside right. Always a dangerous forward, with lots of dash, and shoots well from any position. Very unselfish, and makes good openings for his outside man.

LIEUT. FRANCIS ECKLEY OAKELEY, R.N.
Photo : Russell, Southsea

FRANCIS ECKLEY OAKELEY

SUMMER TERM, 1906.—*Assault at Arms:* Sabres, 1st; Foils, 2nd.

On 4th July he played for the 2nd XI. *v.* Montpelier School. The Royal Naval College won—185 runs to 99. (This is the only time he appears to have played in a cricket match.)

CHRISTMAS TERM, 1906.—Played three-quarter for "Drake" in Term Rugby Competition.

Association Notes.—" A first-class forward, to whom much of our success is due. Plays with great dash, is a fine shot at goal, and makes excellent openings for forwards on each side of him."

Fencing Competition.—Sabres, 2nd; Foils, 1st.

EASTER TERM, 1907.—*Second XV. Rugby Notes:* "F. E. Oakeley. Left centre three-quarter. Obtains cap. At present purely an individual player; must remember that combination amongst outsides is essential; must learn to tackle low."

Hockey Notes.—" Oakeley. Back. A splendid back, who is a sure tackle and a tremendous hitter; has been quite invaluable to our back division."

Athletic Sports.—High Jump (under 15), 2nd Prize; Obstacle Race (under 15), 1st Prize.

Fencing Competition.—Sabres, 1st; Foils, 2nd.

This term he was made a Cadet Captain.

SUMMER TERM, 1907.—*Fencing Competition:* Sabres, 3rd; Foils, 2nd.

CHRISTMAS TERM, 1907.—In the Regatta, F. E. Oakeley rowed in the boat that came in 2nd in the "Drakes" Class Gig Race.

Rugby Notes.—" This term we lose Boyd, Oakeley, Peet, and Eddis, and we shall miss them greatly; but they should all four be a great gain to any ship they may join.

" Perhaps the strongest point in the team this year has been at half, where Oakeley and Boyd, nearly always playing behind winning forwards, have opened out the game in great style for our three-quarters, who very seldom missed a chance of turning an opening to account."

"F. E. Oakeley. Scrum-half. Obtains cap. A very good scrum-working half. If he keeps it up, should go far."

Oakeley's fencing ability was such that his achievements with the foils and sabres at Osborne and Dartmouth deserve a niche to themselves. He was generally first or second, and in fourteen competitions in 1905-7 won 7 firsts, 6 seconds, and 1 third, as follows :—

FENCING.

R.N. College, Osborne.

Summer, 1905, Sabre, 2nd.
Christmas, 1905, Sabre, 1st and Challenge Cup.

R.N. College, Dartmouth.

Easter (Drakes), 1906, Sabre, 1st; Foil, 1st.
Summer (Assault-at-Arms), 1906, Sabre, 1st; Foil, 2nd.
Christmas, 1906, Sabre, 2nd; Foil, 1st.
Royal Naval and Military Tournament, 1906, Cadets under 16 years. Sabre *v.* Sabre, 2nd Prize.
Easter, 1907, Sabre, 1st; Foil, 2nd.
Summer, 1907, Sabre, 3rd; Foil, 2nd.
Royal Naval and Military Tournament, 1907, Cadets over 16 years. Foil *v.* Foil, 1st Prize.

So that it was a very Compleat little Sportsman who went to sea when Oakeley's College days were over. Such a promising youngster was unlikely to escape the critical eye of Engineer-Lieutenant E. W. Roberts, R.N. (Devon and England), and he it was who taught Oakeley most of his Rugby. While Oakeley was a scrum-half to the public, he was described to me by such a famous United Services and England forward as "Dreadnought" Harrison as "about the best forward the Services have got!"

If I was asked to name Oakeley's strongest point, I should say his clever use of his feet in support of his forwards. This feature of his game was often lost sight of by onlookers; but nothing else he did, and he did most things that are in the game of a class scrum-half very well indeed, was quite so intelligently or so instantly done as this. He had the instinct for the game when to handle and when *not* to handle, and was on every count an even better scrum-half than he received the credit for being. Except R. H. Williamson (Oxford University and England), and possibly E. D Caddell (Dublin University and Ireland), and the late E. D. Simson (Scotland), no better scrum-half than Oakeley has played in any XV. of the home Unions in this century, R. M. Owen of Wales not being in the same class as the United Services player on a question of sheer straight Rugby football.

Oakeley played for England in four matches: twice against Scotland in 1913 and 1914, and against Ireland and France in 1914. He was also reserve scrum-half against Wales at Twickenham, January 17, 1914, when the mistake of playing the Leicester halves, Wood and Taylor, was made, and regretted. Oakeley never gave a bad game for England, and was very unlucky not to have played more often than he did; especially in view of the fact that he had first played for the Services when still a midshipman, and so had had early experience of what real first-class Rugby football means. Oakeley was a member of the Royal Navy XV. in the last three Navy *v.* Army matches at Queen's Club, the sixth of the new series, that of March 9, 1912, being the first big Rugby match witnessed by his Majesty King George V. as Sovereign. The Navy won the matches of 1912 and 1913 by 2 goals and 2 tries to 1 goal 1 try, and 3 goals 1 try to 1 goal 1 try respectively, but lost that of 1914 by 4 goals 2 tries to 1 goal 3 tries. These Army *v.* Navy matches are the exceptions which prove the rule, that tall scoring in Rugby football connotes weak defence. There is never a shortage of tackling in either the naval or the military fifteens, though team-defence may sometimes be lacking. It is the fine, free, open, out-to-score type of football played by both sides which makes this match what it is, the best annual game to watch, not excepting the Inter-'Varsity. Friend and foe had a high appreciation of Oakeley's talent, and after his appearance in Paris on April 13, 1914, it was written:—

"England, 6 goals 3 tries. France, 2 goals 1 try.

"En demis, les robustes compères des United Services se conjuguent à la perfection, et on ne sait ce que l'on doit le plus admirer de l'activité d'Oakeley ou de la clairvoyance et de la précision de Davies pour amorcer l'attaque....

"Derrière une mêlée victorieuse, les demis Oakeley et Davies firent ce qu'ils voulurent."

As a man Francis Oakeley was most religious and reverent. The sea teaches that. A brother officer of his told me the following incident, which happened after a great pal of Oakeley's had been lost on a submarine off Plymouth. He had heard the news after a big match at Queen's: "Oakeley took it absolutely fearlessly and quietly," said my friend, "but he was on his knees for over an hour that night before he turned in, and he wasn't asking that he might be spared a similar death, but it was all simply to the end that the men might be spared the agonies of a lingering death. No wonder the men all loved him. He was a fine boy and a very fine gentleman."

It was a strange fate that willed it he should meet a similar end. That he was British when he had to face it, every one who knew him is certain.

Of his Service career the following are the facts: He was one of the second batch of cadets entered under the "new scheme," and went to Osborne, January 1904. He passed out from Dartmouth in September 1908. As a midshipman he served in *London*, flagship of Rear-Admiral Startin, in the Channel Fleet, September 1908; in *Invincible*, Captain Mark Kerr, in the First Cruiser Squadron, March 1909; in *Téméraire*, in the First Battle Squadron, November 1909; in *Warrior*, in the Second Cruiser

Squadron, January 1910; in *Ure*, in the Second Destroyer Flotilla, July 1910; in *Dreadnought*, flagship of Sir William May, in the Home Fleets, September 1910; and in *Formidable*, in the Atlantic Fleet, April to September 1911.

At the end of November 1911 he was made Sub-Lieutenant, and appointed to *Superb* in the First Battle Squadron. In January 1913 he was appointed to *Dolphin* (Portsmouth submarine depot) for instruction, and in the following May was transferred to *Forth* at Devonport, for submarines. In September 1913 he returned to Portsmouth, on appointment to *Arrogant, for C* 17; and at the end of November, in the same year, was promoted to Lieutenant. In September 1914 he was appointed to the *Maidstone, additional for D* 2.

That he was held in the highest esteem the letters received from various brother officers and Rugby club honorary secretaries are eloquent witnesses. I give only the initials of the writers :—

" I was a shipmate of his when he first went to sea in the *Dreadnought*, and as I had been at school with his two elder brothers, I was naturally very interested in him. Even in the early days of his career I could not help noting the great promise he showed—a promise which he more than fulfilled as he got on in the Service. He was the very best type of naval officer, and keen at his work, and equally keen on every form of healthy enjoyment.

" The Navy has lost in him a splendid officer, and his old shipmates have to mourn the loss of a very good friend.

" F. L. L.-S."

From the Rugby Football Union.—" We all feel the loss greatly. Your son had endeared himself to all with whom he came in contact. It may be some consolation under the heavy blow to feel that his death in the service of his country in the hour of great peril is the noblest he could have chosen; also, on this account, his name in the Rugby world will be remembered long after his contemporaries are forgotten.

"C. J. B. M., Secretary."

"I was in your son's term, and he was my first, and best, friend I had at Osborne. I had the utmost admiration for him.
"L. C. R."

"*U.S. Recreation Grounds, Portsmouth.*—Will you please accept the deep regret and sympathy of myself and all the ground employees for the death of your dear son, whose cheery manner and gentlemanly courtesy were so much appreciated by us. "H. M'L., Secretary."

"I shall never forget him, and like to think of him as one of my best friends—one of the very best. "D. J. R. S."

"He served with me for over a year, so I got to know him very well, and it was a sad blow to me when he left. He was liked and admired by every one, and I can assure you he is as great a loss to the Service as he is to you. Personally, I have lost a great pal. "L. M'G.-R."

On the whole, it may be said of Oakeley that, though many players were popular among their fellow-players, opponents, and spectators, few ever so endeared themselves to these as he did. He had all the charm of character which compels our warmest admiration, and the news that he had gone down in a submarine was received with the most genuine pangs of regret. Oakeley was the youngest of five brothers, and his eldest brother, H. E. H., played Rugby for his college at Cambridge and for London Hospital. The first toy of any consequence F. E. Oakeley possessed was a full-sized Soccer ball. Perhaps there was never a younger dribbler than this brave little soul whose memory we all cherish.

RONALD WILLIAM POULTON PALMER

LIEUTENANT RONALD WILLIAM POULTON PALMER, Princess Charlotte of Wales Royal Berkshire Regiment (T.F.), was killed in action in the vicinity of Ploegsteert Wood, Belgium, on May 5, 1915, aged 25. Born at Wykeham House, Oxford, on September 12, 1889, Poulton Palmer was educated at Oxford Preparatory School (1897-1903), at Rugby School (1903-8), and at Balliol College, Oxford (1908-11).

Described by the Headmaster of the O.P.S. as the best all-round athlete who had ever been at the School, Poulton, as he was then, gave early evidence of athletic ability by winning the Long Jump, aged 13 and ten months, with a leap of 16 feet 11 inches; as well as by his performances in the three-quarter line at this well-known Preparatory.

At Rugby (School House) his athletic record included no fewer than three winnings of the Athletic Cup—namely, in 1906, 1907, and 1908. He was in the School Rugby XV. during four years (joint-captain with the late C. C. Watson in the last season), and in the Cricket XI. 1907 and 1908.

At Oxford he was in the 'Varsity XV.'s of 1909, 1910, and 1911. Oxford won all three games. He also played for Oxford against Cambridge in the Hockey teams of 1909, 1910, and 1911. The two former won by Oxford.

He played for England against Scotland in 1909, 1911-13, and 1914 (Captain); against Ireland 1909, 1912-13, and 1914 (Captain); against Wales 1910, 1912-13, and 1914 (Captain); against France 1909, 1913, 1914 (Captain); and the South Africans on January 4, 1913.

While engaged in securing this formidable array of coveted athletic honours Poulton Palmer found time to study for and to pass Examination " A," and gained the certificate in November 1909; and Examination " B," and gained certificate in May 1910.

In addition, he joined the Oxford University O.T.C. on December 12, 1908, resigning on December 12, 1911, with the rank of Cadet Colour-Sergeant.

The foregoing is a bare outline of the athletic and scholastic activities of at once one of the most able, one of the most popular, and one of the most discussed Rugby football players in the history of the game. His introduction to first-class football occurred on the Wandsworth ground on the three-quarter line of the Harlequins in a club match. Much was made at the time of the alleged " discovery " by A. D. Stoop of a promising young player; but a natural player of Poulton's type is never discovered. Such talent forces its way to the front, just as some beautiful flower, refusing to remain below the earth's surface, finds its way into day and sunlight, to bloom for the joy and delectation of all who recognize a rare thing when they see it. In his first first-class game Poulton made a memorable run from near his own 25 line, head thrown back, ball held out in front of him with both hands, his lower limbs seeming to follow his body in a lithe, sinuous style all his own. " This chap is going to make or mar some International teams," said an " old hand," after that game. Never was truer prophecy made, though the makings were rather more noticeable during the next few years—the prophecy was spoken in, I think, the autumn of 1908—than the marrings. Such was Poulton's style when he left Rugby, where he himself had for some time practically constituted the School XV., that he not only mystified the opposition, he mystified his own side as to his intentions. From first to last during his football career this was the flaw in his game, his at first rather delicate defence apart. Most three-quarters who possess the double swerve—and not many do—are in danger of being guilty of what is known as " upsetting " their fellow three-quarters, but when to this property they add a most pronounced byplay with the ball as well, as Poulton did, small wonder that he won a reputation for being a most difficult centre to partner. It was because of this

LIEUT. RONALD WILLIAM POULTON PALMER
Royal Berkshire Regiment

strong weakness, or weak strength, in his game that from the very first time I saw him I labelled him as a wing, and would never admit he was a centre. On this very point I well remember crossing swords with him, in company with the late Lieutenant-Colonel E. R. Mobbs, D.S.O., at Northampton. " I believe you are right," was Poulton Palmer's verdict, " but I mean to play in the centre as long as I am allowed to." The fact was that he liked being in the thick of things, and he felt that on the wing his double swerve was cramped, and that he was in that sense only half so effective in the wing positions. At least that is what I gathered from his own lips as we weighed the pros and cons. A very clear case, which supports my view, occurred in a much discussed incident, which many who saw it will remember, during the South African match on January 4, 1913, at Twickenham. All onlookers will recall that Poulton Palmer cut through down the centre (he was playing left centre), swerved *to the right*, the unexpectedness of this swerve leaving the South African full-back, G. Morkel, standing, and but for an overtaking tackle by E. E. M'Hardy from the South African right wing, would have scored to the right-hand side of goal. The critics, almost with one consent, rubbed it in to C. N. Lowe, England's right wing, for not being " up " for the pass. Discussing the affair afterwards with Poulton Palmer, he said : " It's all very well for them to slate Lowe, what I want to know is what Coates was doing " (V. M. H. Coates was England's left wing three-quarter). I saw my chance, but merely suggested that a wing three-quarter has his limitations, one of them being that he cannot possibly follow all the unexpected moves of his centre, especially one that takes him to the opposite side of the field. Without wings Coates had no chance whatever of being " up " on that occasion. It is, in the light of my estimate of Poulton Palmer's proper place in the three-quarter line, perhaps not a little curious that he should score his greatest success when playing on the wing. That was in the Inter-'Varsity match of 1909, when he scored 5 tries, which is the University match individual record for try-getting. He was left wing that day to C. M. Gilray (New Zealand and Scotland), and H. Martin, on the right wing to the late F. N. Tarr, scored 4 tries, the two wings doing all the scoring for Oxford. The next year, 1910, Poulton Palmer, now in the centre to the late W. P. Geen, scored 2 tries ; and both these players being out of their true positions, Oxford, really much the stronger team, came very near to defeat by scoring 4 goals and a try to 3 goals and a try. My recollection of the first half of that game is that, with Geen in the centre to Poulton Palmer, Oxford would have scored something like five or six tries in the first half, so many opportunities went the way of their left wing. In 1911 Poulton Palmer was Captain of Oxford, who won by 2 goals and 3 tries to nil, their captain scoring a try before he injured some muscle fibres in a thigh. Altogether, in the three years he was present in the Oxford University XV., the University won all three matches against Cambridge, totalling 10 goals and 9 tries against 3 goals and 2 tries, or 19 tries to 5, and of those 19 Poulton Palmer scored 8 himself. Truly a transcendent record, one that in itself will cause his name to be remembered in Oxford University Rugby as long as the game is played there.

To this remarkable individual experience has to be added the figures achieved in the seventeen International games Poulton Palmer took part in. Tabulated the total scores read as follows :—

	Played.	Won.	Lost.	For			Against		
				Goals.	Tries.	Points.	Goals.	Tries.	Points.
v. Scotland	5	3	2	5	6	43	7*	5	49
v. Ireland .	4	4	0	3*	15	59	4**	1	21
v. Wales .	4	4	0	7*	3	43	2*	2	15
v. France .	3	3	0	9	12	81	2	1	13
v. South Africa.	1	0	1	0	1	3	2††	1	9
Total .	17	14	3	24	37	229	17	10	107

* Denotes dropped goal. † Denotes penalty goal.

So far as I can discover, Poulton Palmer scored twenty tries in these seventeen matches; but even if he had not scored one, his International match experience was a most remarkable one, and may be even unique. It was enough to prove him at all events one of the greatest three-quarters of all time. Nobody feared him more than the Welshmen, and well do I remember discussing a forthcoming Welsh match with a Welshman who had not a little to do with the selection of Welsh XV.'s. " We have chosen —— especially because we know he will make Poulton part," was the gist of what he said. They felt over the Severn that if they could force the Oxonian to get rid of the ball the game was half won. In the hands of others it wanted much less watching. They came to Twickenham, Poulton Palmer was in the centre this time, and though —— did his best Wales have still to win at Twickenham.

Apart from his Oxford and International football career Poulton Palmer played frequently for the Harlequins, both as centre and on the wing, and at least once for the East Midlands in the same line as E. R. Mobbs, the fact of his birth at Oxford qualifying him for the E.M. Counties XV., according to the rules of county football. On leaving Reading to learn engineering in Liverpool, Poulton Palmer became one of the very successful Liverpool XV., under the captaincy of his old Oxford friend, the late Lieutenant F. H. Turner (Sedbergh and Scotland), the team including Lieutenant R. A. Lloyd, the Irish stand-off half and captain. Rarely, if indeed ever before, has any club team harboured three International Rugby captains of the same period as Liverpool did in 1913–14. No wonder that the Liverpool team was invincible in the North, and would have made any of the crack Southern club teams travel the whole course to win. During brief holidays in the Isle of Wight Poulton Palmer used to take part in matches there, and his last game of Rugby football before the war was one on that island in April 1914. In the biography of the late F. H. Turner I quote from the beautiful letter Poulton Palmer wrote to me about his old 'Varsity and Club captain, and the closing words of it were truly prophetic. Within a few months the hand that wrote them had been quieted for ever by a sniper's bullet, and Ronny Poulton, as all knew him, had joined his friend on the other side.

One could almost fill a small volume with similar reminiscences in which this attractive player loomed large, but a halt must be called as we turn to the more serious side of the life of one who was at heart a very serious fellow for all his smiling, boyish appearance.

I have already written of Poulton Palmer's first military experiences, ending with his resignation from the Oxford University O.T.C. On going down, however, and going to reside in Reading in January 1912, he took the chance of a commission in the Royal Berkshire Regiment (T.F.) on June 3, 1912, as Second-Lieutenant, and was gazetted Lieutenant July 24, 1913. On Sunday, August 2, 1914, Lieutenant R. W. Poulton Palmer went into camp with the Berkshires near Marlow; but on August 3 they were sent back to Reading, mobilized on August 4, and sent on August 5 to guard the Forts near Cosham. On Sunday, August 9, they were sent to Swindon, and during the course of that week, August 9 to 15, they were invited to volunteer for foreign service. With 70 per cent. of his battalion Lieutenant Poulton Palmer answered this call at once, and went on August 16 to Leighton Buzzard, Bedfordshire, into training. They marched thence to Dunstable, and after a few days were sent to Chelmsford, arriving on August 24, 1914, and remaining in training there until they left for the Front on March 30, 1915. His was a short experience of the horrors of this most horrible of all wars, for he had only about five weeks of it. His last letter, written to his sister, Mrs. Maxwell Garnett, and dated on the day of his death, but obviously written the day before, as he fell at 12.20 a.m. on May 5, runs :—

" Thank you so much for the lovely chocolate which arrived

last night up here. It was sweet of you to write, and also your letters are most welcome. Just as I was proceeding to open them at about twelve p.m., as I was at work all the early part of the night, we had to ' stand to ' as a Brigade order—that meant all being out. It was maddening—three hours messing about doing nothing. Then I got to bed at four, and was woken up and pulled out, because we were being shelled, and it is safer to be under the parapet than in a dug-out. They were shelling a house just in the middle of our trench, which they think we use for sniping (and so we do). But the first four shots hit our trench. The first went right through one officer's dug-out, but luckily he was the one officer on duty, so he wasn't hit. Luck! He'd have been in tiny bits! Another smashed the dug-out of our cook, but he was out too. The house had what was left of its chimney-piece [evidently " stack " intended] removed, and another big hole in the roof. That's about all. Now it's lovely, as I sit in our mess, which is dug down out of sight, but has a lovely back view of the country to the rear—a large root-field, a typical avenue main road to the right, a hill with a ruined château in front. I am getting a bit tired of the view. But it's safer than looking in front."

Two other letters, from brother officers, I am permitted to quote :—

From the late Lieut.-Col. Thorne :—

"Trenches, 5/5/15.

" Ronald was engaged on work of trench repair, in company with Sergeant Brant, and was hit by an enemy sniper at 12.20 a.m. Death, mercifully, must have been instantaneous. This I am sure of, as I reached him a moment after he was shot: he never spoke or moved again, and the Doctor, who shortly after arrived, is of the same opinion. Sergeant Brant did everything that could be done, but it was obviously all in vain. I cannot express what we feel about it, men and all were devoted to him, and there is not one of us who would not have cheerfully exchanged our lives for his. He never shirked a job, whatever the risk was, and he fell, as he would have liked to do, in the execution of his duty. The Regiment has lost one it could ill afford. . . ."

And, dated a day later, from Captain C. R. M. F. Cruttwell:—

"*May* 6, 1915.

" Those of us who have known him for a long while, and loved him, can enter just a little into the grief of his own people. You will have heard the details of his death. It is a great consolation to know that he died painlessly for England, beloved by every one in his Regiment. When I went round his old Company as they stood to, at dawn, almost every man was crying. He will always be an inspiration to those of us who remain. He will be laid in the wood this afternoon in soil which is already consecrate to the memory of many brave soldiers. The oak trees are just coming out, and the spring flowers; and the place would remind you much of the woods round Oxford."

Ronny Poulton Palmer had noble ideas on the equality of mankind, and it is said that when, on the sudden death of his uncle, the late Right Hon. G. W. Palmer, on October 8, 1913, he came into a large income and a deferred life interest in a large estate, one of the first things he said was: " What troubles me is the responsibility of how to use it for the best." He had interested himself greatly before this in the welfare of the employees of Messrs. Huntley and Palmer's factory at Reading, taking part in their sports, playing in the factory XI., and taking their Soccer team for training walks. He hoped some day to start the Rugby game there, and had already taken a lively interest in the Boys' Club of the Parish of St. John's, Reading, before moving north on business connected with the obtaining of engineering experience.

Of himself, Poulton Palmer had extremely little to say. But he was once heard to say that the greatest game he ever played in was the England *v.* Scotland match of March 1914, at Inverleith, when he was Captain of England, and Scotland lost by 2 goals 2 tries to 2 goals (1 dropped) and 2 tries. That was indeed a struggle of "mighty opposites," and at the time of writing these lines the War Record of those two fifteens is: 5 Englishmen and 6 Scotsmen fallen on the Field of Honour, and 2 Englishmen and 4 Scotsmen wounded; while only 4 of the 30 have not been under fire. Apart from this memorable game (the last International played in the United Kingdom) Poulton Palmer considered the greatest games he played in as those against Wales at Cardiff in 1913 in a sea of mud, and against South Africa a few days previously, when he obtained the only try scored against Captain W. A. Millar's South African team of 1912-13 in the four International matches of that " record " tour.

It is, indeed, hard to say "farewell" to such a man. Personally, though I did not know him well, I shall never forget the shock I experienced when, strangely enough, I saw the placard at Waterloo Station announcing Poulton Palmer had fallen. There, where I had gone so often on my way to see him play, it was terrible first to become aware of the loss our world of games and its chief game had suffered. Ronny Poulton Palmer can never be forgotten; such men do, indeed, live for ever, enshrined in hearts which have learned to love them even if only at a distance.

One feels instinctively that it might have been while thinking of Poulton Palmer that the late Captain Basil Hood wrote those moving lines :—

"Some one called England so,
'This young, fresh England'; he, at the Mermaid Tavern,
Spoke so; and one who listened answered him:
'By three words hast thou prettily conjured
A picture of smooth Thames and green pasture;
That hath the very sound of schoolboy feet
Rushing through meadow grass—this young, fresh England.'
And the other laughed, and leaned across the table
To touch his friend, lifting himself a little
To mark his humour; saying: 'I tell thee, friend,
When thou and I lie dead three hundred years,

Unto this England shall new breath be given—
Salt of the Sea—borne by the winds of Heaven;
And young, fresh England shall stand up awake,
To spend her youth for youth and freshness' sake!'"

For Ronald William Poulton Palmer was the worthiest exemplar in our day of this young, fresh England which the dramatist pictures.

JAMES PEARSON

PRIVATE JAMES PEARSON, 9th Royal Scots, fell in action at Hooge, Belgium, on May 22, 1915, aged 26. He joined the Army in August 1914, and left for the Front on his birthday, February 24, 1915.

James Pearson, born February 1889, went to George Watson's College in 1896, started playing cricket in 1899, and in that season and all others till 1904 (his first year in the 1st XI.) he made at least one score of over 50. He was in the 1st XI. for four seasons, 1904–7, and won the batting average on two occasions, 1905 and 1907. During 1907, while playing for the Former Pupils XI., he had the satisfaction of making his first century (102 not out, against Leith Caledonian). In the football season of 1905–6 he was persuaded by some of his school friends to take up Rugby. He did so, and during his first year an accident to Milroy, the famous half, saw him get a place in the 1st XV. as a half. The next year he was in the side as a three-quarter, which proved to be his real position. During the summer of 1907 he carried off the School Championship at the Athletic Sports, being placed in the 100 Yards, 440, the Hurdles, Throwing the Cricket Ball, and the Long Jump. After leaving the school he played regularly for the Watsonians at both cricket and football; he missed only two cricket matches for them, and that was when playing for Edinburgh v. Glasgow, and only missed one Rugby match, owing to an attack of water on the knee. In seven seasons of Wat-

PRIVATE JAMES PEARSON
9th Royal Scots
Photo: Ayton, Edinburgh

sonian cricket he won the batting average on either three or four occasions. In 1914 he topped the Watsonians' averages with the highest that had been for a great number of years—namely, 52. His Rugby International matches were as follows: I., E., 1909; F., W., I., E., 1910; F., 1911; F., W., S.A., 1912; I., E., 1913. Against France in 1911 he dropped a goal, and against France in 1912 he dropped a goal from a penalty, and scored a try. When he first played for Scotland he weighed just over 9 stone with all his clothes on, so that stripped he must have been a good bit under 9 stone, which is an extraordinarily light weight for an International centre three-quarter. He was very keen on Seven-a-Side football; but only had the opportunity of playing on four occasions, on each of which, however, he was on the winning side. He was a regular competitor at the Annual Sports in the F.P. events, and with the exception of one year he always won at least once. In his last year, 1914, he was second in the 100 yards and first in the half-mile, both from scratch. In the half-mile he covered the first quarter in $57\frac{2}{5}$. Very keen on golf, he had not much time for it. In 1913 he joined the Edinburgh and Leith Corn Merchants' Club, and in his first competition he won the scratch prize. Pearson played in only two golf competitions in his life, the aforementioned and another in the same club, when he was beaten, after a tie, for third prize. All outside sports he loved—tennis, badminton, fives, and curling. In a letter his Colonel wrote of him to a friend in Edinburgh: "He was as popular with the men of my battalion as he was at Myreside." James Pearson was killed by a shot from a sniper.

There is no doubt that Pearson was a very fine centre three-quarter indeed in Club football; but whether or no it is admitted in Scotland, he never really shone in International football. The reason is not far to seek. He was too light. For a centre three-quarter nine stone fully clad is an absurd weight, and so this gallant Scot was always struggling against an overwhelming handicap when it came to International fray.

What possible chance could he have of coping successfully with a rush of Irish forwards, or of Welsh miners and policemen, or of stopping a John Birkett or a Failliot in full stride ? Scotland won six and lost six of the dozen games in which Pearson took part, these including two wins and a defeat by France. Small light players can be great successes as wing three-quarters in International football, as C. N. Lowe proved in almost every match he played in, but it is beyond human power to be so in the centre at eight stone something. For all that, worse players have been seen in that position in the Scottish XV.; and taking this handicap fully into account, the fairest verdict on Pearson as an International centre is that he was very nearly a wonderful player.

LOUIS AUGUSTUS PHILLIPS

SERGEANT LOUIS AUGUSTUS PHILLIPS, Royal Fusiliers, was killed in action near Cambrin, France, on March 14, 1916, aged 38. Phillips was born at Stow Hill, Newport, Monmouthshire, on February 24, 1878. He was educated at Monmouth Grammar School, afterwards serving his articles with Messrs. Huberston and Fawckner, architects, and being elected A.R.I.B.A. He started practice in 1907. When war broke out he joined the Public Schools Battalion Royal Fusiliers in September 1914, and went to France on November 16, 1915. He was shot through the chest while out with a wiring party on the night of March 14, and is buried in Cambrin Churchyard.

" Lou " Phillips, as he was known by everybody, was one of the most versatile games-men Wales ever owned. He played both cricket and water-polo, and started his Rugby football career by playing for Monmouth Grammar School. Later his work at half-back with Llewellyn Lloyd for Newport and for Wales became an historic partnership. He gained his place in the Newport 1st team in 1897–8—the year in which J. J.

SERGEANT LOUIS AUGUSTUS PHILLIPS
Royal Fusiliers
Photo: Siedle, Cardiff

Hodges, R. T. Skrimshire, and other well-known men came into prominence. Phillips played at scrum-half four times for Wales— namely, against England, Scotland, and Ireland in 1900, and against Scotland in 1901. In the latter match he damaged his knee, and the injury put an end to his International football career.

As a golfer Phillips was Amateur Champion of Wales in 1907 and in 1912, and went further outside Wales than any of his compatriots, as he was runner-up for the Irish Championship in 1913, and was beaten in the sixth round for the Open Championship in 1914. He was a bachelor, a most reticent man, and, as one who knew him very well has told me, " nobody talked less about his own athletic deeds than he did ; while he was as true as steel, kind-hearted, loved by children and animals, and a sportsman in the best sense of the term."

Wherever Welsh half-back play is discussed among Rugby men the name of L. A. Phillips is always spoken of as one to conjure with. And, indeed, he was one of the great scrum-halves of all time.

ROBERT LAWRENCE PILLMAN

CAPTAIN ROBERT LAWRENCE PILLMAN, 10th Battalion Royal West Kent Regiment, died of wounds near Armentières, on July 9, 1916, aged 23. Born at Sidcup on February 16, 1893, he was educated at Merton Court, Sidcup, and Rugby School (1907– 11), where he was a forward in the 1st XV. in 1910, and also got his XXII. in 1910. He was a brother of the famous Blackheath and England forward, Captain C. H. Pillman, Dragoon Guards ; and his single appearance in the English XV. was against France in April 1914, in the last International match played before the War. When hostilities broke out, Captain Pillman enlisted in the 10th Battalion Royal West Kent Regiment on

September 1, 1914, trained at Colchester and at Ludgershall, became Lance-Corporal, and then got his commission in the same Battalion in July 1915. Was promoted Captain in January 1916, and went to the Front in France in May 1916. He volunteered for Brigade bombing officer, and was leading a raid on an important part of the enemy's trenches when he was mortally wounded. One of his brothers writes to me in eloquent words, that will go home to the heart of every reader :—

" Attached herewith are letters from brother officers which speak for themselves. Their testimony proves that he maintained in his military career that same open-hearted, generous nature that made him such a dear brother and pal."

Thus, F. W. Waydelin : " Your son's death has cast quite a gloom over the Regiment. He was liked and admired by every officer, N.C.O., and man, and we could ill afford to lose him. He was always cheery, and set a good example of pluck. He was doing a very courageous deed when he was hit."

And A. Wood Martyn : " It is the greatest grief to us all, and myself in particular. I was very near when he was shot, and was able to help him to a shelter when the doctor came, when I had to leave, but sent Coke to do what he could for him, and he died shortly afterwards. Had he survived, I fear the shot in his thigh would have maimed him for life, as it was the result of a ricochet bullet."

John R. Coke was with him during his last plucky moments. " I went to him directly I heard he had been hit," he wrote, " and stayed with him to the last; everything possible that could be done for him was done, and he died as he lived out here, like a man and a brave soldier. I have lost my greatest friend, and a boy I loved as my own brother; so just how you must feel, whose own son he was, I can well imagine."

We must not trespass further in this hallowed private correspondence concerning one who might have had his commission

CAPTAIN ROBERT LAWRENCE PILLMAN
10th Batt. Royal West Kent Regiment

Photo : Tear, Ipswich

some time before he took it, but refused to take it until the three friends with whom he enlisted got theirs also. A beautiful nature shone out in this act alone; for in those, as in most, days it was pleasant to escape from the roughing it of life in the ranks to the comparative luxury of existence as a commissioned officer. During Pillman's training as an officer he was sent to the Staff College, Camberley, where it was only natural that a Rugby, Blackheath, and England forward would be in great request for leading the morning runs which formed part of the training. And when the day came for work of a particularly dangerous character, Bob Pillman at once volunteered, although he might have left the task to junior officers. His thoroughness was shown when he selected fifty of the men, who also had volunteered, and trained them himself for some weeks on a specially prepared replica of the German trenches which had to be raided, so that on the day they seemed to be going over familiar ground. The young officer had already had considerable raiding experience, and on one such adventure a soldier being gassed Bob Pillman carried him to safety on his back. On the night of his death he had determined that the raid should be effective, but he never had a doubt as to the great risks to be run. It was to be a raid of some hours' duration, as they had to get through much wire entanglement. This some half-dozen of them had succeeded in doing, and it was while he was waiting on the German parapet for the patrol to pass down the trench that he was hit by a shot fired by a German soldier coming over the parados. Pillman ordered his men to retire, and managed to struggle back himself to our trenches, where he died in a few hours.

Thus died one of the finest of our youngsters, a boy of whom Dr. White, the head of his firm (Pillman had taken his Intermediate exams for a solicitor's profession), wrote to his father: " He was one of the finest lads who have gone to fight, body, heart, and brain. Oh! the pity of it. He had all the promise of a good and great man."

Off the Rugby field Bob Pillman had proved that when he became too old for the more strenuous game he was very likely to make his mark on the links. He had won the Gold Medal of the London Solicitors' Golf Club, as well as the first-class handicap of the Sidcup Golf Club. Nor must I forget that he was a member of the pack of the " London " fifteen, which was one of the two to defeat the great South African team of 1912-13.

Of his prowess in the Rugby game one of the best judges of it who ever lived has written—I refer to R. L. Aston (Tonbridge, Cambridge, Blackheath, and England)—in the following terms :—

" Bob Pillman, younger brother of the famous Charlie, gained his International colours v. France in 1914, and but for his untimely end and the War would have undoubtedly played in more Internationals. He was not of the same type of forward as his brother, but always played very hard, and was quick on the ball—he was rather light for an International pack, but this fact brings into greater prominence his many virtues as a forward. He took pains always to be in good condition, and could be relied upon to do his full share of work in the scrum and in following up outside it, while his tackling was also very sound. ' Never say die ' was his motto in football as in war, and England can ill afford to spare so fine a fellow."

From a dug-out on the Somme " C. H." wrote me concerning his younger brother, in these modest terms :—

" At Rugby School R. L. Pillman played for the 1st XV. and also represented the school at Fives. Leaving school he played for Blackheath, and with F. S. Stone, Sykes, and Craven formed the basis of the best pack of late years. R. L. Pillman was a big and strong forward, who was very quick and neat for his weight. With F. S. Stone he shared the honours for always being up to get into the front rank, and as hookers they were unsurpassed. They were especially good in this respect when playing against

Welsh sides, when loose head was a thing that had to be got to do any good. As a tackler R. L. Pillman was great, his play being always very, very hard, but never foul, and in some of the matches that were played this hard play was the deciding feature of the match. R. L. Pillman played for England against France in the last International played, and I believe played very well indeed. As a golfer he was very good, reaching the scratch mark and playing most consistently."

Captain R. L. Pillman was, in my opinion, only at the very threshold of a long career as an International forward. He was only just of age when he played against France, and was at that time getting a very sound grounding in the art of scrummage play with the Blackheath pack, with men like Lieutenant-Colonel W. S. D. Craven, D.S.O., and his brother, C. H. Pillman, as mentors and exemplars. It is not until a man has approached the middle twenties, as a rule, that he really knows anything about this game, or cricket, the rare genius of the Vassall-Macleod-Maclear-Lowe type excepted. Pillman had the constitution, the pluck, the honesty of purpose, the brain, and the faculty of playing downright hard football all the time, that is never missing from the football character of a really good forward, to support my suggestion that 1914 was for him the beginning of a long period studded with English Caps, to appear later like stars to brighten his old age and to carry his memory back to the golden hours of Youth and Vigour, when man crashed at man in mimic war and rivalry as keen and as fierce, though less deadly, than that of this ghastly War, with its futile slaughter and destruction of manhood most glorious. And, now, it is Bob Pillman who is the memory; but a memory all who ever saw or knew him will not cease to cherish.

CHARLES MEYRICK PRITCHARD

CAPTAIN CHARLES MEYRICK PRITCHARD, 12th Battalion South Wales Borderers, died at No. 1 Casualty Clearing Station in France on August 14, 1916, of wounds sustained during the night of August 12-13, aged 33. Pritchard was born at Newport on September 30, 1882, and was educated at Newport Intermediate School. He played for the Long Ashton, Bristol; Newport Intermediate and Newport Clubs; and was Captain of Newport, for which he played for many years. His first International match was Wales v. Ireland, in 1904 at Belfast, when Ireland won by a goal-kick, 1 goal 3 tries to 4 tries. After that this grand forward became practically a fixture in the Welsh XV., playing against England, Scotland, and New Zealand in 1905; England, Scotland, and Ireland in 1906 and 1907; South Africa in 1906; France in 1910; and England in 1908 and 1910—or fourteen matches in all. He was without exception one of the finest forwards who ever played for Wales. His ceaseless and quite indefatigable energy was a feature of every match he played in, whether for his club or his country, and he played himself to a standstill in the memorable game with the New Zealanders. While it is true that Pritchard was often a back-row forward, nobody could truthfully accuse him of " winging," as the heavy work had absolutely no terrors for him. He had the true tackle, hard and low, and very tenacious. At the line-out, whether he or his nearest opponent got the ball, there was generally something definite done. His game was as true as a bell, like his nature, which was unfailingly cheerful and full of exuberance. He made hosts of friends among opponents and fellow-players alike; and though no forward of his day played a game more full of fire, nobody ever saw Charlie Pritchard guilty of anything but the cleanest, straightest Rugby. His death was deeply deplored wherever he had played in the four Unions.

CAPTAIN CHARLES MEYRICK PRITCHARD
12th Batt. South Wales Borderers

Photo: Wykeham, London

It was in 1915 that Pritchard took his commission in the 12th South Wales Borderers, and leaving for the Front on June 5, 1916, he soon got his Company. For him the experience of active service was not of long duration. The act for which he was mentioned in dispatches, and in the performance of which he received his mortal wounds, was described officially as follows :—

" Captain Pritchard was in charge of a raiding party on the night of August 12–13, 1916, the object being to secure a prisoner. He led his men with the greatest dash and bravery, entering the enemy trenches at the head of his party. He was almost immediately wounded in the wrist, but nevertheless continued to encourage and direct his men. He himself took one of the enemy prisoner and forced him to ascend the ladder, following him over the parapet. He was then again badly wounded, and handed the prisoner over to another officer of his party. He was finally brought back to our parapet in a state of collapse, owing to his many wounds. The success of the enterprise was largely due to his gallant leadership and devotion to duty."

For this, which was signed by the Lieutenant-Colonel Commanding the 12th South Wales Borderers, Alexander Pope, he was recommended for the Military Cross by Brigadier-General A. S. Prichard, 119th Infantry Brigade. Major-General H. Ruggles Brise, Commanding 40th Division, wrote on the report : " I should have recommended this Officer for the D.S.O., but he has, unhappily, died to-day of his wounds. I recommend that he be mentioned in dispatches."

The news of his dangerous wounding reached Mrs. Pritchard on August 13, and two days later came the dread telegram. The blow was softened a few days later by receipt of a most kindly letter from his Commanding Officer, from which I have been permitted to cull these extracts :—

" Had he lived he would, without doubt, have received the

decoration. He was always as brave as a lion, and he died as he would have wished, a truly glorious death fighting for his country in a great cause. It is not given to all of us to die in such a haze of glory."

His Brigadier-General wrote : " We all admired him, especially those who knew him best, and deplore with you the loss of such a brave soldier."

Captain Pritchard was conscious when brought into our trenches and able to ask : " Have they got the Hun ? " and when they said : " Yes, he's all right,"—" Well, I have done my bit." And those were practically his last words. They were certainly characteristic.

The South African International, Major J. E. C. Partridge (Newport, Blackheath, and Army), has written the following warm and thoroughly well-deserved appreciation of Charlie Pritchard :—

"He was a very powerful forward, who played his hardest bang up to 'no-side.' I have never met a man who played more in the spirit of the game. He played one of his greatest games against New Zealand at Cardiff in December 1905. Pritchard was Captain of Newport—for whom his first match was in Llewellyn Lloyd's year against Swansea—for three seasons. He was a fine example of what a British sportsman should be, and was loved by all who came in contact with him. He was so strong, and yet did not know his own strength. One of his most cherished possessions was a set of jerseys of every International, Colonial, and County team he had ever played against, and whenever he got up a team for a charity match he turned them out in these jerseys. He was a fine fisherman and shot. I have heard that in the raid in which he was mortally wounded, I believe by a German officer, Charlie knocked down two of the enemy with his fists. He died as he had lived, playing for his side to the last."

JOHN EDWARD RAPHAEL

LIEUTENANT JOHN EDWARD RAPHAEL, Duke of Wellington's West Riding Regiment, attached King's Royal Rifle Corps, was born in Belgium in 1882. He lies buried in Belgium, having died on June 11, 1917, of wounds sustained on June 7, aged 35. He was the only son of the late Mr. Albert and Mrs. Raphael, and was a cousin of Major Sir Herbert Raphael, M.P. for South Derby. Educated at Merchant Taylors' School, whose best all-round athlete by far he was, Raphael went to St. John's, Oxford, as a History Scholar in 1901, having played in the XV. and XI. from 1897–1901, and been Captain of both in 1900 and 1901. He represented his school at Aldershot in fencing, and was also an accomplished swimmer. At Oxford he played for the XI. three times against Cambridge at Lord's, scoring 130 in 1903, and two years later failing by only one run to achieve another century. He found time to become President of the Oxford University Swimming Club. Getting his football Blue in 1901, he played four times against Cambridge at Queen's Club as a centre three-quarter, on the winning side in 1901 and 1903, the losing in 1904, while the other game was drawn, a goal and a try each. Between 1902 and 1906 he won nine International Caps for England—namely, three each against Wales and Scotland, and one each against Ireland, New Zealand, and France. In 1903 and 1904 he did not play once for England. Meanwhile he played cricket for Surrey during the four years 1903–6, and was Captain of the XI. in 1904. Later he went on tour with a football team in the Argentine. The foregoing is ample evidence of great athletic versatility, such as would have sufficed to satisfy the demands on the energy of most young men between the ages of nineteen and twenty-seven, but John Raphael had very serious views of life, and was far from being content with the ephemeral laurels of athletic success. Proof that he had political ambitions was shown when he became President of the Palmerston Club in 1904–5, and he strongly advocated women's suffrage at the Union. He entered Lincoln's Inn on going down in 1905, and was called to the Bar in 1908. He made a bid for Parliament, when he fought Croydon unsuccessfully in the Liberal interest in 1909. A tour round the world in 1911–12 he thoroughly enjoyed, and came back and played for his beloved Old Merchant Taylors on their glorious turf at the Old Deer Park, Richmond, whether as three-quarter or as full-back, almost as well as ever, though then in the thirties. It is noteworthy that one of his last appearances at Oxford was when, at an Essay Society, he engaged a German Rhodes Scholar and an Austrian Pole in a three-cornered discussion of much interest, and not without significance in the light of subsequent events. Raphael was the organizing secretary of a movement for promoting societies for the study of " War and Peace."

As a player Raphael's style was a model of clean, straight, typically English play. He impressed one as just the type one would choose for young boys to go to watch that they might exercise their imitative powers. Those who did so were sure not to go far wrong. The defect in his game was a tendency to inconsistency, and to roving. Perhaps it was this latter fault which induced the selectors to deem it a virtue and to play him " as a rover " against the New Zealanders at the Crystal Palace in December 1905. Surely never in an important game was a good player more completely wasted than on that memorable afternoon. I have a distinct vision of John Raphael's tackling that day—the number of times he had to tackle the man who had just passed the ball was extraordinary, for there was nobody else to tackle, and he had to tackle. It was really a most peculiar feature of a big match, and Raphael was in no way to blame. He was, indeed, ubiquitous, but the New Zealanders got their five tries as though he was non-existent; indeed it seemed as though two or three more " rovers " would not have altered the result. It is not to

LIEUT. JOHN EDWARD RAPHAEL
Duke of Wellington's West Riding Regiment

Photo : Bournemouth View Co.

be supposed that such a mentally equipped man as John Raphael would participate regularly in any game simply for the physical exercise. He studied this grand game of ours, and by the time he had added the experience of two or three International matches to his large store of games-knowledge, it is the bare truth to quote in his case the trite and oft-abused saying, that what he did not know about Rugby football was not worth bothering about. Though trite, the phrase is but a dangerous half-truth, as there is always something left in this highly intelligent game to " bother " about. I feel rather sure that though he had pondered its problems John Raphael did not admit finality had been reached. He, like all sensible players, was always learning and ready to learn; in this, again, he was a model for our schoolboys, some of whom are a little apt to imagine that the wearing of the School 1st XV. cap connotes complete knowledge of all there is to know about the Rugby game. Raphael's study had the all-important result that his play was generally, almost invariably, very sound. When he failed, he failed attempting the right game. His target in defence was the man with the ball; and in attack it was to pass the ball to the man whom he had decided was the most likely to be free to do something with it in the event of his acceptance of the pass. Nobody ever saw John Raphael run up to the full-back with a fellow in attendance, and then try to score the try himself. No question of selfishness or unselfishness entered into his pass on such occasions to his team-mate. He knew it was Rugby football to pass, so he passed. That sums up his game. His faculty for going for the man with the ball it was that was responsible for the feature of the game at the Crystal Palace already alluded to. His insistence on this primary rule of all defence compelled the New Zealanders engaged by him to part with the ball. Their good play in not parting until the last possible moment of time it was that caused Raphael to be left so often with the man-without-the-ball. The only alternative was to bluff, and he knew the New Zealanders could also bluff! But I saw him bluff such an old soldier as his once fellow Oxonian, A. D. Stoop, into making a pass too soon. Stoop was bearing down on Raphael, then playing full-back, with John Birkett handy to Stoop's left—the line ten yards distant. There was never, granted the pass correctly given and taken, a greater certainty of a try being scored. But no try was scored, and Raphael actually floored Birkett with a man-and-ball tackle worthy of Gamlin at his best. This was how he did it. Judging his time and distance with almost uncanny accuracy—and knowing that Stoop would be sure to pass—he dashed at Stoop as though to tackle the man-with-the-ball, but broke off his dash after the first step and went straight for Birkett. Stoop, deceived by the first sign of a dash at him, passed the ball, which reached Birkett practically simultaneously with Raphael! It was the most perfectly managed bit of defence by a full-back, confronted by two good and experienced attackers, I have ever seen. Just about this time Raphael was in the running to play for England as a full-back, a thing not generally known. For the selectors were then wavering between W. R. Johnston of Bristol and S. H. Williams of Newport — an Irishman and a Welshman!—for the English full-back position. And they decided in favour of the Welshman, though there was at least one Englishman, albeit born in Belgium, who was as good as either.

Concerning Raphael's Army career I think it would not be unfair to state that he was a shining example to all pacifists, being one himself. For in the first month of war he was one of a body of sixty Old Merchant Taylors who marched to the headquarters of the Hon. Artillery Company to enlist. He had travelled, and read, and he knew. He was not long in getting a commission, and was gazetted to the West Ridings in December 1914. Unselfishness, if I may say so, was the keynote of the young officer's service. He saw to everybody else's wants—whether it was a hot meal, a cricket bat, or a football—before his own. His football inconsistency was shed, but he still clung in the right sense to his "roving" propensities, for he became A.D.C. to the G.O.C., "ran" the sports and games, was Mess President and Camp Commandant; and he would never allow that his Division was second to any other. His men adored him, it is needless to add.

How John Raphael looked death fairly and squarely in the face—for he had time to do this—was precisely how any one who knew him would have expected him to, and that is unselfishly. His beloved Division had taken a German stronghold with great success, and with three others John had gone to inspect the position just won. Captain Eric White it is who tells the simple yet noble story :—

"There were four of us together," he wrote to Mrs. Raphael. "John, Captain Quare, our G.S.O. 3, my servant, and myself. We were just leaving a dug-out, and John and my servant were in front. I was immediately behind them, and Captain Quare was still in the dug-out. The shell burst only a few feet in front of us. I was more or less knocked over, and when I recovered myself my servant ran up to me saying he was hit. I took him into the dug-out to see if he was bad or not; and after some moments I heard John say in a perfectly natural voice, ' Will some one come here a minute ? ' I went outside and found him lying near the door, obviously wounded. Captain Quare immediately went out to find stretcher-bearers and a doctor, while I, with the help of another man, carried John into the dug-out; and I started to dress the wound. . . . So far I have confined myself merely to a statement of facts; but, above all things, I want to impress upon you how extraordinarily pluckily he behaved. I don't think he ever suffered much pain, but he was, of course, very uncomfortable and had experienced a great shock; nevertheless he never made a murmur or complaint. While he was being bound up he asked several times after my servant. . . . I saw him three times in the Casualty Clearing Station after that, and on each occasion he was bright and cheerful. He never talked about himself . . . but was very concerned about his servant, his groom, his horses, and everything else except himself. I have seen many men in many parts of the world under all sorts of conditions, but never in my experience have I been so impressed by such a magnificent display of sheer pluck and unselfishness."

Later it was found necessary to operate on his wounds, which were very severe in the chest and back. During the operation the trouble was found to be more serious than had been expected, and although he was perfectly conscious for some hours after the operation, he never seemed to recover, and at five minutes past ten on the night of June 11, 1917, John Raphael died. He was buried next day at 2 p.m. in the Military Cemetery at Remy, a mile from Poperinghe, General Lamford, G.O.C., and many others being present at the final scene.

And thus one of the most popular and best loved of our Rugby Internationals crossed the vale and joined the fine company of the best and bravest of our blood, who awaited him and beckon to us Yonder. We who knew him knew him as a great big healthy boy full of the *joie de vivre*, with seemingly not a care in the world. It might have been of John Raphael that R. L. Stevenson was thinking when he wrote:—

> "All that life contains of torture, toil, and treason,
> Shame, dishonour, death, to him were but a name.
> Here, a boy, he dwelt through all the singing season,
> And ere the day of sorrow departed as he came."

LEWIS ROBERTSON

Captain Lewis Robertson, Cameron Highlanders, died of wounds on November 3, 1914, sustained on the previous day at the First Battle of Ypres, aged 31. He was twice wounded, the

CAPTAIN LEWIS ROBERTSON
Cameron Highlanders
Photo : Lafayette, Dublin

first time not seriously, after which he insisted on returning to his men, when he was mortally wounded. He was buried in the garden of the Convent of the Blessed Virgin in Wennick Street, Ypres, as the Germans were shelling the cemetery that day.

Born on August 4, 1883, at Hawthornden, Captain L. Robertson went when ten years old to Cargilfield, and in 1898 to Fettes College, Edinburgh, whence he passed out into the Royal Military College, Sandhurst, in December 1901; passing out thence with honours in December 1902, and joining the 1st Battalion Cameron Highlanders in May 1903 at Fort George. His regiment was transferred to Dublin in 1905, and it was then that he played for Monkstown. At Fettes he played during his last season for, and was a member of, the 1st XV., for which it has often been said that he never got his colours, and in the Army found ample scope for the exercise of his keenness on games and athletic pursuits, being especially keen on gymnastics and bayonet fighting. He passed at Hythe, then took a course of mounted infantry training. He afterwards increased his knowledge of the military art at Woolwich, at Enfield, at Tidworth, and at Aldershot, where he went through a course of gymnastic training, and was, in 1911, appointed Assistant Inspector of Gymnasia to the Eastern Command, and was stationed at Shorncliffe. He worked exceedingly hard while holding this appointment, which he did when war broke out, and there was probably no better, and certainly no more keen, officer in the Army in this particular sphere of Gymnastics and Bayonet Fighting.

During all this time Robertson never lost an opportunity of playing Rugby football. As a consequence of the life he led, backed by his own thoroughness and earnestness of purpose, he became, as Major H. C. Harrison, R.M.A. (Old Edwardians, United Services, Navy, Army, and England), once said to me, " Quite the hardest man to come up against I ever met on the football field. He used to go through every game with teeth clenched, often muttering to himself to spur him on. He was a terror to run up against, as hard as a nail and a fighter through and through, until he was absolutely stopped." Such testimony from such a quarter speaks for itself, as Harrison is not a critic who praises without excellent reason. Captain Robertson was a playing member in turn of Monkstown, London Scottish, Edinburgh Wanderers, United Services, and the Fettesian-Lorettonians, with whom he went on many tours at Christmas. He played for London Scottish for ten seasons, and in six successive years for the Army and Navy at Queen's Club, and was Captain of the Army XV., which in the last match played, that of March 1914, beat the Navy. It was typical of his fine, modest character that on one occasion when for some reason, probably connected with overwork, he did not feel that he was fit for such a match, he offered to stand down from the captaincy of the Army XV., and thus to give up also the honour of being presented with his team to His Majesty, because he considered it in the interests of the Army XV. that he should not be included. But let Major Rainsford-Hannay, D.S.O., tell the story. Major Rainsford-Hannay, as Hon. Secretary of the Army Rugby Union, has done more for the game in the Army than any individual off the field; his will be an even busier task after the Peace, when Rugby football is made compulsory in every regiment, as it naturally will be. Major Rainsford-Hannay wrote to me in these terms:—

"Lewis Robertson was one of my greatest friends. My youngest boy, who was born on August 23, 1914, is called after him, and he was to have been his godfather. As regards any details of his soldiering life I can tell you very little. I do know that he was shot through the shoulder, and insisted on going back to his company after the wound had been dressed. He was then wounded again, this time mortally. He could not be taken away, and had to be left where he was till night. He talked and spoke quite cheerfully after being hit the second time. He died at, I think, the Convent of the Blessed Virgin, Ypres, and is buried in the garden. As regards his games I can tell you very little that you do not already know. He was the hardest working forward I ever met, and for that reason rarely showed up in a theatrical way. He was always where the work was hardest, and anything in the shape of winging was abhorrent to him. It was on account of this that people, who never saw him do anything spectacular, used to think he was not a really great forward. He was certainly the chief factor in turning out the Army pack of 1914. From the very first he took a strong stand against anything in the shape of 'winging,' and always said that if a forward couldn't push as well as run he was no use to him. I can give you an incident which shows what a really great sportsman he was. Lewis had played for the Army ever since the matches against the Navy were started in 1907. Speaking from memory, I think he played in every match but the first. At any rate he held the record for number of games played, not only Army and Navy, but for all Army matches. In 1913 he was elected Captain. The 1913–14 season was to be his last, and his great ambition was to wind up his football career as Captain of a winning Army side against the Navy. Shortly before the match H. C. Harrison became eligible for the Army team, owing to his having been given a shore job. He was unquestionably a better leader than Lewis, who was handicapped by short sight. One day Lewis came to me, and said, 'Look here, I think I ought to stand down from the side this time. The "Dreadnought" is a much better leader of forwards, and I am getting a back number. I'll resign the captaincy, and let him take it on and lead the forwards.' He was quite prepared, in what he thought were the best interests of the team, to stand down altogether and give up what he had looked forward to for years. Of course we refused to let him go. He was well worth his place on form, so we compromised. Harrison led the forwards, and Lewis captained the team. I mention the incident, as it was so typical of him. We worked together for years for the Army XV., and never had a cross word. He was a regular attendant at committee meetings—often at great personal inconvenience, and nobody has done more for Rugby football in the Army. If I had to write his epitaph, I think I could do it in four words :—

" ' A VERY PERFECT GENTLEMAN.' "

Lewis Robertson went twice to play at Bordeaux with the Army XV. got together by Major Rainsford-Hannay. During the years 1908-13 he played nine times for Scotland, having, for such a rare worker, the peculiar experience of playing his first International match in March 1908, and his next in February 1911. Again he was left out until the following year against Wales, when he played in the most disastrous defeat Scotland ever sustained from the Welshmen—that of 3 goals (1 dropped) and 6 tries to 1 dropped goal and 2 tries—at Edinburgh, in February 1912. Thereafter he played in every match of 1912, including that against the South Africans on November 23rd, and all three matches against the Home Unions in 1913, his last International being that " close call " at Twickenham of a try to nil win for England.

As he was seconded when war was declared, Robertson was sent to the depot at Inverness, and afterwards to Aldershot; but not for long, as he crossed over to France on September 26, 1914, to fight on the Aisne. He was promoted Lieutenant in 1909, and was gazetted Captain on January 16, 1915, to date from September 30, 1914.

Ranking high among the great forwards of modern times, Lewis Robertson's name will be handed down along the generations of Rugby men to come as " *Chevalier sans peur et sans reproche.*" No man who knew him on or off the field will dare question his right to that.

ANDREW ROSS

SERGEANT ANDREW ROSS, 29th Canadians, "Tobin's Tigers," was killed in action on April 6, 1916, aged 36. He was the eldest surviving son of Mr. Andrew Ross, *Ross Herald*, and was educated at Mr. Henderson's Private School in Edinburgh, where he was born, and afterwards at the Royal High School. He soon became noted at school as an all-round athlete, and excelled at swimming. Having a craving for the sea, he was apprenticed at sixteen on the *Glenfyne*, sailing from Dundee; and it is noted of him that the voyage round the Horn to Iquique quite satisfied for the time being his seafaring appetite, and he returned to school for another year. He became then apprenticed to an engineering firm, and while there played for the F.P. team of his old school, soon gaining such a reputation as a fast and courageous forward that in 1899 he played in the Inter-City for Edinburgh *v.* Glasgow. For the previous ten seasons Glasgow had won this great annual game; but on December 2, 1899, the spell was broken, when the Edinburgh pack included Mark Morrison and Andrew Ross, Edinburgh's victory being modestly acclaimed as being due to the dearth of first-class players in the West. But Ross did not confine his energies to land. Led by W. G. Lockhart of Portobello, a number of wetbobs persuaded the Scottish Amateur Rowing Association to institute a championship on the Firth of Forth for four-oared jolly boats. On July 6, 1901, four crews started—namely, the Stirling Amateur Rowing Club, in that year the champion outrigger crew of Scotland; the Portobello Amateur R.C.; the Portobello Eastern Amateur R.C.; and the East of Scotland R.C. of Leith. The last named won by about five lengths, the crew being: bow, J. Fordie, 11 st. 9; 2, Andrew Ross, 12 st. 4; 3, W. L. Lockhart, 12 st. 11; stroke, A. Smith, jun., 10 st. 9; cox, G. Watson, 6 st. 11.

At the end of his engineering apprenticeship Ross again went to sea, became a marine engineer, and took out his chief's certificate. He visited the ends of the earth from Iquique to Tokio. He had rare adventures, and in South America his courage was tested more than once in his dealings with "greasers" of all nationalities, some ferocious, others truculent. He nearly died of yellow fever in Rio; in the Bowery he and three companions narrowly escaped a diabolical plot when a trap door failed to work to time. His knowledge of the pipes led to a quaint scene in Cuba, where the manager of a sugar plantation, hearing he could play them, sent round the fiery cross, and every Scot for miles around was soon on the spot. Hundreds of negroes sat round for nearly two hours as young Ross strode up and down playing national airs. The journey to and from the plantation was done on a special train—a puffing-billy engine, drawing one truck that had neither ends nor sides, the passengers' legs banging against the vegetation as they crept along soaked to the skin. But such a life made and kept him superlatively fit for Rugby football, so, when he was home in 1904-5, he played again in the Inter-City at Hamilton Crescent, Glasgow, Edinburgh winning 6-3. The same day he was chosen to play for the Cities *v.* Rest, and his form in that game, on January 14, 1905, fully entitled him to be chosen to play against Wales at Inverleith on February 4, 1905, in which, I remember, he showed up extremely well, though Wales just won by 2 tries to 1, their style of play in that game causing considerable comment. Ross kept his place, but Ireland won the next match on February 25, 1905, at Inverleith, by 1 goal and 2 tries to 1 goal: Basil Maclear, H. Thrift, J. C. Parke, E. D. Caddell, and T. H. Robinson of the Irish back division, being too strong for the Scottish backs, of whom L. M. Macleod, E. D. Simson, P. Munro, A. B. Timms, and W. T. Forrest were easily the best that day. But Scotland won the next match, at Richmond, for which Ross naturally kept his place. England was beaten by 8 points to nil, and I wonder how many of those points were due to the sheer pluck of Ross? He had two ribs cracked and one broken

SERGEANT ANDREW ROSS
29th Canadians
Photo: U.S.A. Studios, London

soon after the start. He changed places in the scrum, stuck it out to the end, and caught the night mail. A huddled figure sitting over the fire in the dining-room met the astonished gaze of his family on the Sunday morning. He was hustled off to bed and well lectured by the doctor on the risks he had run. A few weeks in bed was the punishment. Four years later he was in the Scottish team on February 6, 1909, against Wales at Inverleith, Scotland losing by a goal to a penalty goal; and against Ireland on February 27, 1909, when Ireland won by a penalty goal to nil. That was his last International match. After being assistant-engineer at the Edinburgh Municipal Electric Station for some time he must needs go a-rovin' again, and we find him next at Vancouver. When the Call came he was on the confines of the Arctic Circle, but he started south at once, and I must quote now from his war correspondence :—

"*November* 29, 1914.—We arrived in Vancouver from Albert Bay on the 14th of this month, and have started training. . . . In this Second Canadian Contingent most of the men are splendid shots. At 200 yards yesterday A Coy. were shooting. Twelve men made the highest possible, and about 70 per cent. of the Coy. did not drop more than five points. I had eight bulls and two inners. . . . The work in camp is hard, but we all like it, as we have to get into good condition for the British Army."

Here spoke the Rugby player who knows the value of physical condition.

Again: "HASTINGS PARK, VANCOUVER, January 8, 1915.— A man feels that it's worth his while giving up his life to save millions of homes, such as ours, from the fate of poor old Belgium. . . . We don't want to have to stay too long in England drilling, so it is with a jolly good will we go into our drills here. You find that nearly every man has his drill book in his tunic pocket, and reads it up at odd moments." He was a week in hospital at Devonport on arrival in June 1915, owing to an injury to his back while skylarking on the voyage, and after ten days at home he returned to camp, and wrote, July 30, 1915 : " I go up to London on Sunday morning in the team representing Canada, to compete in the regimental sports at Stamford Bridge." And so to the Front in September 1915, whence on the 28th he wrote : " Our line varies from 30 to 250 yards from the Germans. . . . The Germans occasionally give us a ' hymn of hate ' in the shape of shrapnel morning and evening. The star shells at night are fine. In fact, if you keep your head down and listen to the crack of the rifles, and watch the incessant stream of star shells, you would think you were at a Pain's firework show." On November 23, 1915 : " We got a prisoner the other day who told us that London was in ruins, and that Great Britain was starving for want of food. We couldn't get grain into the country, as the Kaiser's submarines had command of the sea, and there were going to be big riots all over England and Scotland. We have great sport with the Bavarians, who are opposite us just now. We can get their goat every time. We never run a dodge till they get on to it like the English regiments do. For instance, this morning we got a bunch who were wondering what those damn Canadians were doing. What we did was this. We lit a fire in the trench and put plenty wet wood on it. That made a big smoke. Then two men made all the row they could, shouting at each other and hitting an empty biscuit tin with sticks. The result was, Fritz easily located the row by the column of smoke, and all the Fritzes within hearing peeped round their sandbags to have a look, and as every one in our trench was on the lookout, it was the last look for most of them."

And so his letters run on, always on the cheerful note of a thorough sportsman in the pink of health, as witness : " December 18, 1915.—We expect some fun any minute, as the Germans are using gas. The scones were fine." Can any foreign army expect to beat such cheery folk as the type that writes such letters ? A gas attack in being, a more serious attack expected, and—" the scones were fine!" And on January 15, 1916: "Fancy Xmas Day in hospital [this was due to a whiff of gas, E.H.D.S.] with mulligan and a slice of cold duff for dinner. Eggs cost 3½d. each here, and when I came out of hospital I had six fried. They were good." Some of us in these islands will endorse this verdict when next we enjoy a similar experience. The sportsman in him welled up again to the surface in his letter describing his first attack with the bayonet, but I refrain from quoting. And thus to his last letter, dated April 4, 1916: "You will see by the papers that there's lots of fighting where we are at present, and just now we are in the German trenches, so have a busy time. . . . I'd like to see you all again. . . ." And then, from the corporal of his section: "On the morning of the 6th April we were serving together in the trenches. While attending devotedly and most courageously, under very heavy artillery fire, to our wounded men, he was himself hit, and falling over a man he was dressing, died instantly. Quite reckless as regarding his own life, he exposed it, and gave it to save, as his quick attention undoubtedly did, the lives of a great number of our men."

Andrew Ross's Commanding Officer wrote: "He was killed while doing his duty like a man, on the morning of 6th April. No man could do more. He was a splendid character, and was loved alike by his officers and men, all of whom feel his loss most keenly." It has since been disclosed that Ross was wounded before he was hit finally, but continued on duty until killed.

"I with uncovered head
Salute the sacred dead,
Who went, and who return not. Say not so!
'Tis not the grapes of Canaan that repay,
But the high faith that failed not on the way:
Virtue treads paths that end not in the grave:
No bar of endless night exiles the brave;
And to the saner mind
We rather seem the dead that stayed behind."

JAMES ROSS

PRIVATE JAMES ROSS, London Scottish Regiment, was reported wounded and missing after the battle at Messines, October 31, 1914, and as nothing further has been heard of him he has been assumed to have been killed on that date, aged 34. Born on February 15, 1880, at Rutherford, Roxburgh, Ross was educated at Cargilfield (1888-94) and Fettes College, Edinburgh (1894-99). He was in the XV. at Fettes in 1895-99, and Captain of it from 1897-99, a most remarkable record. The cases of a School captain of Rugby football for three years are very rare. He was also in the XI. and the Hockey XI. J. Ross possessed five Scottish International Caps, as he played for Scotland against England, Ireland, and Wales in 1901; being a member of one of the most famous International XV.'s, as it was certainly one of the very best, in history; and against Wales in 1902, and England again in 1903. He was a sturdily built, very hard-working forward of the short and heavy type. He played a great deal for London Scottish, of which club XV. " Jummy " Ross was Captain in 1901-2 and 1904-5. A good all-round outdoor man, he could hold his own at golf, fishing, and shooting; and he used to take a stroll before breakfast to the top of North Berwick Law and back, by way of keeping fit, when there in the summer. " Jummy " had no previous military training except that obtained between August 29 and September 15, 1914, on which latter date he went to France. He was a most popular man wherever he went, and grief was indeed great and hearts heavy when the sad tidings came through that he was missing.

PRIVATE JAMES ROSS
London Scottish Regiment

REGINALD OSCAR SCHWARZ

MAJOR REGINALD OSCAR SCHWARZ, King's Royal Rifle Corps, died on active service in France, of influenza, aged 43. Educated at St. Paul's School and Christ's College, Cambridge, he got his Blue as a half in 1893; but did not get his Cap until in 1899 he played against Scotland, and two years later against Wales and Ireland. Oxford won his only 'Varsity match by 1 try to nil, and England lost all three Internationals in which he took part; so that his appearances in big football were not so fortunate as to result, as so good a player and splendid a companion deserved should be the case. He was a good sound player without being brilliant. It was as a bowler of the off-break delivered with a leg-break action that he became world famous, and it may be placed on record here that he never had an equal in making a ball break from the off on a perfect wicket. The pitch was never prepared upon which he could not make the ball break from the off, in his best day, before an elbow injury deprived him of most of his power in this respect. He did not break the ball from leg as well, as has more than once been stated in print; and during his great tour with the South African team in England, Scotland, and Ireland in 1907, he did not take one wicket with a leg-break, though heading the bowling averages of the best bowling team of this century with 137 wickets for 11·7 runs each. For South Africa against an England XI. at Lord's, in 1904, he had a great match, getting Ranjitsinhji's wicket in both innings, scoring a century, and taking 8 wickets for 106 runs, " England " losing by 189 runs.

As was only natural, he was at once in khaki when the War broke out. He was in South Africa at the time, and served through the South-West African campaign before coming back to England to take his commission in the K.R.R. He was wounded in France, and won the Military Cross. It came as a great shock to his many friends when his name appeared in the casualty lists, and it was known that he had died of influenza in France, after having gone right through the War from the beginning to its last few days. There never was a more popular double International than Reggie Schwarz, who made friends wherever he went owing to his charming and frank disposition. I spent a lot of time in his company so long ago as 1891, and again in 1904, 1907, and 1912, and he was always the same whether the South Africans had just won an important game or had had a severe beating. He always recognized to the full that—

> "The Game is more than the players of the Game,
> The Ship is more than the crew."

GEORGE MAURICE VICTOR SELLARS

PRIVATE GEORGE MAURICE VICTOR SELLARS was a member of the First Auckland Infantry Battalion, and was killed in the fight for Messines Ridge on June 7, 1917. While assisting to carry a wounded comrade back to the dressing-station a shell blew his shoulder and side to pieces.

George Sellars was selected as a front-rank forward in the New Zealand team that toured in California in 1913, and was a member of the New Zealand Native team that toured Australia and New Zealand in 1910, under the management of Mr. W. T. Parata. He also played for the North Island against the South Island in 1910. He was born in Auckland and educated at the Napier Street School. He joined the Ponsonby Football Club as a third-grade player in 1905, but before the season was over he was promoted to the Seniors. He captained the Ponsonby Club team, and was a member of the Committee of the Club for several years, being always a popular player. He represented the Auckland province in its inter-provincial matches continu-

MAJOR REGINALD OSCAR SCHWARZ
King's Royal Rifle Corps
Photo: Sport and General, London

PRIVATE GEORGE MAURICE VICTOR SELLARS
Auckland Battalion, N.Z.

ously from 1909 until the time of his enlistment. For his weight (11 st. 10 lb.) he was considered one of the best forwards who have ever played in New Zealand. A shipwright by trade, Sellars was also an enthusiastic yachtsman, sailing several different yachts to victory on numerous occasions. He was also handicapper for the Victoria Cruising Club, Auckland, for a number of years.

RONALD FRANCIS SIMSON

LIEUTENANT RONALD FRANCIS SIMSON, R.F.A., was killed in action on the Aisne on September 14, 1914, aged 24.

He was the first Rugby International to fall in this war.

Simson was born at Edinburgh on September 6, 1890, and was educated at Edinburgh Academy from 1897 to 1909, and at the Royal Military Academy, Woolwich, in 1909 and 1910. He was in the Edinburgh Academy XV. and XI. in 1907–09, and Captain of the XV. in 1909. He gained the Calcutta Cup for athletics when he won the hundred yards, the hurdles, the quarter-mile, the high and long jumps. At Woolwich he was in the XV., and won the Silver Bugle for athletics, taking the hurdles, quarter, and long jump. He played for the Army *v.* Navy at Queen's Club in 1911–13. His play in the Army *v.* Navy match of 1911 secured for him his International Cap for Scotland as a centre three-quarter against England, when Scotland lost by a goal and a try to two goals and a try, Simson scoring one of the Scots' tries. He was a fine tall centre, with excellent hands and long raking stride, and a very keen nose for a chance of a try. Some rated him an individual player only. But he was far from being that. He had the *flair* for the cut-through and for doing something with the ball in the way of making an opening before parting with it to his wing, as was the custom with some of our overrated modern automata. Woolwich and the Army and Edinburgh

Academy knew how good he was, and how very unjust the label "individualist," when applied, as it was in his case, to one who was very closely allied to that *rara avis* the born centre. Other fine players, and especially stand-off half-backs and centres, have suffered from the same sort of uninitiated criticism—that which does not recognize that players in these two positions exist mainly to make openings, and that in the making of an opening even the very best of players must frequently be tackled in possession. Simson was worth a great many more than one international cap, neither of the centres, who were given the preference over him in 1912, 1913, or 1914, being better all-round players than he, if, indeed, even his equal.

Of Simson the man, one who knew him very intimately, but who desires to be nameless, has kindly written for me the following appreciation :—

"'Ronnie' Simson, for so every one called him at school, was a universal favourite. The ordinary Scottish boy is reserved and hates to show his feelings. He seems rather ashamed to smile, and only does it under severe provocation. But 'Ronnie' was quite different; he was bubbling over with mirth. If he met you in the street he chuckled; if he was caught by his master with his work unprepared, he could hardly restrain his merriment; if he was violently stamped on by the opposing forwards, he came up shaking with laughter; on the one occasion he made 100 at cricket (and not a very bad one either) he came in almost convulsed. He was so modest that he did not realize that his play had anything to do with it, but it seemed to him the most amusing thing in the world that there could be bowlers so bad that he could get 100! And so he remained after school, always cheery and a tonic to those of a less buoyant disposition. And yet at the same time there was a real solidity in his character at bottom, though a casual observer might not have observed it. All would have recognized his charm immediately, but it needed a longer

LIEUT. RONALD FRANCIS SIMSON, R.F.A.
Photo : Lafayette, London

acquaintance to recognize his sterling worth. For a schoolmaster, who has seen all the boys he has liked best appear one after the other in the list of killed, it is impossible to think that so many lives of such great promise would be taken away, unless they are to be transferred to a better sphere and one of wider usefulness."

Of course Simson played often for the London Scottish and for the United Services, which makes his single appearance for Scotland the more remarkable.

In 1910 he was gazetted to a commission in the gunners, and he went to France with the first division that left England in 1914. His death was instantaneous. He was riding forward as reconnoitring officer, to select a new position for his battery, when a shell burst right under his horse, killing both. It is not by any means because he was the first Rugby International killed in this war that R. F. Simson will be long remembered and regretted. For he was as fine a character as he was a player, and I for one shall always consider myself lucky to have seen him in full stride on the football field. It was my good fortune to see him score both for the Army and for Scotland, and the sight was a sheer delight.

LANCELOT ANDREW NOEL SLOCOCK

SECOND-LIEUTENANT LANCELOT ANDREW NOEL SLOCOCK, 10th Battalion Liverpool Regiment, was killed in action at Guillemont, France, on August 9, 1916, aged 29. Born at Wootton Warren, Warwickshire, on Christmas Day, 1886, Slocock was educated at Marlborough College from 1900–4. He was in the Marlborough XV.'s of 1902 and 1903, in the Hockey XI. of 1903, 1904, and in the Cricket XI. of 1904. He played for England against Wales, Ireland, and Scotland in every match of 1907 and 1908, there being not the slightest doubt during the Welsh match of 1907, his first International, that England had found one of the forwards of all time. That was the famous game at Swansea when, knowing nothing about the peculiar needs of the particular game of " a place for every forward and every forward in his place," the English eight were at sixes and sevens within a quarter of an hour of the start, and never, in fact, played as a pack. Their pace was the pace of their slowest member, and Welshmen have a way of detecting the weak spot in their opponents' armour and of playing on to it. One of the few of the English eight who came out of that turmoil with honours was Noel Slocock, and until an injured knee, and his own disgust at the selection of the English pack against Scotland in 1908, combined to end his active interest in the game, there was not a better all-round forward in the United Kingdom than he, who was certainly the best Rugby football player who ever left Marlborough. He was Captain of the English XV. in that match against Scotland, when England, who were really the better side on the day, lost by 3 goals (2 dropped) and 1 try to 2 goals, partly owing to the way two members of the pack let the side down. I have never forgotten Slocock's disgust, and I must say it was justified. He had no place in his creed for any one who did not play downright hard football from kick-off to "no-side," and a very severe critic of himself as well as of others, he would allow no excuses for any one who shirked. There was no branch of forward play in which one could fault Slocock unless it was in dribbling, at which, because he was tall and heavy and dashing, he was less able than he was at the rest of the game. He was a terror for work in the tight, a fine man at the line-out, grand at following up, and never let go of anything he once got a hand on to. The number of points his side were "down" had no particular interest for him unless to spur him to even greater exertion. If there is one thing more certain than another in the matter of the deaths of the glorious men whose names adorn these pages, it is that there was a grim and terrible struggle where Noel Slocock fell—that is if, as is

SEC.-LIEUT. LANCELOT ANDREW NOEL SLOCOCK
10th Batt. Liverpool Regiment

Photo : Medrington's Ltd., Liverpool

probable, it became a hand-to-hand affair. If such was the case the enemy knew they had got a Briton on business in their midst. A giant in stature, with large limbs and hands to make his figure the symmetrical and beautiful thing it was, Slocock in battle must have conjured up visions to those who saw him of the Berserks of old of whose deeds with battle-axes we have read. If he died in a hand-to-hand he was fortunate, for he would have chosen it so—he would have despised to be laid low by a bullet started on its deadly mission a mile away. He was of that type which we, who knew him, knew instinctively when he went to war that we should not meet again on this earth. There are many such in this noble Roll, and among the greatest of them there is no doubt Noel Slocock holds a high place. It was no fault of his he was not sooner in the battle-line. He had an important business appointment, which meant much travel between Lancashire and the States, and at that time, 1914, it was no light matter just to fling down the reins, disorganize somebody else's big business, and march to war. The fact that he took a commission in September 1915 proves that he had moved in the matter of being with the rest of the playing Rugby world and all the physically fit body of Rugby men who are past playing age, some time before he joined the Army. He was in France in January 1916, and was "missing" in the same action, or near it, where the late Lieutenant-Colonel E. R. Mobbs, D.S.O., another of the same type of player and patriot, was severely wounded; and actually in the same fight after which the popular little Yorkshireman, Jack King, was reported "missing." The affair cost us two of the biggest-hearted forwards who ever entered a scrum; and if we know anything, we know that both of them gave the very fullest expression to the time-honoured description, "good in the tight work," in their final scrum.

But if L. A. N. Slocock had not gained honours on the Rugby field he would, had he had time, have secured them at cricket. He was a splendid fieldsman and a good sound bat, with plenty of attack in his game. I know if he could have spared the time he would have played, and have done well, for Lancashire. They were prepared to play him, as I wrote to A. N. Hornby about him, and his reply left no doubt upon this matter; but business, as it has in so many cases, and rightly so, intervened. Although I knew him fairly well personally, I was very glad to get the following appreciation of him from one who knew him a great deal better than I did. He wrote :—

"Few people really understood L. A. N.—he was reserved, but always cheerful and had a keen sense of humour. He led a very simple life in early years, and prior to going to Marlboro' showed no signs of developing any sporting powers—he had never played Rugby before going to Marlboro'. Yet, in 1903, he was a member of the finest XV. Marlboro' ever had. This XV. defeated Wellington and Clifton in hollow fashion. He was a great scorer for his house at cricket, and generally scored a century in the house matches. He was also a very fine hockey player, and would have represented either University had he gone up.

"In later years he spent six months in America every year, but managed to spend the summer in England. As a Club cricketer he was invaluable, and for Liverpool *v.* Manchester made 81 in less than twenty-five minutes, and 115 in an hour and a half. In the South of England he seldom made less than 50, and rendered Marlow great support in the last two seasons before the War.

"His two best tries at football were for Lancashire *v.* South Africans, 1906, and for England *v.* Scotland in 1908.

"He leaves one boy, Anthony, who is the exact likeness of his father."

That this fine specimen of "young, fresh England" may grow up to be as good a man and a sportsman as his splendid father will be the wish of all who remember Noel Slocock at play or at work. He has an example not given to all youngsters, for his sire was a man among men.

ROBERTSON SMYTH

MAJOR ROBERTSON SMYTH, M.D., Dublin, R.A.M.C., died in London on April 5, 1916, from the effects of exposure on active service in France, aged 36. He was born at Banbridge, Co. Down, Ireland, and was educated at Dungannon Royal School and Dublin University. Here he was only in his second year when he gained a place in the 1st XV. He played regularly until in 1902-3 he was elected Captain of the team. In 1903 he won his Irish International Cap against England and Scotland, and then went with the British team to South Africa during our summer of 1903. In seventeen of the twenty-four matches of that tour Dr. Smyth took part, scoring four tries, besides being Captain of the team. In 1904 he won another Irish Cap against England. His time at Dublin University having now ended, he played for the Wanderers, and was in their XV. which won the Leinster Senior Cup. His love for the game was well known, but I dare say everybody does not know that while he played for Dublin University for five years he never failed to turn out for a single match during the whole of his first four seasons there. A remarkable record, evidence alike of his keenness, his popularity, and his ability to stand the racket of first-class football. He was Captain also of the Hospital team that won the Hospital Cup. All this while work was not permitted to be shelved. In 1903 he became a resident pupil, and in 1904 he took his medical degrees, including M.D., and also passed the examination for entrance into the R.A.M.C. He was appointed House Surgeon for Sir Patrick Dun's Hospital in 1905, being seconded by the War Office, so that he might take up that appointment. Joining the R.A.M.C. in 1906, he went to India in 1907; and sticking to the great game got up a team at Ambala to beat the 1st D.O.W. West Riding Regiment, at that time many times winners, and I believe holders of the All India Rugby Cup. His team, which included the late

Captain E. D. Simson, "Nimmo," the famous Scottish scrum-half, and Captain T. H. Robinson, R.A.M.C., the Irish half-back, and also Captain F. George, Connaught Rangers, who had played frequently for Dublin University, beat the champion regimental team. When war broke out Captain R. S. Smyth, as he was then, went to France in September 1914, and served continuously until December 1915, when he was invalided home soon after having been gazetted Major. In January 1916 he was mentioned in dispatches by Lord French for distinguished service in the field. Not long after his ill-health compelled retirement from the Army, to die in London; a life given up for King and Empire as certainly as that of any hero killed leading a charge. As a man and a companion Robbie Smyth, as he was known, was always deservedly popular. He had the lovable disposition and engaging personality which make and keep friends. This, and his love of all forms of outdoor sport, but especially of physique and character building Rugby football, endeared him to a very large circle of the best type of sportsman. His was another splendid career cut short long before its full powers had bloomed, and in his play and in his own life he was an outstanding example of the kind to emulate which must be the desire of future generations of Britons.

ALBERT LEWIS STEWART

MAJOR ALBERT LEWIS STEWART, D.S.O., Royal Irish Rifles, attached Machine Gun Corps, was killed in action at Glencorse Wood, Ypres Sector, Belgium, on October 4, 1917, aged 28. Born at Belfast, Ireland, on February 19, 1889, Stewart was educated at Royal Belfast Academical Institution (1902–7). He was in the School 1st XV. 1903–7 (the first year as full-back, the other years centre three-quarter). He was awarded the School Honour Cap for best play, 1905–6, and was Vice-Captain of the

MAJOR ROBERTSON SMYTH, R.A.M.C.
Photo : Debenham, Southsea

1906-7 team. In 1905-7 he played centre three-quarter in the Schools " Inter-provincial " Ulster v. Leinster (the former winning each time). In a critique on the 1st XV., by an " Irish International," in the School Magazine of 1907, he was described as " the outstanding back of the side. Is strong and heavy, and has a useful turn of speed. Takes and gives his passes well, and is a fine kick. Makes lots of openings, and can himself go through on occasion. He is equally happy in attack and defence. When play is in his opponents' half he gets the ball from ' touch ' in a refreshing way. Can place-kick, as is evidenced by the fact that he converted 6 out of 8 tries in the Ulster Schools Cup Semi-final. Knows the game thoroughly."

During the 1906-7 season he kicked 24 goals.

He was in the Cricket 1st XI.'s of 1904-6, and showed good form as a batsman and was a thoroughly reliable fielder, according to the School Magazine, 1906. In swimming he was in the School Relay " four " which competed without a single defeat in the Ulster Inter-Schools Flying Squadron races of 1905 and 1906. He was " Number 2 " of the team (" Number 1," the captain, being Walter J. Drummond, who afterwards broke the Irish 100 Yards Record, and also won the 100 Yards and 220 Yards at the Ulster Championships, and was chosen for British Olympic Team, 1912). Stewart passed the examination for Royal Life Saving Society's Medallion in 1906.

In Gymnastics he was, in 1904, in the team which won the School Junior Gymnastic Competition; and he was a School Prefect, 1905-7.

On leaving school Stewart joined North of Ireland Football Club, and at once was given his place as centre three-quarter in the 1st XV., playing in all the seasons of 1907-14. Half-way through the season of 1914 all the clubs in the Province cancelled the remainder of their matches so as to devote more time to drilling—practically every Rugby man being a member of the Ulster Volunteer Force to resist Home Rule. Stewart was awarded the N.I.F.C. Honour Cap in 1908-9, and in 1911-12 he was Vice-Captain, and in 1912-14 Captain of the Club. He represented Ulster in the Inter-provincial match against Munster in 1908-9, and v. Stade Français, 1908-9. He went with the team as first reserve for Ireland v. Scotland and v. Wales, 1908-9, and played for Ulster team v. South Africans, 1912-13; for Ulster v. Leinster, 1912-13, and v. Munster, 1912-13. He played for Ireland v. France, 1913; Ireland v. Wales, 1913; and Ireland v. France, 1914. He was chosen v. England, 1914, but owing to the drilling of the U.V.F., of which he was a Company Commander, he declined.

On the running track Stewart ran in the colours of the North of Ireland Club, and won several prizes at sprint distances. Amongst his successes was the Old Boys 220 Yards, from scratch, at his old School Sports in 1910. He was magnificently built, being 6 feet 2 inches in height, and nearly 14 stone in weight. He was a member of the Committee of the Irish Rugby Football Union.

Immediately war was declared Stewart, who was a Chartered Accountant by profession, volunteered in the 10th (South Belfast) Battalion Royal Irish Rifles, in 36th (Ulster) Division, and was given a commission as Second-Lieutenant. The Battalion was in training at Newcastle, Co. Down, and shortly afterwards removed to Ballykinlar Camp, Co. Down, where it remained till May 1915, and then went to Seaford, Sussex, and later to Bramshot, to leave on October 1, 1915, for the Front in France. In the spring of 1915 Stewart was promoted Lieutenant, and became Machine Gun Officer to the Battalion. After the Ulster Division's advance on Thiepval on July 1, 1916, he was promoted Captain, " mentioned in dispatches," and recommended for the Victoria Cross. Soon afterwards he was attached to the Machine Gun Corps, and appointed to command the 22nd Machine Gun Company. In January 1917 he was promoted Major, and in the summer was again " mentioned in dispatches." In December

MAJOR ALBERT LEWIS STEWART, D.S.O.
Royal Irish Rifles (att. Machine Gun Corps)

ALBERT LEWIS STEWART

1917 his name appeared in the *Gazette* as having been awarded the D.S.O., which, alas! he did not live to receive.

In a letter Brigadier-General Julian Steele wrote :—

"I have been his Brigadier for just a year, and during that time have been in very close touch with him. Not only have I lost a most excellent and brave soldier, but also a most delightful companion, and I feel it will be impossible to replace him. I cannot express all I feel. . . ."—*24th October* 1917.

A fellow officer in the Royal Irish Rifles wrote: "I saw him on the night of July 1, 1916, when he came back, after being over all day in the German trenches, where he had done such splendid work. He was completely worn out, as he had had a terrible time all day, but he was himself again in the morning of the 2nd." It was for his deeds that day that he was recommended for the V.C.

His Company Sergeant-Major wrote: "He was one of the bravest men in France; his thoughts were of his men always, and I am certain that when he met his death he was doing what he wouldn't ask one of his officers, N.C.O.'s, or men to do. I am asked by the N.C.O.'s and men who served under him in his old Company to say this."

Major A. L. Stewart was, on all counts, a grand Irishman, of the most patriotic, loyal type. His death has created a gap in the life of sporting Ireland that will indeed be difficult to fill.

His Headmaster has written the following appreciation of him for this volume, and I publish it as received :—

"Lewis Stewart was five years at 'Inst.,' from 1902–7. He was not, therefore, one of the boys who come to a school for one year or, at most, two years; who contribute little to the school, and have not the opportunity of carrying much away from it. He was long enough a pupil to acquire the spirit and tradition of the place. To this influence he reacted sympathetically; and he made a large return to the School for whatever advantage or stimulus he received from it. He had too many interests as a boy for the teachers to expect him to tread the narrow path of the mere ' swotter.' He was not only a born athlete and sportsman, but in his School days he had several hobbies which he prosecuted with success. He was at the same time distinctly a boy of great intelligence and capacity. He was at the School for a time during some portion of which he found himself with such fellow-pupils and sportsmen as Captain A. Gallaher, D.S.O., Captain A. N. M'Clinton, M.C., Captain W. A. Anderson, Second-Lieutenant C. B. Pyper, the Rev. Sidney M'Gaffin, the late Captain S. M'Clinton, and the late Second-Lieutenant J. Austin."

STEPHEN SEBASTIAN LOMBARD STEYN

LIEUTENANT STEPHEN SEBASTIAN LOMBARD STEYN, Royal Field Artillery, fell in action in December 1917, aged 26. His father was a cousin of President Steyn, Orange River Free State. Steyn was educated at the Diocesan College, Rondebosch, and at University College, Oxford, whither he went as a Rhodes Scholar in 1909. He was probably a better player as a wing three-quarter during the season of 1910–11 than at any other time; and the omission made by the Oxford University authorities in not playing him against Cambridge was accentuated when the Scottish Football Union, quite satisfied—as indeed they had every right to be—that he had Scottish connections and sympathies, played him in March 1911 against England in the first Calcutta Cup match ever played at Twickenham. There have been few instances either of a player getting his International Cap before getting his Blue, or of a player who has been an undergraduate at Oxford or Cambridge being an International and not a Blue. Nine months after playing for Scotland Steyn got his Blue, and

LIEUT. STEPHEN SEBASTIAN LOMBARD STEYN, R.F.A.
Photo: Sport and General, London

STEPHEN SEBASTIAN LOMBARD STEYN

played on the winning side against Cambridge. He played once more for Scotland, against Ireland this time, in the winter of 1912; and after playing again for Oxford, this time on the losing side, 1912, the remainder of his first-class football was played with the Guy's Hospital XV. He was studying medicine when war broke out.

"Beak" Steyn, as he was known to his intimates, was a most amusing fellow. He always saw the funny side, and was in consequence a capital man to have in a team. Going up to Oxford as a Rhodes Scholar from South Africa—his family were connected with the late President Steyn, but the Oxonian's mother is a Scots lady—Steyn was very soon popular. Of course, he was soon in both the Cricket and Rugby teams of University College, and was also a member of the Shakespeare Club at University. He got his Scottish International Cap before his Blue, and it was his play against the South Africans in 1912 for Oxford, when the visitors only just won, though expected to win comfortably, that had much to do with that result. His knowledge of the Taal came into play here, as Oxford had another South African, L. R. Bröster, playing scrum-half, so that when the visiting halves gave each other the tip in Dutch as to their intentions, at least two of the Oxford backs were ready for them—especially round the blind side, where the defence of a wing three-quarter is so essential. In the same 'Varsity XV., that of December 1912, with Steyn were the late W. P. Geen, killed in 1915; the late E. F. Boyd, killed in 1914; the late W. M. Dickson, killed in 1915; G. B. Crole, reported missing and then prisoner in the late autumn of 1917; and E. G. Loudon-Shand, wounded in 1915 and 1917. "Beak" was an extraordinary shot with a cricket ball, his powers of throwing being in great demand with chunks of bread across the quad when a scout with a full tray offered an irresistible target! It was said of him, he could fling a roll across the quad into almost any window named. Not perhaps an accomplishment which comes under the heading of either indispensable or worthy of imitation, but one which serves in those far-off golden days of youth, when animal spirits effervesce and help to make life bright and bearable. " Beak " Steyn was a cheery soul who had no enemies, and who will be long remembered.

WALTER RIDDELL SUTHERLAND

SECOND-LIEUTENANT WALTER RIDDELL SUTHERLAND, 8th Battalion Seaforth Highlanders, was born at Hawick on November 19, 1890, and was killed by a shell at Hulluch on October 4, 1918, aged 27. When the call to arms resounded through the British Empire in 1914, and was freely responded to in all the Scottish Border towns, Sutherland was among the first to offer his services. He enlisted in the Lothians and Border Horse Yeomanry in September, and, in the following July, he transferred to the 14th Battalion of the Argyll and Sutherland Highlanders. With it he proceeded in May 1916 to France. In January 1917 he was invalided home, suffering from dysentery. On being discharged from hospital he went through a course of nine weeks' training necessary for non-commissioned rank. On its conclusion he applied for a commission, and proceeded to Pirbright, where he underwent his Cadet training. He was then gazetted Second-Lieutenant in the Seaforth Highlanders, and, after a short stay at the depôt of that regiment, he proceeded to join the 8th Battalion in France.

Sutherland was soon in the fighting line, taking part in the memorable affair at Buzancy, where the 15th Division covered itself with glory. He was fortunate to come through without hurt. Writing home to his father after the event, he incidentally revealed the fierce nature of the struggle when he informed him that he was one of the four unwounded officers out of eighteen to emerge from the fighting line. In almost the last letter home he gave a racy account of Athletic Sports held at an Instruction

SEC.-LIEUT. WALTER RIDDELL SUTHERLAND
8th Batt. Seaforth Highlanders

Photo: Murray, Keswick

Camp, in which he took part, greatly distinguishing himself, more particularly in the running events, by winning almost every item.

The manner of his death was that, such was his anxiety to be with his men after a period of rest, he hired a bicycle to cover the distance separating him from them. Passing through the village of Hulluch, a stray shell from the enemy reached his vicinity—" a bow at a venture "—and he was killed, not leading his men as he would have desired, but, nevertheless, in just such a manner as he had lived, doing his duty. Sutherland had received his education at Teviot Grove Academy in his native town, and at the time of his enlistment was training for a Sanitary Inspector in the office of the Burgh Engineer, Hawick.

Reared in an atmosphere where sport of all kinds was a frequent topic, and in a town and district where outdoor sports were vigorously pursued, it was not surprising that, as a boy, Walter Sutherland not only evinced a keen interest, but showed a rare aptitude in all games. At his School sports he was successful in all the events for which he entered ; and, in the School cricket and football teams, he was looked upon as the leader of his side. It was the latter game for which he showed a decided preference.

Shortly after leaving school, and while his contemporaries were ploughing their way through Junior ranks, Sutherland became a member of the famous Hawick " Greens." At that time the club counted many well-tried players of all-round ability, and included such players as R. H. Lindsay-Watson, William Burnet, and Willie Kyle, the hero of a score of International Caps. He proved that he was worthy of the confidence reposed in him, and soon became recognized throughout Scotland as one of the coming three-quarter backs. Slim of build, but symmetrical of figure, Nature had not dowered him with great proportions; but he possessed speed of the highest order, abundant resource, and the necessary coolness for adapting himself to any circumstances

which might crop up. His success in Club matches was instant and phenomenal, and in his early years with the team he had the satisfaction to see Hawick occupying the position of Joint Champions of Scotland. He was a prolific scorer, and the following records will show what a tower of strength he must have been :—
1909–10 : scored 13 tries, kicked 12 goals ; 1910–11 : scored 16 tries ; 1911–12 : scored 21 tries, kicked 8 goals ; 1912–13, scored 14 tries ; 1913–14, scored 8 tries in eleven games.

At the age of nineteen he reached the height of every Rugby footballer's ambition, and was chosen to represent his native country. It was a great honour for one so young, but there was no doubt he deserved his place. The honour was repeated thirteen times, including the famous matches against the South Africans and France. How well he acquitted himself in these encounters is a matter of history. It is the barest truth that he never played a poor game ; and, while his companions might feel a little nervy as the important contests approached, Sutherland was cool and collected. Two displays in his series of Internationals stand out prominently, and were pre-eminently his finest exhibitions ; and one does not know which to admire most —his dashing display of running and tackling against England at Twickenham, or his masterly defence at Cardiff against a strong Welsh side. Of his display in the former match, no greater tribute could be given to any player than that paid by Mr. Dallas, then President of the Scottish Football Union. At a meeting of the Council after the match, he said : " I cannot help referring to the extraordinarily fine display given by W. R. Sutherland in the recent match against England. It was Providence and Sutherland that saved Scotland that day from a much greater defeat." His International match record reads : England, 1910, 1911, 1912, 1913 ; Ireland, 1913 ; Wales, 1910, 1912, 1913, 1914 ; France, 1911, 1912, 1913 ; South Africa, 1912.

On the running-track Sutherland's speed was shown to full advantage, and here also he earned both a local and national reputation. His principal honours included the 100 Yards and 220 Yards Scottish Border Championship in 1911, 1912, 1913, 1914. He carried off in two successive years the 100 Yards Sprint at the Berwick-on-Tweed Harriers Sports. He won the 220 Yards Scottish Championship, and set the seal on his fame by being chosen to represent Scotland against Ireland in 1911–13, running second the first year; and, in the second, after a most magnificent race, by sheer pluck defeating the Irish Champion, Shaw, in the fast time of $22\frac{1}{2}$ seconds. Writing to Lieutenant Sutherland's father, H. M. Finlay, Esq., Secretary, Irish A.A.A., says: " I cannot forget the race he ran against Shaw in the 220 Yards at Belfast." D. S. Duncan, Esq., Secretary, Scottish A.A.A., wrote: "He will never be forgotten by Rugby and Athletic Scotland."

For the bulk of the foregoing information I am much indebted to Mr. Walter Hume, Headmaster of Trinity School, Hawick, who adds :—

"It is not, however, the enumeration of his brilliant deeds on the football and athletic fields that forms the chief claim to the high esteem in which Walter Sutherland was held. He stood for all that was best in whatever he did. He early recognized that all outdoor sports were for recreation merely, and are not the serious business of life, and it was in that spirit and with that aim in view that all his energies were directed. He proved by his life that the two were not antagonistic, but were co-essential, and that in games many lessons were to be learned which would prove of the utmost benefit in after life. With that ideal before him, his play was always bright, natural, honest, and aboveboard. He scorned to do a mean action. He had no occasion to resort to trick or stratagem; his play was, like his life, clean and wholesome. After the most stubborn or exciting contest no action of his ever left a sting behind. He made no enemies. Beloved by troops of friends, who admired him as the truest type of sportsman, he added a charm and freshness to the game, and his movements were followed with the keenest interest, the execution of which could always be followed by the merest tyro as by the most critical. He had enjoyed success, and naturally loved victory; but he also knew how to acknowledge defeat, and no one was more ready or more generous to admit gifts in worthy opponents. Success made no unwelcome inroads on his character; empty self-esteem he had none; modesty reigned supreme. He knew that success in this direction was but ephemeral and elusive. At the height of his fame he was still the same bright, unassuming character, loyal to his home, his friends, and native town. His boyish disposition remained with him to the end. His four years of military life were spent just as in civil life, in carefully blended work and play. He was always ready and in perfect condition for the performance of any work which duty demanded. By so many lovable ties had he endeared himself to the followers of the Rugby game, that his death was looked upon as a personal loss. For those of us who had followed his career, and had watched its development, it is hard to realize that one who so recently had walked the streets of the old Border town, who was held in such affection by its youth, whose bright smile and cheery nature were like rays of sunshine, had gone and would never again adorn its peaceful life. In all he achieved, the reward he most appreciated and cherished was the affection of his friends and admirers. The memory of such a life, with so many just claims to remembrance, will always stand out as a permanent inspiration and a bright example to all who may follow the Rugby game.

> "'Qui procul hinc, the legend's writ,
>   The frontier grave is far away;
> Qui ante diem periit
>   Sed miles, sed pro patriâ.'
>   NEWBOLT."

"Since writing the foregoing," continues Mr. Hume, "a

note-book was found among Lieutenant Sutherland's belongings at home, in which he jotted down his successes in succeeding years. The following are quotations from it :—

"'*Season* 1908-9.—Started playing for Hawick 2nd XV. Played two matches, then got place in first team. Nearly eighteen years of age. Played all season. The best game of the season was against Edinburgh 'Varsity, when we were 10 points down, and 15 minutes to go; ultimately won by 13 points to 10. Joint-Champion of Scotland with Edinburgh Watsonians.

"'*Season* 1909-10.—Played in all the Scottish Trial Games, and was chosen for the Scottish team as reserve against Wales and England. Game against Wales was my first, and my club-mate, W. E. Kyle's, last. He was the oldest and I was the youngest player in the side. Played right wing to Angus at Wales, and left wing to Pearson against England. Scotland beaten in both games.

"'*Season* 1910-11.—Played for Scotland against France and England. Played right wing to Buchanan against France, and right wing to Cunningham against England. Scored my first try for Scotland. Scotland beaten in both games.

"'*Season* 1911-12.—Captain of Hawick team. Had a good season. Played for Scotland against France, Wales, and England. Played right wing to Angus against France and Wales, and right wing to W. Burnet against England. Scored twice against France, and once against England. Scotland beat France and England, and lost to Wales. Game against England was the most exciting ever played in. M'Callum and Scottish forwards won the game.

"'*Season* 1912-13.—My best season. Captained South of Scotland against North. Played for Scotland against South Africa, France, Wales, Ireland, England. Was only three-quarter to play in all Internationals. Played left wing to Angus against France and Wales. Left wing to Pearson against Ireland. Right wing to Angus against South Africa. Right wing to Loudon-Shand against England. Played right centre against England half the game, owing to Loudon-Shand getting hurt. My finest game.'

" The notes finish here, but he played against Wales in the memorable match in which he was hurt, and took no further part in International contests."

If I may add my personal opinion, it is that, next to the late L. M. Macleod, Sutherland was the soundest three-quarter Scotland has produced in this century. Never showy, he was always doing something useful, and should never have been left out of the national team from the day he was first chosen to play for it. A straight, clean player, Sutherland's every action was above suspicion. He played the Rugby game as it is meant to be played, and in this particular respect the Border country can be, and assuredly is, very proud of its three representatives in this magnificent Roll of Honour—Lieutenant J. L. Huggan, of Jed Forest, Major W. T. Forrest, of Hawick, and Second-Lieutenant W. R. Sutherland, of Hawick—for the game of each was

" *Sans peur et sans reproche.*"

FRANCIS NATHANIEL TARR

LIEUTENANT FRANCIS NATHANIEL TARR, 1/4th Leicestershire Regiment (T.F.), was killed in action near Ypres, Belgium, on July 18, 1915, aged 27. Born in Derbyshire on August 14, 1887, Tarr was educated at Stoneygate School, Leicester, and at Uppingham (1902-6). He was the most distinguished three-quarter who ever left Uppingham School, and one of the two best, Gregor Macgregor being the other, that School can claim. At Uppingham Tarr was a three-quarter in the XV., and was Captain of Games. On going up to University College, Oxford,

LIEUT. FRANCIS NATHANIEL TARR
1/4th Leicestershire Regiment

Photo: Orr, Woodford Green

in October 1906, he did not get into the XV. in that season; but he played against Cambridge in the centre in 1907 and 1908 with H. H. Vassall, and in 1909 with C. M. Gilray, when with H. Martin on his wing, and the late R. W. Poulton Palmer on Gilray's, Cambridge had nine tries scored against them, five by Poulton, as he was then, and four by Martin. It was in this match, 1909, that Tarr sustained a broken collar-bone. In spite of this great wing three-quarter match, it was when Tarr was partnered by Vassall that centre three-quarter play at its very best was seen. Indeed, their partnership was the feature of those two seasons, and certainly the best seen at either University since the four three-quarter game came in vogue. Like Vassall, Tarr had perfect hands for accepting passes, and perfect judgment alike in the choice of time and manner of delivery of the final pass, which is the hall mark of the really good centre. Rarely, if ever, did either of these players make a bad mistake in choice of action when it came to a question of whether to pass or to punt. Both were much faster than they appeared to be, possessing long strides, and both had that peculiar faculty of appearing to do little or nothing, while most of the time they were doing a very great deal. In this way they were not appreciated by the peculiar selectors of their time, and generally failed to please the many uninitiated critics who recognize good play chiefly in showy nothingness. Tarr was a deadly tackler, and a very fine judge indeed of the right game to play.

Elsewhere in this volume I have written of the immortal try scored by the late Lieutenant-Colonel E. R. Mobbs, D.S.O., with Tarr's most able help, against the Australians at Blackheath, in January 1909, and will not here add to what I have written save to say that it was a try that will live as long as International Rugby matches are played; for it was, in truth, one of the very best ever scored, being perfect in execution from the moment Tarr first received the ball to the moment Mobbs touched it down for a try.

Another try in which Tarr was much concerned also lives. Cambridge went up to Queen's with a smashing reputation in December 1907. They would win so easily, said some of the above-mentioned critics, that when it became known that they had won the toss and had taken the high wind, it scarcely seemed worth while to kick-off! For more than twenty-five minutes of the first half Oxford were penned to their half of the ground, mostly in their own 25, largely due to the touch kicking of K. G. Macleod with the wind; but no matter how their forwards heeled and their half-backs passed, neither Macleod nor any other of the alleged invincible Cambridge backs could do anything against the clever spoiling and sound tackling opposed to them, and especially that of the two Oxford centres. Half time was at hand when, from a scrum on the Cambridge side of the Oxford 25, R. H. Williamson fed G. Cunningham. The ball was soon in Tarr's hands. He very deftly drew Macleod before passing to Vassall. Half a dozen tremendous strides and Vassall had drawn the Cambridge left wing near the half-way line and given the ball to H. Martin, who scored after a run of nearly sixty yards, the Cambridge full-back, the late R. C. C. Campbell, being only able to watch him score. Tarr's quickness and cleverness in removing the chief danger from the opposition—although Macleod could do " evens," he had, of course, no chance with Vassall and Martin after having been successfully drawn by Tarr—it was that had most to do with this score. The extraordinary quickness and perception of the right moments to pass displayed by the Oxford centres was such that though there were players of the calibre of Macleod (Scotland), F. C. Pyman (Durham County), V. M. H. Coates (Somerset and England), and C. C. G. Wright (Kent and England), on the Cambridge three-quarter line, not a finger was laid on either Vassall or Martin! Centre play can soar no higher. And yet, such was the myopic selection work of those days, Tarr played but four times for England, one of these occasions being six seasons after the above match—in which, by the way, the invincible Cambridge XV., though with half a gale behind them during the first half, lost by 1 goal and 4 tries to nothing!—while Vassall was chosen only once. Tarr continued to play year in and year out as well as ever, for either Leicester or Headingley and the Midland Counties, and, except when injured or ill, was all the time easily one of the two best centres in England, and, after the retirement of Gwyn Nicholls of Wales, and H. H. Vassall's departure to Nyassaland, one of the two best in the United Kingdom. Had he been Welsh, Irish, or Scottish born Tarr would have possessed something like twenty International Caps; but a prophet has little honour in his native country, they say, and so this highly intelligent and able player, so very sound in defence, so clever and piercing in attack, was overlooked time after time. It is true that he was asked to play in a fifth International match—that against Ireland in the season of 1908-9—but, for reasons there is no need to enter into here, he declined the honour. Take his football one day with another, no better centre three-quarter has played for England in this century than Frank Tarr.

A keen Territorial before the War, Tarr was gazetted to his Regiment on May 11, 1913. When war broke out he trained at Luton and at Bishop-Stortford, and became machine-gun officer for his Regiment, going to the Front at the end of February 1915. He was Acting-Adjutant at the time of his death. The details of how and where he fell are given in the following letter to his mother from Lieutenant-Colonel R. E. Martin, the Officer Commanding his battalion :—

" He had gone across two fields," wrote Colonel Martin, " from where we are in underground shelters, to the shelters of the 5th Lincolns, to make some arrangements with their Adjutant. While he was there the enemy began to shell the place. He went into one of the shelters to wait until the shelling was over. While he was sitting inside it a shell burst a few yards away, and a piece came in through the doorway and struck him on the head. He died at once, and the doctor assures me that he would suffer no pain.

"He is buried in a grave near by, where a number of soldiers lie who have been killed here. The Brigade Chaplain read the service and all the officers of the Battalion were present, as well as the machine-gun men whom your son had trained, and of whom he was in charge, up to the time when he began to act as Adjutant. The grave will be marked and a cross will be put up by the Graves Registration Committee, who have official charge of that work. We will have as nice a wood cross erected as we can get made here.

"I have been in constant association with your son during the last few weeks, since Captain Dyer Bennett was wounded and he took over his duties as Acting-Adjutant. He was a peculiarly attractive fellow, and as loyal and conscientious an officer as any colonel could wish to have under him. I had a great regard for him, though my close association with him was comparatively short, and I shall mourn his loss profoundly on personal grounds, in addition to my regret at losing a most valuable officer. His name had gone forward for promotion to the rank of captain.

"I hope you will allow me to express my profound sympathy with you in your overwhelming loss. The burden of this war falls with peculiar weight upon those who are left at home to bear the loss of those who are taken out here; we who are in the middle of it have the constant and exacting demands of our work to fill our minds. I know from my personal experience how keen is the sense of loss in spite of this constant distraction, and I would beg you to accept my most sincere sympathy, and to assure you that your grief is shared by every one here who has served with your son.—Believe me, yours very truly,

"R. E. MARTIN."

Lieutenant F. N. Tarr was articled to Messrs. Owston, Dickinson, Simpson, and Bigg, Solicitors, of Leicester, and was a B.A. of Oxford University.

ALFRED SQUIRE TAYLOR

CAPTAIN ALFRED SQUIRE TAYLOR, R.A.M.C., attached Highland Light Infantry, was killed attending wounded near Ypres, Belgium, on July 31, 1917, aged 28. He was educated at Campbell College, Belfast, from 1902-7, and at Edinburgh University, where he graduated M.B., B.Ch., in 1914. At School he won the Honour Cap for Rugby football in 1906-7, and at cricket in 1905, being Captain of the XI. in 1906. At Edinburgh he was Captain of the University XV. in 1911-12, having played for it in 1909, 1910, and 1911 also. Captain Taylor played for Ireland against England, Scotland, and Wales in 1910, and against France in 1912 as a centre three-quarter. He played also for Ulster against the Stade Français in 1912. Joining the Army in October 1914, it was not long before he was at the Front in France with the R.A.M.C., serving there throughout 1915. In 1916 he served with them in Mesopotamia, whence he was invalided home; but on recovering he offered his services again, and was sent to Flanders in 1917, and was attached to the H.L.I. in the Ypres sector. While dressing the wounds of a brother officer in the front trenches, both he and patient were killed. Of him Colonel Pollock, R.A.M.C., wrote :—

" He was one of my best medical officers, a very gallant officer and a good friend. His death is a great loss to the Division."

The Officer Commanding the Battalion of Highland Light Infantry to which Captain Taylor was attached wrote: " I cannot speak too highly of his work on that morning before he was killed. He had a very keen sense of duty, which he always performed so well. I personally had a great liking for him: he was always cheery under all circumstances."

And another tribute read : " His death will be mourned by hundreds of men all over the world, as he was extremely popular."

Captain Taylor was a member of Malone Golf Club. As a Rugby player his attack was better than his defence, for he had plenty of pace and was a fine kick. When he fell Ireland lost one of her best sons, and one who will be long mourned wherever he was known.

CHARLES GERALD TAYLOR

ENGINEER-CAPTAIN CHARLES GERALD TAYLOR, R.N., was killed by gunfire in the fighting top of *Tiger* during the action at the Dogger Bank on January 24, 1915, aged 51. He entered the Navy as an engineer student on July 1, 1885, at Portsmouth, and then at the R.N.C., Greenwich, receiving a commission as assistant-engineer, dated July 1, 1886. His first ship was *Carysfort*, which he joined May 1887, being invalided home from the Mediterranean station in May 1890, suffering from malaria. He served in turn on *Gossamer, Impérieuse* (three years on the China station), *St. George, Banshee,* and *Quail.* Commendation was expressed on the paying off of *Impérieuse* for the satisfactory state of her machinery. For five years after leaving *Quail* he was on *Renown* for service in Halifax Dockyard, and while there was made Chief Engineer, becoming, under the new nomenclature, Engineer-Lieutenant, on his return to England in March 1903, when he was appointed to *Aurora*. Transferred in August 1904 to *Racer* for duty at the R.N.C., Osborne, and promoted Engineer-Commander in December, receiving about this time an expression of their Lordships' cordial recognition of the energy and capacity he displayed as a member of the Committee on the Extension of Training of Officers New Scheme. Captain Taylor went to sea again in *Cumberland* (cadets' training ship), September 1907, and in April 1908 was appointed to *Espiègle* for service at the

CAPTAIN ALFRED SQUIRE TAYLOR, R.A.M.C.
(Att. Highland Light Infantry)

Photo: Baker, Newcastle-on-Tyne

R.N.C., Dartmouth, again receiving commendation from the Lords of the Admiralty. On February 10, 1911, he was appointed a member of the Royal Victorian Order, 4th class. From March 1911 until September 1914, when he joined the Staff of the Vice-Admiral Commanding the first Battle Cruiser Squadron, Captain Taylor served in *Hercules* and at the R.N.C., Keyham, Devonport, as Engineer-Captain in command.

The foregoing is a sketchy outline of a very busy and useful professional career. But like most naval officers the late Engineer-Captain C. G. Taylor was a splendid athlete in his day. He was, apart from his great ability at Rugby football, a fine pole jumper and a good cricketer. I cannot do better than quote from the Rev. F. Marshall's well-known book on the Rugby game. There it is written: " Three famous players came to the front in 1883, one of them being C. G. Taylor. C. G. Taylor was one of the cleverest men in the kingdom with his feet. He was originally an Association player of some note. His first Rugby experience was with the Royal Naval Engineering College at Portsmouth. Taylor was asked to play for a scratch Welsh team against the 'Varsity at Oxford. He played a clinking game, and scored the only two tries obtained against the then redoubtable Oxford team. He was immediately afterwards chosen for Wales, and played in most of the International matches. He was one of the most extraordinary players who ever played, as he retained much of his old Association style of play; indeed, he was one of the very few players who went in for flying kicks, and hardly ever failed to bring them off—a style of play then, as now, much deprecated. He was very fast and a good kick."

Engineer-Captain Taylor's appearances for Wales were nine in number—namely, *v.* England, 1884–5–6–7; *v.* Scotland, 1884–5–6; and *v.* Ireland, 1884, 1887.

Two of his brother officers who knew him well for many years —namely, Engineer-Captain E. W. Roberts, R.N. (Devon, United Services, and England), and another, who wishes to remain merely

" W. P. H."—have written for me the following sympathetic appreciations of this remarkable sportsman. I give in full what they wrote :—

"C. G. Taylor," wrote the old Devon and England forward, "was originally a Soccer player, and a very good one at that. He is referred to in a book (published before '95) in this manner: 'Never fly-kick on a Rugger field unless you are a C. G. Taylor, and there is but one.' I believe I am right in saying that he is one of the *very* few people who tried to, and actually was successful, in kicking a few 'field goals'—not allowed nowadays. He played for Wales as a three-quarter when there were only three, and also for Wales, I believe, in their first match with four. He was then wing to A. J. Gould. He has told me many times about his old Rugger days, and I am sorry my memory isn't better; but perhaps you have the means of verifying what I say—this is somewhere about 1887. He was also a member of Blackheath, and played many brilliant games for them. At this time he was a Naval Engineer Student at Portsmouth. The United Services played very few matches in those days, but, of course, he always assisted them when they had a match on. During the time he was playing for Wales, he was said to be the finest drop-kick in the United Kingdom. He was also Champion Pole Jumper of Wales. Pole jumping in those days was a great sport. In after years he was Chief Engineer of Halifax Dockyard (Nova Scotia), and on one occasion, when the athletic sports of the year were being held—he, Taylor, was one of the judges—after the pole jumping the winner gave an exhibition jump. Some one asked Taylor what he thought of it, whereupon Taylor took off his boots and coat and easily cleared the bar! He was also very good at cricket, and having a good eye he broke many a bowler's heart, being a hard hitter. He went to the Mediterranean Station after leaving Portsmouth, and there contracted Malta fever, which nearly finished him. When Engineer-Officer of a torpedo boat

ENG.-CAPTAIN CHARLES GERALD TAYLOR, R.N.
Photo: London Stereoscopic Co.

based on Bermuda, he distinguished himself during a gale, and it was almost entirely due to his efforts that the boat got to harbour; in fact, the Commander-in-Chief, Admiral Fisher (now Lord Fisher) had given her up for lost. It was due to his splendid services on this occasion that Admiral Fisher got him appointed as Chief Engineer of Halifax Dockyard, and afterwards had him appointed to Osborne College at the beginning of the new scheme of entry and training for officers of the Navy. It was very largely due to him—for he was not only a brilliant man professionally, but also most charming, full of common-sense and tact, in fact a great leader of men—that this new scheme turned out the great success it did. From Osborne he followed the scheme to the R.N.C., Dartmouth, and then to the R.N.C., Keyham, of which place, as Engineer-Captain, he was in command at the time war broke out.

"On the outbreak of war he asked the Admiralty to give him a sea appointment, which they did as soon as possible. At the time of his death in *Tiger* he was Engineer-Captain of the Battle Cruiser Squadron."

" W. P. H." wrote :—

"If one might attempt to express his personality in two words, it might be done by saying he had a 'big heart,' both in the football sense and in the sympathetic understanding he had for every one he knew. It was this latter quality, together with the touch of humour which was never far from the surface, which enabled him to carry out his intentions against often considerable opposition. He was unconventional in the sense that he never troubled to plagiarize other people's idiosyncrasies or methods (witness his astonishing drive off the tee !), and he didn't care to see other people doing so whether in regard to games or other matters. He liked people to be direct, as he was himself, and he had a very definite aversion to the supporters of red tape and all other obstructionists. He was a very 'bad one to beat' in any enterprise he had embarked on. I remember once playing him at racquets when he was badly out of practice, whilst at Dartmouth; I won the first rubber, but he got the second, though he was tiring. He wouldn't stop though, but took the third also, purely and simply through wearing me down, though I was quite moderately fit. For the next two or three days Taylor could scarcely walk for stiff joints and blistered feet."

The late Engineer-Captain C. G. Taylor was indeed, on all counts, one of the old brigade who was very bad to beat.

REGINALD TAYLOR

CORPORAL REGINALD TAYLOR was killed on June 20, 1917, by shell-burst on the Western Front, aged 28. The officer in charge of his Company wrote to his parents:—

"It will be some small consolation to you to know that Taylor was killed while carrying out his duty. We had just returned from work we were carrying out, and he was taking his section back when the enemy started shelling again. I have known him practically ever since he joined up with us, and cannot speak highly enough of him as a soldier and a man. He was always cheerful and bright, under even the most adverse circumstances, and a splendid example to the men under him."

Taylor was born at Hillsborough, six miles from New Plymouth, on March 23, 1889. He was educated at Inglewood State School, where he commenced his football career, playing for the redoubtable Waimate Club, Taranaki, for several seasons; and then for Kaponga, of which team he was Captain. In due time he won his place in the Taranaki representative team, playing for the North Island in 1913, and played for New Zealand against the Australian team that toured the Dominion

CORPORAL REGINALD TAYLOR, N.Z.

in 1913. The season before he left New Zealand he played for the Clifton Club, enlisting from Waitara. He left New Zealand with the Sixth Reinforcements. In all departments of the game—New Zealand and Taranaki representative and as a Club player—Taylor was always known as a clean player and a clean liver. He had the entire confidence, the highest esteem, and the good-fellowship of all with whom he came in contact. Having made the supreme sacrifice for his King and Country, his name and fame are not likely to be forgotten by his numerous chums and admirers. Taylor came of a good fighting stock, and his father was sergeant in the 57th Regiment—the "Diehards."

HORACE WYNDHAM THOMAS

SECOND-LIEUTENANT HORACE WYNDHAM THOMAS, The Rifle Brigade, fell in action on Sunday, September 3, 1916, at the Battle of the Somme, aged 25. Educated at Bridgend County School (1900–5), Monmouth Grammar School (1905–10), and King's College, Cambridge (1910–13), where he took his B.A. and Second Class Honours in the Historical Tripos. Thomas played for Cambridge University against Oxford University in 1912, and for Wales in 1912 and 1913. But for injury he would have played in another inter-'Varsity match. He was a very fine attacking stand-off half with a very quick change of foot, excellent hands, a good pass, and a keen intuition of the right game to play. His departure to take up a business appointment cut short what would have been, I feel sure, a long appearance in International games. He had "arrived" in Welsh football at a time when that country was deploring its dearth of class players in the back division; and as Thomas, without being numbered among the great tacklers, had defensive ability considerably stouter than is usually seen in Welsh stand-off half-backs, it is probable that, barring injury, he would have been undisputed holder of that position in his National XV. for several seasons. Alike as a player and as a man Thomas was extremely popular. Indeed, I feel diffident about paying this small tribute to his memory in the face of the following extracts which I have been privileged to make from letters received by his parents :—

Thus, from his first School : " He was the finest character we ever had here."

From the Provost of King's College : " His whole career was one to be proud of ; " and again, " I remember when we first saw him at King's, after he was tried for his choral scholarship, we all said we must have him in the College. It was not only his voice; it was his bearing of gay modesty that won upon us; and ever since he kept his place in our hearts."

Cases of premonition are often quoted: a good instance is that of young Thomas, concerning whom two strangers to each other wrote to his parents, the one: " I had a charming letter from him, dated August 30, telling me that he was going on a very dangerous job, and really saying ' Good-bye ' "; and the other : " My excuse [for writing] is that your son knew I was one of his real friends, and wrote to wish me ' Good-bye ' two days before he was killed."

And Thomas's last letter home, written at the same time as those to the persons above referred to : " I am not afraid of Death at all, I feel a clean conscience. My life has been a truly happy one, thanks to you all from the bottom of my heart."

Only a clean British boy can pen beautiful words such as these. They are akin to that simple inscription, straight from the heart of a French soldier, found scribbled on a bomb-proof shelter, I believe before Verdun :—

> " To earth, my body ;
> To God, my soul ;
> To France, my heart."

SEC.-LIEUT. HORACE WYNDHAM THOMAS
Rifle Brigade

As an example to future generations that of this brilliant young Welsh-Cantab stands out as a beacon. He would, indeed, have gone far in the world.

RICHARD THOMAS

COMPANY SERGEANT-MAJOR RICHARD THOMAS, 16th Battalion Welsh Regiment, Cardiff City Battalion, was killed in action at Mametz Wood on July 7, 1916, aged 35. He was educated at Ferndale Board School, Glamorganshire, and was a member of the Glamorganshire Constabulary. One of the earliest Welsh Rugby Internationals to join the Colours, he was unable to get away from his police duties to enlist before January 16, 1915, when he went into training at Colwyn Bay with his regiment until August. He completed his training, when his battalion was moved to do so, with the Welsh Division at Winchester, the whole Division being drafted to France in December. Promotion with " Dick " Thomas, as Wales best knew him, was very rapid, his police and football training and experience standing him in good stead; so from Private Thomas in January we find him Company Sergeant-Major in March of the same year. That he played a Rugby man's part in the fight we may be sure, and he was alongside the officer commanding his Company (Captain Herdman), leading an attack, when he was shot through the head, Captain Herdman being severely wounded, and the regiment losing about half its effectives in this affair. Thus died a very gallant and popular son of Wales, upholding the honour of his country, his calling, and the great game, by meeting his fate in the position every Rugby player fain would meet it—right in the forefront of an attack.

It is in no captious spirit I write that Wales has had some fairly hefty and tough men in her pack from time to time. Burly and hard-bitten sons of the hills most of them, caring little or nothing for physical hurt whether to self or opponent. And one of the toughest, and the fairest, of these was "Dick" Thomas, who, as one of his friends has written me, "could always take a knock without moving a hair; this served him as well in the police force as on the football field." Thomas had the national aptitude for the game, and did not play long for the junior team of Ferndale before Penygraig, one of the leading Glamorgan League teams, drafted him into its pack. Very soon afterwards he played, in 1904, for Glamorganshire v. Monmouth. Joining the police in November of that year he was posted to Mountain Ash, and during his ten years' service in the Force he played regularly for Mountain Ash, for Bridgend, and for the Police team, except during 1906–7, when appendicitis interfered with his football career. In 1906 he played in the famous Welsh defeat by the South Africans at Swansea, and then fell out, owing to his illness, of first-class football until he got his Welsh Cap again in 1908, against Ireland and France, and the following season against Scotland. These were his only International Caps, four in all, three of them obtained after his operation. He played in all twenty times for his county, including in this number the dropped goal to a try defeat at Swansea from the New Zealanders, when he was one of the most prominent men on the field. Thomas was the handy-man of the Police Force XV., in which he gave his pace and individualistic tendencies full rein. For them he generally played half or three-quarter, and this experience was most obviously useful to him when playing for Glamorganshire or for Wales. One of his greatest friends, Mr. T. D. Schofield, of the Welsh Rugby Union, has kindly responded to my invitation for a note on Company Sergeant-Major Thomas, with the following sympathetic tribute. He writes :—

"Of the large army of heroic Welsh Rugby players who have laid down their lives on the altar of sacrifice in this world-wide war for righteousness, liberty, and justice, I can assign no greater

COMPANY SERGEANT-MAJOR RICHARD THOMAS
16th Batt. Royal Welsh Regiment

prominence to an individual on the 'Scroll of Fame' than to Company Sergeant-Major Richard Thomas, of the Cardiff City Battalion of the Welsh Regiment. 'Dick' Thomas, as he will always be remembered by followers of the Rugger code in Wales, was, without doubt, one of our gallant little country's best and most versatile Rugby players. His rightful position, both by physique and natural aptitude, was in the pack; but his all-round abilities were such that he came to be regarded as the 'emergency man,' to be drawn out of the front division to defend any rear position from half-back to full-back when serious attack was threatened. I shall never forget that memorable night, in the summer of 1916, when one of his colleagues in the Glamorgan Police Force came to my house with the distressing message, 'Come down to town immediately; poor Dick Thomas has been killed.' It was such a great shock to me. I thought of the invaluable services he had rendered to the Mountain Ash Club, the Glamorganshire Rugby League, Glamorgan County, Glamorganshire Police, the Principality of Wales, and last, but not least, as Captain of the Bridgend Rugby Club. He was a keen, but genial sportsman—the life and soul of any team. Gentle by no means, he, nevertheless, never failed to play the game properly. He would take and give hard knocks. A hard-working scrimmager, he was no less prominent in the open. He was a fearless tackler, and had the happy knack of adapting himself to any circumstance of emergency. Perhaps his great value as a player is best summed up by the remark of a member of the Monmouthshire Rugby League, who once said: 'The Monmouthshire League team would sooner face any man than Dick Thomas, the fiery chariot.' By his own sterling qualities Dick Thomas was the means of winning many a game off his own bat, so to speak. Of the many games I saw him play, one which stands out most prominently in my mind was that between New Zealand and Glamorgan County at Swansea, when Glamorgan were very unlucky in losing by a dropped goal to a try. Dick Thomas's performance on that day was head and shoulders above that of any other forward on the field. I think I am betraying no secret when I say that he was a warm favourite with all members of the Welsh Rugby Union Selection Committee, and it was only an attack of appendicitis which prevented his inclusion in the Welsh International team on many more occasions than he did appear. He was a man beloved by both players and spectators, and his loss to the Rugger Code in Wales is as irreparable as it is greatly deplored. He died as he had always lived, a great hero."

T. D. S.

"BRIDGEND, *December* 1, 1917."

GERALD THOMPSON

PRIVATE GERALD THOMPSON, 5th Battalion South African Infantry, fell in action in East Africa on June 30, 1916. He was born at Carnarvon, Cape Colony, and educated at Rondebosch High School. He was a member of Captain W. A. Millar's (Coldstream Guards) South African team of 1912–13, which created a record by winning all four of its International matches in the United Kingdom. Of that giant pack, the finest pack of forwards that was ever seen on a football field in the opinion of many, Thompson was one of the two best. In all respects he was a very great forward indeed; but, naturally, better on hard than on soft ground, as Colonials must be in the great majority of cases. Thompson played against Scotland, Ireland, and Wales on that tour. For myself, I have never seen a better individual performance than his on that frost-bound pitch at Lansdowne Road, Dublin, on November 23, 1912, when Ireland were routed to the tune of 4 goals and 6 tries to nil. Only a few have I seen to equal that all-round display. Thompson played like one possessed, and as though the Irish XV. were like a lot of unpractised schoolboys. It was a memorable performance on a never-to-be-forgotten afternoon when we saw South African Rugby on a pitch as hard as its own home pitches at its best. Thanks to the kindly assistance of J. G. Hirsch and H. W. Carolin, two old friends of the 1906-7 South African team, I have been able to obtain from South Africa, from the pen of Mr. B. Dods of the Somerset West Rugby Club, the following sympathetic appreciation of the former Somerset West forward. Mr. Dods writes :—

" Possessed of a shy, gentle, and equable disposition, 'Tommy' was a very lovable fellow. His ready and pleasant smile, his quiet unostentatious manner, and his easy good nature endeared him to all with whom he was associated. He was 'Tommy' to every one. The fame he achieved as a 'Springbok,' and on the football field generally, in no way altered his manner or character. His was a character that would remain steadfastly the same under all circumstances. His appearance and manner at once impressed one with a sense of reliability, and a more intimate knowledge of him confirmed that impression, and convinced one that at all times and under all circumstances he could be absolutely relied upon. Physically he was strong, mentally he was sound, and temperamentally he was generous and steadfast.

" When war broke out he immediately joined up, obtained a commission, and served to the end of the campaign in South-West Africa, when the Commando to which he was attached was disbanded. The ink on the notices calling for recruits for service in East Africa had hardly dried ere he presented himself, and was drafted to the 5th South African Infantry, and proceeded with that regiment to the field of operations. He did not wait to obtain a commission ; he was prepared to serve in any capacity. He fell in action at Kangata. His conduct before the action was characteristic of the type of man he was. He had reported sick, and had been advised to join the wagon transport. Instead of taking advantage of this privilege—and only those who served in East Africa can appreciate what it meant to be allowed to ride on a wagon—he quietly resumed his place in his Platoon and carried on. While the action was in progress he heard that his brother had been wounded. Without thought for the risk to himself, anxious only about his brother, he exposed himself. A bullet penetrated his neck, and before many minutes had elapsed his big heart had ceased to beat, and his brave and generous spirit had winged itself to that bourne of the true and brave that is beyond human ken.

" ' Tommy ' possessed the essential qualifications of a Rugby player—great physical strength, good staying power, patience and pertinacity ; his sense of fairness, his equable temperament, and his aversion to all that savoured of the illegitimate on the field rendered him an ideal player : a tower of strength to his side, morally and physically.

" The average Scot is thrifty in the bestowal of praise. If such praise as he does bestow exceeds ' Oh ay, it's no' bad,' the object on which it is bestowed is worthy of it. Of Tommy it was said by the Scots players that ' he was one of the finest forwards that had ever been seen in Scotland.'

" Those who knew him well are not likely to forget him. His personality was such as to leave a lasting impression. They will regret his loss, but they will derive pleasure and pride from the knowledge that he was their friend, and that their belief in him was not altered by his life or by his death."

ALEXANDER FINDLATER TODD

CAPTAIN ALEXANDER FINDLATER TODD, 1/3rd Norfolk Regiment, died of wounds sustained at Ypres, Belgium, on April 20, 1915, aged 41. Born at Forest Hill, London, on September 20, 1873, Todd was educated at Mill Hill School (1885–92), and at Cambridge University. He was in the XV. at Mill Hill, of which Lieutenant-Colonel T. W. Pearson, the Welsh International, was

CAPTAIN ALEXANDER FINDLATER TODD
1/3rd Norfolk Regiment

ALEXANDER FINDLATER TODD

captain in 1888–89. Others in that team were C. E. Fitch, Cambridge University XV. 1889, and J. B. Jackson of the Middlesex County XV. Todd was in the team for the next three seasons, and Captain of it for the last two. He was also in the School XI.'s of 1889–92, keeping wicket. On going up to Caius College in 1892, he played against Oxford in 1893–95 as a forward, Oxford winning the first by a try to nil, while the second was drawn, a goal each, and Cambridge won the third by a goal to nil. Five seasons later, having played regularly for Blackheath in the meanwhile, he got his English Cap against Ireland and Scotland, the Irishmen losing at Richmond by 2 goals (1 dropped) and 2 tries, to 1 dropped goal, and the Scottish match being drawn, no score, at Edinburgh. At Cambridge his chief contemporaries were W. E. Tucker and F. Mitchell, and during the period 1895–1900 he captained Kent, went on several Barbarian tours, and with the United Kingdom team to South Africa. He played a lot of cricket for Berkshire and for London County Cricket Club, and was a very fine wicket-keeper indeed when in practice.

"Toddles" saw quite a fair amount of active service. He served as a Captain in Roberts' Horse in the South African War for a year and nine months, and was wounded during the action at Diamond Hill. At the outbreak of this War he joined the 3rd Battalion Norfolk Regiment, and although he was offered his majority if he stayed in this country, he preferred to go to France as a subaltern. This he did in the first week of October 1914, and was in the trenches before the month was out. He was gazetted Captain in April 1915, just about the time he fell at Hill 60. Such is, I fear, a rather inadequate outline of the fighting career of a good, straight Briton of the type that makes us proud to be of the same race. "Toddles" had no enemies. His friends could not be counted. He played both these great games of Rugby football and cricket to the last ounce, for all they and he were worth. He was one of the very best of opponents to meet when you had made a duck at cricket, as he made you feel your trouble was his, and not as is so often the case, that your failure was a fit subject for his gloating or cynical joy. In short, to no man I have met on many fields of sport did the oft abused term sportsman more straightly apply than to this great big delightful boy, merely to know whom was one of the pleasures of existence.

FREDERICK HARDING TURNER

LIEUTENANT FREDERICK HARDING TURNER was killed in the trenches near Kemmel on January 10, 1915, aged 26. Born on May 29, 1888, in Liverpool, Turner was educated at Greenbank, at Sedbergh School, Yorkshire (1902-7), and at Trinity College, Oxford (1907-10). He was Captain of football and of cricket at Sedbergh, and of Rugby football at Oxford, for whom he played against Cambridge in 1908-10—the first match being drawn at 1 goal each; the second, " Poulton's match," a win by 4 goals and 5 tries to 1 try; and the third a win by 4 goals and 1 try to 3 goals and 1 try. Turner played for Scotland against England, Ireland, Wales, and France in every match of the three seasons 1911-13; against the South Africans in 1912; and against England and Ireland in 1914, gaining fifteen Caps in all. That he was a sound, hard-working, honest forward is certain. The best note on his football I have ever read was that which was written to me by the late Lieutenant R. W. Poulton Palmer, who, if anybody did, knew Turner's game thoroughly. This is what he wrote to me in the last week of January 1915 on hearing of the death of his University and Club captain :—

" The death of F. H. Turner has been a sad blow to his many friends, and to one unused to writing character sketches it is indeed hard to put down on paper the effect that his cheering presence had upon those with whom he was acquainted. Thousands of those who have watched his play in 'Varsity, Club, and

LIEUT. FREDERICK HARDING TURNER
Liverpool Scottish
Photo: Moffat, Edinburgh

International matches must have realized the strength he was to his side, quite apart from his own individual efforts, which were of a very high standard.

"I have played behind many packs of forwards, but never have I been so free from anxiety as when those forwards were led by Fred Turner. Those who saw last year's England v. Scotland match could realize what an anxiety to his opponents his peculiarly infectious power of leading was. His play, like his tackle, was hard and straight, and never have I seen him the slightest bit perturbed or excited; and in this fact lay the secret of his great power of control. His kicking ability is well known, and his tenacious determination to stick it was well shown in the 'Varsity match of 1909, when he returned to help his scrum when in great pain, with one knee useless owing to a displaced cartilage. Off the field he was the same. Whether one saw him at his home, at his old school (Sedbergh), at the 'Varsity, or walking on the hills, his face always showed his cheery satisfaction with the world at large. At any moment he would burst into that cheery and infectious laugh. He was always ready to take his part in any harmless practical joking, on tour or elsewhere. His loss is part of the heavy burden of war; and England, in defending her honour, will have to face the loss of the very best of her sons."

It is impossible, in my opinion, to improve upon this description of F. H. Turner in the football field, beyond saying he was one of the great forwards of this century, and certainly of higher value to his side than the mere onlooker, who sees so little of the game after all, generally realized.

Turner was in business in Liverpool when war broke out, and being already in the 10th Battalion Liverpool Scottish, he joined them at once, and was gazetted Lieutenant just before leaving for the Front on November 1, 1914. In France and Belgium he was evidently the same cheery modest soul, the hardships of war making of him an even more invaluable companion than he was during or after a losing game of football. His letters home tend to prove this; and he was particularly anxious to do something to moderate the tendency, then rather general and perhaps not unnatural, to exaggerate everything done by our grand fellows at the Front during that most exacting and testing of all times, the first year in the trenches. To this end he wrote once :—

" We are not yet the finest battalion in the British Army, nor have we absolutely annihilated the Prussian Guard ; all we have really done is to take our share in the discomforts and in some of the dangers of the campaign without grousing."

Turner had the highest admiration for the Regulars and what they endured, and had he lived would not have been numbered among those of short memory, who have forgotten the deeds of the " Old Contemptibles " almost to the extent of trying to belittle their doings, without guns and shells and a hundred other necessaries, by comparison with the fine work of our later fully supplied and equipped forces. In this regard he wrote to his old master at Sedbergh :—

" We are still going strong out here, and manage to keep our heads above water, though at times we are hard put to it to do so, I can tell you ! It is a man's life out here, and it agrees with me splendidly. I have never felt fitter in my life ; in fact, I could very nearly run the whole length of the old footer field at school uphill without breaking down, which, you will admit, would be a performance of some merit.

" For goodness' sake, don't believe all the yarns you see in the Liverpool papers about us. True we have had some hardships, and not a little discomfort, but it has been a picnic by comparison with what the Regulars went through. They are a magnificent lot, and one admires them more and more every day."

And so, a short two months of hard work, amid all manner of

FREDERICK HARDING TURNER

dangers, and this splendid specimen of our race met his end in the following circumstances, as told by a brother officer :—

"Freddy had been putting some barbed wire out in front of the trench, and after breakfast he went down to have a look at the position. Twice he was shot at when he looked up for a second. He then got to a place where the parapet was rather low, and was talking to a sergeant when a bullet went between their heads. Freddy said : 'By Jove, that has deafened my right ear,' and the sergeant said, 'And my left one, too, sir.' He then went a shade lower down and had a look at the wire, and was shot clean through the middle of the forehead, the bullet coming out at the back of his head, killing him instantly. The same man had evidently been following him all the way down the trench, and he ought not to have looked up for a bit, as a man walking along a trench can be seen by the enemy every time he passes a loophole. We got him down to —— that night with great difficulty and buried him in the local churchyard in pouring rain. The grave, though baled out in the evening, was 18 inches deep in water. However, it is quite the best cared-for grave in the churchyard, and looks very pretty, with a nice cross put up by one of the other regiments in the brigade, and also a very nice wreath."

To his bereaved parents, his father's end having been hastened by the loss of such a son, another brother officer wrote :—

"Others will tell you of his superlative qualities as a soldier. Never have I met a truer, straighter man than he, or one braver or more modest. He was a *man* all through—and he was such a dear good chap as a pal. We shall never forget him."

Nor, may I add, will any lovers of Rugby football who ever had the pleasure of seeing him play, whether for his School, his Club, his 'Varsity, or his Country.

Rugby football was not his only game. He was at one time

in the running for his Cricket Blue, being a forcing batsman; about the best bowler Sedbergh ever had, as he could bowl a very good "googlie"; and like most Rugby players a good fieldsman. But the more vigorous game was his love, and at it he excelled as do only very few.

ALBERT LUVIAN WADE

LIEUTENANT ALBERT LUVIAN WADE, 17th D.C.O. Middlesex Regiment, attached 6th Trench Mortar Battery, fell in action at Oppy Wood, Arras, on April 28, 1917, aged 32. He was born in Glasgow, and educated by a private tutor, and afterwards at Dulwich College, from 1896–1904. He was in the Dulwich XV. from 1902–4 as scrum half-back, and Captain of it in the season 1903–4. From 1904–8 he played for the London Scottish, and from 1908–13 for the Old Alleynians, of which he was Captain from 1909–13. He played for Scotland against England in 1908 at Inverleith, Scotland winning by 3 goals (2 dropped) and 1 try to 2 goals. Like practically the whole world of physically fit Public School boys, Wade joined his Majesty's Forces in the first week of war, with the 13th Kensingtons. He was transferred to the Inns of Court O.T.C. on November 14, 1914, and given a commission on April 15, 1915, in the 17th D.C.O. Middlesex Regiment. He went to the Front in September 1915, and was promoted Lieutenant on March 28, 1916. In December of that year he was attached to the Trench Mortar Battery, to meet a soldier's death five months later. Bertie Wade's body was never recovered. His T.M.B. went beyond their objective, actually penetrating into the third line of German trenches, in which Wade fell. The strong counter-attack which followed rendered it impossible to bring in our casualties.

Such was the fine, keen finish of this cheery young soul. Wade was of the very best type of British Public School boy. His character was stamped on his smiling face, and was of that

LIEUT. ALBERT LUVIAN WADE
Middlesex Regiment (att. 6th Trench Mortar Battery)
Photo: C. E. Butler

straight, clean nature that makes a man a favourite even among men who have never been within speaking distance of him. It was my privilege to know the little man. It would be infringing on the truth to describe him as a great scrum-half, for he was not that, but he was well worth his Cap and had the good luck to be behind winning forwards in what some thought ought not to have been his only International game. That match was memorable, in that it was the only big one I can recall in which two tries were scored from an in-pass by a wing to his centre. H. Martin was not fast enough on the wing for K. G. Macleod (his centre), nor had he the hands to take Macleod's " shot " passes. But he managed to do so at least twice, and to get the ball back again to Macleod, whose fielding and speed did the rest, and exposed the lack of team-defence on the English side at the same time. It was largely due to Wade's celerity and agility at scrum-foot that the Scottish backs saw so much of the ball that afternoon. In club football Wade did a great deal for the Old Alleynians in keeping the side together, and in other ways. A clever fellow, Bertie Wade showed promise as a black-and-white artist, and when the Old Alleynians XV. toured in Bordeaux and Agen at Easter 1912—instead of at Frankfort-on-the-Main as usual—Wade replied in French to the formal welcome at the Café Américain of the officials of the Sporting Union Agenais. In these and countless other ways he endeared himself to his fellows. I cannot make extracts from the numerous letters concerning him which it has been my great privilege to be permitted to read, but one remark, from an Old Alleynian writing to Wade's father, must be permitted : " It is something—it is a great thing—to leave a memory like his, and I hope that the thought of it may comfort you in your deep sorrow." For myself, the little man with the cheery smile will ever be a most pleasing memory.

From the pen of Wade's great friend, the Old Alleynian Stanley H. Cross, M.C., comes the following touching tribute, which I have been asked to give as it stands :—

"We were sitting outside our dug-out, my Company Commander and I; the mail from home had just come in, and both of us were deep in the contents of letters and newspapers. 'Haven't I often heard you speak of a great pal of yours named Wade, well-known Rugger man, wasn't he?' I looked up at the sound of Captain T——'s voice, and seeing that he was reading *The Times*, an icy fear stole into my heart as I replied, 'Yes, what's up?' 'Sorry, old man, he has gone under; here's a notice about him.' The bright spring afternoon seemed to grow darker at his words, and I went off to a quiet spot I knew of, just to have a good think about the best pal I ever had. It was on the football field we first met, the place where so many lifelong friendships have been formed. What a fine little player he was! Splendidly built and very strong, he could stand any amount of knocking about, and as a tackler was absolutely fearless. Better perhaps in defence than in attack, where the critics would have it that he was a little prone to run across, he was a deadly player near the line. Woe to the opposing half who did not keep a sharp eye on the blind side when Wade was about—he would whip round the scrum, and, using his solid compact strength for all it was worth, would be over the line like a shot. Yes, a fine player and splendid, cheery captain of a side, who always came up with his well-known smile from the very roughest handling. He was one of the best-tempered players I ever met, and in him the Old Alleynians and Middlesex have lost a player whom it will not be easy to replace. He gained one International Cap, being in the winning Scottish Fifteen *v.* England at Inverleith in 1908. His play that day was quite sound if not brilliant; and he has often told me how handicapped he was in his position, where it was necessary to get off the mark quickly, by the frozen state of the ground.

"My thoughts wander on to the many happy times we had enjoyed together, both in England and his beloved Paris. Wade was a black-and-white artist of no mean merit, and, as in everything he undertook, he threw himself into his work with all his might. How he loved the old Latin Quarter!—every nook and corner of which he knew by heart; and how he was beloved by the long-haired, untidy-looking denizens of that fascinating spot, all of whom knew the spruce-looking little Englishman who had come into their midst! I have a letter before me, as I write, that tells me how touched he was at the welcome he got when he went to revisit the old haunts on his first leave from the Front. 'They all remembered me,' he wrote, ' and all seemed so pleased to see me again, that it fairly brought the tears to my eyes;' but then, he adds, ' I always was a sentimental ass.' Personal magnetism and charm of manner were perhaps his greatest assets. There was another side to Bertie Wade's nature that very few knew, but knowing it, could only love and reverence him the more. A fine officer, and plucky as you make 'em, as his brother officers and men who saw him fall will tell you. Surely one of the best that the great game of Rugby football has given in old England's cause."

WILLIAM MIDDLETON WALLACE

LIEUTENANT WILLIAM MIDDLETON WALLACE, 5th Rifle Brigade, attached Royal Flying Corps, was killed in action in the air, at Sainghin, near Lille, France, on August 22, 1915, aged 22. Born at Edinburgh on September 23, 1892, Wallace was educated at Edinburgh Academy from 1899–1912, and King's College, Cambridge, 1912 to July 15, 1914. He was the full-back of the Academy XV. in 1909–12, and was one of the most versatile schoolboy athletes of his day. He was Vice-Captain of the XV. in 1912, and in the XI. in 1909–11; and Captain of it in 1911, being the wicket-keeper. He won the Bradburn Shield for the best all-round athlete in 1910; the Burma Cup for the highest number of wins in the School Sports in 1912; the Fives Cup in 1910. He was in the Gymnasium Eight in 1911; created school records in the High Jump—5 feet 5 inches—in 1911, and in

Throwing the Cricket Ball, with 105 yards 6½ inches, in 1912. On going to Cambridge he gave such a cool and finished performance in the Freshmen's match, that there was no doubt before half time who would be the 'Varsity full-back against Oxford. This he was in 1912, and in 1913, in spite of a severe wrist injury in the Lent Term of 1913 when playing at Newport. His confident style, splendid fielding, and long kicking with either foot, led naturally to his inclusion in the National XV. of Scotland; and he played against England in 1913 and 1914, and against Wales and Ireland in 1914. Of him it used to be said, that he was too cool, too daring, over confident. As something may be, and generally is, said about every really class full-back the game has ever known, Wallace's place in this gallery was revealed in the accusation. That was his way—he did everything, from driving a motor to wicket-keeping, as though nothing mattered and as if nobody was quite so good at it as he. This was not due to conceit, but to sheer self-confidence of the right type. Wallace had no superior as a full-back in the United Kingdom during 1912–14.

It was said at the time of his death, which occurred while he was engaged in photographic reconnaissance, when he was shot down by anti-aircraft gunfire, that he was the first undergraduate to go into action. Whether this is actually true or not it is impossible for me to say, but there cannot have been many before him, as he left for France on August 30, 1914. He was gazetted to the Rifle Brigade on August 15, and was in training at Sheppey until 30th August. He served with the 1st Battalion Rifle Brigade, with the 4th Division, till February 13, 1915, and was present at the Battle of the Aisne, at Frelinghien, and at Ploegsteert Wood. He became an observer in the R.F.C., No. 2 Squadron, 1st Wing Royal Flying Corps, on February 14, 1915, till the day of his death; and fought at Neuve Chapelle, Aubers, rue d'Ouvert, and several other actions in the Armentières-La Bassée area. Became senior observer in his squadron, and was promoted Lieutenant on July 21, 1915.

LIEUT. WILLIAM MIDDLETON WALLACE
5th Rifle Brigade (att. Flying Corps)

Photo: Drummond Young and Watson, Edinburgh

From the Academy *Chronicle* of October 1915 I have been permitted to cull the following appreciation of him :—

"His success as an athlete was partly due to his natural ability at all games, but more especially to the inherent qualities of his character. First and foremost, I should put it down to his great self-reliance and coolness—qualities which were apparent in him, not only when playing games, but also in the course of his everyday life. . . . None who ever saw him play will easily forget his beautiful touch-kicking or his reliableness under difficulties; but what impressed the spectator most was the fact that he was always cool and collected, that nothing seemed to put him out, and that he never knew when his side was beaten."

Such qualities are essentials in a high-class full-back, and that Wallace possessed them to a marked degree no eye-witness of any of his games can deny. His was an athletic form and a method which will long endure in the memories of us all.

PHILLIP DUDLEY WALLER

SECOND-LIEUTENANT PHILLIP DUDLEY WALLER, 71st Siege Battery, South African Heavy Artillery, was killed by shell fire near Arras on December 14, 1917, aged 28. Born at the Limes, Odd Down, Bath, Waller became identified with Newport and Welsh Rugby as a regular member of the Newport 1st XV. There is no doubt he was a very clever forward in the loose, and especially at the line-out, but the thick of the scrummage had few attractions for him; and he was not a noticeably good defensive player, for a first-class forward his tackling being at times rather superficial. He played in every match of the 1909 season for Wales, and again, in 1910, against the Australians and France. After that he went to South Africa with the team from the British Isles which toured there in 1910, and played in twenty-three games of a tour containing twenty-four matches. Settling in Johannesburg, Waller continued to play football, but his style did not quite fit in with that which is the outstanding feature of the South African forward game. But he was still a useful member of any average team in the loose when he came over as a gunner in the South African Heavies in 1915, and played in their team, which beat an excellent side of wounded and convalescent New Zealanders at Queen's Club in the winter of 1916, to lose the return match a few weeks later, at the Athletic Ground, Richmond. That was Waller's last first-class match. He went to the Front shortly afterwards, and having won his commission, fell in the fight at such a time that the announcement of his death preceded by a day his gazetting as full Lieutenant.

Concerning Waller's career since his schooldays the following are the facts : He was apprenticed, in 1906, as an engineer to the Alexandra Dock, etc., Railway Co. Here he was under Thomas Pearson, the well-known Welsh International of the nineties, and was introduced to the Newport Club. After a few games with the Newport third team, he was promoted to the second, and after a season with them obtained a place in their first team, and in 1907 he played for Somerset County, under his birth qualification. Waller joined the Service at Cape Town in August 1915, as a gunner in S.A.H.A. Battery, commanded by an old football antagonist, Major H. C. Harrison, the English International. He trained at Bexhill-on-Sea, and went to the Front in February 1916, where he obtained his commission for distinguished services in the field in May 1917. Waller was killed outright by the shell which also killed his Major. His late Commanding Officer, Major Rann, wrote to his father :—

" I knew him from the time of his enlistment in Cape Town, and was certain, after a time, his ability and personality would soon work for his promotion. As his Battery Commander I was glad when he could be recognized by the distinction of a com-

SEC.-LIEUT. PHILLIP DUDLEY WALLER
S.A. Heavy Artillery

mission in the field, and not only that, but be allowed to remain in his old Battery."

In 1910 Waller left for South Africa as a member of the British Rugby team. He played with distinction in all the matches except one. At the conclusion of the tour he was persuaded to remain in South Africa, and he settled in Johannesburg, where he became a member of the Johannesburg Wanderers Football Club. He captained their 1st XV. for three seasons. He obtained an appointment as engineer under the Johannesburg municipality, which he only relinquished on joining up.

JAMES HENRY DIGBY WATSON

TEMPORARY SURGEON JAMES HENRY DIGBY WATSON, R.N., H.M.S. *Hawke*, was drowned when that vessel was torpedoed by a German submarine on October 15, 1914, aged 24. He was born at Southsea, and was educated at King's School, Canterbury, from 1899–1906; at Edinburgh Academy from 1906–8; and at Edinburgh University from 1908–13. He was Captain of the Edinburgh Academicals as a centre three-quarter in 1912–13, and had been, of course, in the 1st XV. at both King's, Canterbury, and Edinburgh Academy. He played for Blackheath and for London Hospital either at centre or wing three-quarter or stand-off half, but generally at centre three-quarter. He had the unique distinction of being reserve three-quarter for Scotland in 1912–13, the season before that in which he did so much as right centre of the English three-quarter line to win the match, though it was won by only one point, at Inverleith. He represented Scotland against Ireland at Athletics, winning the Long Jump with 22 feet 9½. He won the High Jump at Edinburgh Academy every year he was at school, and later on he won the Edinburgh University Middleweights Boxing Competition. I find I have omitted another honour in the possession of this versatile athlete, for he was also in the Edinburgh Academy XI. Some little time before he appeared in the Blackheath XV., those of us who travel about and see football other than that on London grounds were aware of the great ability of " Bungy " Watson as a three-quarter back. The first time I saw him play was on the wing of the Edinburgh University XV., when beaten at Oxford; and I left the Iffley Road ground wondering what had happened to the Scottish selection committees that Watson had not yet played for Scotland, in spite of an admitted dearth of class three-quarters. It was about the time France beat Scotland at Colombes, near Paris, after which game one of the Scots selectors told a friend of mine: " The fact is, we haven't got a class three-quarter in Scotland," which was inaccurate so far as Watson was concerned. There was a story, spoken generally in jest, that one reason why Watson never got his Scots Cap was because, during a Calcutta Cup match at Inverleith, he sat near the Scottish Selection Committee and cheered everything the Englishmen did! But there was certainly a feeling against him for International fray on the ground that his play was too individualistic in tendency; that he wasn't really fast enough for an International wing, which was true; and that owing to his individualism—not selfishness, never that in his case, but just sheer *joie de vivre*, " I've got the ball, I'm jolly well going to do something with it before I'm downed " kind of thing—he could never be an International centre. In theory this is all sound enough, but in practice " Bungy " proved during his three matches for England (Scotland, Wales, and France in 1914) that one can have a great deal too much theory. His case is akin to that of the batsman who is told he mustn't, he can't, cut off the left leg, and who, thereupon, goes in and plays a match-winning innings of 50 odd runs, 20 of these from cuts off the left leg! " Bungy " Watson's Rugby was played in his own way. In my experience of him he always played best on the wing; for I saw him give some shocking passes when in the

TEMP. SURGEON JAMES HENRY DIGBY WATSON, R.N.

Photo: Brown, Helensburgh

centre, where a player who does that can never be tip-top. On the other hand, I saw him play splendidly for Blackheath v. Harlequins at stand-off, where "hands" are so essential. Major H. C. Harrison, D.S.O., tells me he never knew a back who did so much with the ball as "Bungy" could; and nobody would question Harrison's right to express an opinion, for he is more than a good player, he is a student of the game and its illimitable points. Watson would have had at least one other Cap, as he was prevented by accident from playing in the Irish match of 1913–14, for which he had been chosen. My recollection of him is that he was essentially a very live force on the football field: a player bound by no hide-bound convention, but whose methods were, on the whole, thoroughly sound. His attack was his best defence, but this is not to say he could not tackle. In fact he jibbed at nothing; but I think that the close, experienced observer of "Bungy" Watson's football will agree with me, that he remembers more of him threatening the enemy's lines than keeping his own intact. He was from all counts a delightful companion, and what sportsmen sum up as a real good chap. He is certainly in a congenial company now.

DAVID WESTACOTT

PRIVATE DAVID WESTACOTT, 16th Platoon, D Coy., 2/6 Gloucester Regiment, fell in action on August 28, 1917, aged 35. Educated at Grange National School, Cardiff, Westacott was one of the first Welsh Rugby Internationals to join the Colours, which he did on November 15, 1914. After training at Woolwich he went to France in February 1915, returning for his first short leave a year later. His next return was when he came back wounded on August 23, 1916, when, after he had had ten days at home in November, he was stationed at Maidstone and Sittingbourne for eight months, and then returned to the Front to meet a soldier's death. To his widow came the following note of sympathy from the Officer Commanding his Company :—

"I much regret to inform you of the death in action of your husband, Private Westacott, of my Company. He was killed by a shell in the support trenches on the 28th of last month. Death was instantaneous. He was buried in the proper manner the following day. I am very sorry indeed to lose him. He was a fine man, and one of the mainstays of the platoon. I had heard of his athletic fame, and he certainly died as he lived, a true sportsman. Please accept my most sincere sympathy.
"(Signed) C. M. HUGHES GAMES,
"O.C. 'D' Coy, 2/6 Gloster Regt.
"B.E.F., *September* 2, 1917."

I have, unfortunately, not been able to obtain any particulars of Westacott's football career, but he was a forward who played well enough in the Cardiff pack to win a Welsh Cap against Ireland in 1906, in that memorable game won by Ireland at Belfast, when playing "two short" during the last quarter of an hour—both their half-backs, Lieutenant-Colonel E. D. Caddell, R.A.M.C., M.C., and Major W. B. Purdon, R.A.M.C., D.S.O., being off the field injured.

JOHN GEORGE WILL

LIEUTENANT JOHN GEORGE WILL, Leinster Regiment, attached Royal Flying Corps, was killed during an air fight on the Arras front on March 25, 1917, aged 24. He was educated at a private Preparatory School and at Merchant Taylors' School from 1906–11, and Downing College, Cambridge, from 1911–14. At school he was for one year in the XI. and for three in the XV. as stand-off half; he won the School Quarter Mile in 53⅔ (the school record), and also the Hundred, the Half, the Long Jump, and the Hurdles. At the Public School Sports he won the Quarter and the Hundred,

PRIVATE DAVID WESTACOTT
2/6th Gloucester Regiment

and there is no doubt that in his best days he had ideal football pace, which is so often the case with quarter-mile runners. On going to Cambridge he played in the trial games at left wing three-quarter; but in his first year, 1911, as stand-off half against Oxford. In 1912 and 1913 he played at left wing three-quarter in the Inter-'Varsity, and it was in that position he played for Scotland in 1912 in all matches, and in 1914 in all matches except against France. He was Captain-elect of Cambridge for 1914, and would have led them against Oxford in December of that year but for the war.

Will joined the Honourable Artillery Company in August 1914, and went to the Front with them in September 1914. He took a commission in the Worcesters in March 1915, and was transferred to the Leinsters in April 1915. Wounded near Hooge in August 1915, he joined the R.F.C. in November 1915, going out to Egypt as Observer in November 1915. Returning to England in June 1916 to take his Pilot's certificate, Will was an Instructor at Dover during the winter of 1916–17, returning to France in February 1917. He was promoted Lieutenant in August 1916.

On March 25, 1917, Will was attacked by twelve German Albatrosses while escorting an observing machine. On his return journey he went to the assistance of a comrade who was in trouble, and drawing the enemy's fire, enabled his friend to escape, while his life was sacrificed in the noblest possible way.

There was somehow something very appropriate in the thought of George Will as a flying man. It suited the slender figure we had so often seen scudding along with the ball, often held in both hands, at such a high speed, albeit with an effortless gait, in the striped jersey of Cambridge. Flight seemed part of this very trim-built athlete. What a great wing he was in his best day, before a dicky knee and ill-health took some of the sharpness out of his game! Well do I recall a wonderful try he scored against a representative Swansea team at Cambridge somewhere about 1912. Playing on the left wing as usual, he actually scored the try in the right-hand corner, a sight not often witnessed in the case of a match against such a highly combined and well organized team as the first XV. of one of the leading Welsh clubs. Will's great pace enabled him to run along behind the line of advancing three-quarters, and to take Lowe's pass as though Lowe had been right centre and Will right wing. I remember well the surprise of the opposition, who were considered, and not without justice, to be past masters in the art of team-defence. There was also a memorable match on the St. Helens Ground, Swansea, when Wales won by 4 goals (2 dropped) and 1 try to Scotland's 2 tries, both scored by Will. That was in 1912, when some Welshmen regarded Will as the best wing in the four Home Unions at that time. Not a great kick by any means, Will had good hands, and at his best a great nose for the shortest way to score, which, for all good wings, is, in the vast majority of cases, hard for the corner flag. Will's last match was in the season of 1916–17, when he turned out at centre three-quarter for the Public Schools Services team against the Army Service Corps team, composed mainly of Northern Union professionals. But centre was never his place, and being short of practice and training it was not a very enjoyable match for him. His partner on that afternoon was D. L. Monoghan (Uppingham, Rosslyn Park, and Manchester), who also has given his life for the best of all causes. A most popular little man Will was: certainly one of the outstanding players among wing three-quarters of this century.

JOHN LEWIS WILLIAMS

TEMPORARY CAPTAIN JOHN LEWIS WILLIAMS, 16th Battalion Welsh Regiment, died of wounds at No. 5 Casualty Clearing Station in France, on July 12, 1916, aged 34. Born at Whitchurch, near Cardiff, on January 3, 1882, J. L. Williams's first experience at football was with the Association Code, having

LIEUT. JOHN GEORGE WILL
Leinster Regiment
Photo: A. Hester, London

gained his Colours at Cowbridge Grammar School, where he was educated. His first attempt at the Rugby game was with the team at his home, Whitchurch, in which he played left wing three-quarter, a position which he maintained throughout his brilliant career. His sure tackling, fielding, and kicking, combined with a deceptive turn of speed, and, above all, a capital swerve, soon attracted the attention of the critics in Wales. Newport was the first Club to extend an invitation to him to play in first-class football, and Williams played for both the second and the first fifteen of that Club. Being engaged in business at the Coal Exchange, Cardiff, in 1903-4 he joined the Cardiff Club. In his first season, as partner to R. T. Gabe, he scored 10 tries and dropped 1 goal. In 1904-5 and 1905-6 he was the leading try-getter in the Cardiff team, in the latter season making the splendid total of 35 tries. This was a memorable season for Cardiff, when no inter-club match was lost, the only loss being that against the New Zealanders by 2 points (10-8). Williams's combination with Gabe will live in the memory of Welshmen. He scored many remarkable tries, and that one against the South Africans for Cardiff will never be forgotten by those who witnessed it. In 1908-9 Williams captained the Cardiff Club. He was a member of the British team which played in New Zealand and Australia, and during the tour wrote several articles to local newspapers. He played eighteen times for Wales, and was Captain of the Welsh XV. against France in 1911. He was also a member of two unbeaten Welsh fifteens, those of 1908 and of 1909. Williams played in the following matches for Wales: *v.* South Africa in 1906; *v.* England, Scotland, and Ireland in 1907; *v.* England, Scotland, Ireland, France, and Australia in 1908; *v.* England, Scotland, Ireland, and France in 1909; *v.* Ireland in 1910; and *v.* England, Scotland, Ireland, and France in 1911.

The late Captain Williams joined the Royal Fusiliers (Public Schools Battalion) on September 24, 1914, in training at Ashtead, Surrey; got his commission as Second-Lieutenant in the 16th

Welsh Regiment (Cardiff City Battalion) in December 1914, and proceeded to Colwyn Bay for training. He was promoted First-Lieutenant in February 1915, and to Captain in March. He spent April at Chelsea Barracks undergoing a special course, and left Colwyn Bay with his Battalion for Winchester (Hazely Down Camp) in August 1915; after which he went to the Staff College, Camberley, for a special course, eventually proceeding to France on December 1, 1915. He was wounded while leading his men in an attack on Mametz Wood on July 7, 1916, and died of his wounds on July 12, 1916, at the Casualty Clearing Station. He lies buried at Corbie Communal Cemetery.

Williams was at his best a very fine wing three-quarter, certainly the best seen in Wales since the retirement of E. T. Morgan and W. Llewellyn. Indeed, his only serious rival as a wing was the late Major Bryn Lewis (Swansea and Cambridge University), who had the misfortune to be a much better performer off than on a Welsh ground. Williams's game was that of a true lover of sport, and not only west of the Severn, where the affection for a good player of Rugby football falls little short of worship, will " Johnny Bach " be long remembered and mourned.

RICHARD DAVIES GARNONS WILLIAMS

LIEUTENANT-COLONEL RICHARD DAVIES GARNONS WILLIAMS, 12th (Service) Battalion Royal Fusiliers, fell in action at Fosse 8, Loos, on September 27, 1915, aged 59. Born at Llowes, Radnorshire, on June 15, 1856, Garnons Williams was educated at Sully, Glamorganshire (1862); at Magdalen College School; at Trinity College, Cambridge; and at the R.M.C., Sandhurst. He was in the Rugby team of Magdalen College School as well as of his College at Cambridge. He played in Club football for Newport, and in the year in which he played for Wales against England (1881) he played for Wales also, under Association rules,

CAPTAIN JOHN LEWIS WILLIAMS
16th Batt. Welsh Regiment

LIEUT.-COL. RICHARD DAVIES GARNONS WILLIAMS
12th Batt. Royal Fusiliers

Photo: Elliott and Fry

stipulating when asked to fill a gap in the Welsh XI. that he should play as goalkeeper, which he did. Lieutenant-Colonel Garnons Williams won many athletic prizes at School, at Cambridge, and at Sandhurst. He was always very proud of having been a double International, and in the same year; and it was always a pleasant recollection with him that as a boy and a young man he was never out of training. This magnificent patriot retired as Major from the 1st Battalion Royal Fusiliers in 1890, having served with the Regiment for seventeen years; and during the South African War as Depôt Adjutant at Hounslow. When the present War broke out he rejoined his old regiment in September 1914 at the age of fifty-eight, went into training for a year, and out to France in September 1915, in which month he was killed in action when in command of his Battalion. He would have chosen no other end.

CHARLES EDWARD WILSON

CAPTAIN CHARLES EDWARD WILSON, the Queen's Royal West Surrey Regiment, Légion d'Honneur, was killed in action on the Aisne on September 17, 1914, and was the third Rugby Football Internationalist to fall in this War. Born at Fermoy, Co. Cork, Ireland, on June 2, 1871, he was 43 at the time of his death. He was educated at Dover College, and later became famous as a forward in the Blackheath pack at the time of such well-known players as Commander P. M. Royds, R.N., Major R. F. A. Hobbs, D.S.O., and Major P. Maud, R.E., when C. Dickson was captain. In the Queen's Regiment with him, and playing at the same time, were the Internationals Lieutenant-Colonel R. O'H. Livesay, D.S.O. (Blackheath), and Major R. H. Mangles, D.S.O. (Richmond); and but for the fact that regimental properties in these days are mostly stored, I should be able to give here a photo of the three Internationals together—a little record of its own of which the Queen's is justly very proud. Captain Wilson was a solid scrummager, one of the hard-working type, and he got his only Cap against Ireland at Richmond in 1898. It has been stated that his International career was cut short by an accident sustained at Exeter, when playing for the South v. North, when he broke a leg. But the letter I quote below from Dr. W. Ashford (Exeter, Devon, St. Thomas', and England), who was running by his side at the time, and to whom Wilson was about to footpass the ball, dates the accident very definitely. Dr. Ashford's version of a rather remarkable incident is as follows: " Wilson broke both bones in his leg in the second North v. South match, played at Exeter, in the season 1897–98. I think the match was played after Xmas. Wilson played in both North v. South matches of that season. The first one was at Carlisle, when South won by 3 tries to a dropped goal and a try. The South won at Exeter by 5 goals and 3 tries to nil, although the North had eleven present or future Internationals! I was close to Wilson when the accident happened, soon after the commencement of the game. He was dribbling the ball, Brettargh dived for it, and I believe Wilson tripped over his shoulder. Wilson, as you know, got his Cap against Ireland in the following International season. I should describe him as a thoroughly honest scrummager, good tackler, but not very brilliant in the open. I don't know his weight, but I always thought him on the light side for Internationals."

Captain Wilson served on the Staff during the South African War, and took part in the Relief of Ladysmith, the actions at Colenso, Spion Kop, Vaal Kranz, Tugela Heights, Pieters Hill, and the operations in Natal. He was mentioned in dispatches, and received the Queen's medal with two clasps and the King's Medal with two clasps. After returning from that war he played a few times for Blackheath, and on going out to India he relinquished the honorary secretaryship of the Army Rugby Union. So recently as 1913, on discovering that his regiment had no team

CAPTAIN CHARLES EDWARD WILSON
Queen's Royal West Surrey Regiment

Photo: Haeking, Vancouver

entered for the Army Cup, he set to work at once to raise a side, although at forty-two men are past their prime for cup-tie matches, and played full-back himself. It is recorded that in one of the games he scored a try himself from that position. Though he was a Blackheath and England forward, Wilson had now and then deputized at half for his brother officer Livesay.

FRANK R. WILSON

LIEUTENANT FRANK R. WILSON was a member of the Auckland Infantry Battalion, New Zealand Division. He died on September 19, 1916, from wounds received in action in the Battle of the Somme the previous day, aged 31 years. Wilson's company was holding a trench which they had captured at Flers on the night of 18th September, when a high explosive shell struck the parapet, wounding him very severely in the head. He was removed to a dressing-station, but expired shortly after, and was buried in Dernancourt Communal Cemetery Extension, France. He was the son of Mr. and Mrs. John Wilson, of Pompallier Terrace, Ponsonby, Auckland. He was educated at the Ponsonby School, Auckland Grammar School, and Auckland University College, and at the time of enlisting was a master at Newton West School. He left New Zealand with the Sixth Reinforcements with the rank of Sergeant, and received his commission on the field in France. He first saw service on Gallipoli, and was selected as one of the last fourteen New Zealanders, under Lieutenant J. M'Kenzie, to leave the trench facing the Turks at the evacuation.

At the early age of eleven Wilson made his *début* on the football field, playing three-quarter for the Ponsonby School team which won the Championship in the inaugural year (1897) of public school football in Auckland. Three years later found him included in the Auckland Grammar School XV. as a five-eighth, the school having a season of success. After graduating through the junior and third-class grades, Wilson became a senior player in 1905, scoring three tries in his first appearance for the Ponsonby team. The next year he won a place as three-quarter in the Auckland representative team, playing in all the four games of the year. His form was maintained for the following four seasons. In 1907 he toured New Zealand with the Auckland team, and the following year left his old love Ponsonby and joined University, being a tower of strength to the students. He was selected for all the representative matches, including the one against A. F. Harding's British team. In 1909 Wilson got a step nearer to a Dominion footballer's coveted goal, playing for the North Island against the South at Wellington. He reached the highest pinnacle obtainable in 1910, when he was selected to represent New Zealand for a tour in Australia. Unfortunately, he got little opportunity of justifying his selection, an injury in the first match against New South Wales preventing him from playing again on the tour. Returning to Auckland he was selected to play for his province against the American team.

Wilson's activities, however, were not confined to Rugby football. As a cricketer he was also very successful, being a reliable batsman, and making many hundreds. He captained the Ponsonby team when it won the Championship in 1914–15. As an amateur runner he was considered one of the fastest sprinters in Auckland of recent years. He won the Grammar School Old Boys' Race (150 yards) in 1904 in the record time of 15½ seconds (since unbeaten), and again in 1907. He was also a strong swimmer, and acted as starter to the Ponsonby Swimming Club. To complete the list it may be said that at lawn tennis he was also a very good player.

And then, the nature of the man. The following extract from a letter, addressed to Wilson's parents, received from Chaplain-Captain G. H. Gavin, is permitted :—

LIEUT. FRANK R. WILSON
Auckland Battalion, N.Z.

"We ought not to be sorry on his account, I am sure, but rather thank God for his noble example in both life and death. From his letters, which fell to my lot to censor, I learned something of the good, manly influence he exercised over his young boy admirers in Auckland. May memories of Frank Wilson ever be an inspiration to them."

Among the many noble fellows who have so unselfishly offered up their lives in the defence of the Empire, few will be lamented more in the Dominion of New Zealand than Wilson. His name alone, among adults as well as children, was a synonym for all that was clean and manly in sport. For years he was the popular hero of the Auckland football public, more particularly among the class who form the keenest critics of all—the schoolboys. In all his successes on the Rugby field he was never selfish, and herein lay the true value of his example to the younger generation, for Frank was never the one to sacrifice the success of his side for personal glory. Then, again, his extreme versatility made him eminently suited for a teacher—a teacher who loved his boys and believed firmly in the "sound mind, sound body" principle. Many a promising athlete can look back gratefully to the early training he received from Wilson. More than one mother has been heard to remark: "I could wish for nothing better than that my boy should follow in Frank Wilson's footsteps." And now a heroic death has closed the bright young life of him who could never stoop to a mean or paltry action. No more fitting epitaph could be written to his memory than this: "He was indeed a man."

JOHN SKINNER WILSON

LIEUTENANT-COMMANDER JOHN SKINNER WILSON, Royal Navy, H.M.S. *Indefatigable*, fell in action at the Battle of Jutland, on May 31, 1916, aged 32. He was First-Lieutenant and Torpedo-Lieutenant. He was a son of Sir David Wilson, K.C.M.G., and was born at Trinidad on March 10, 1884.

J. S. Wilson was appointed cadet in the *Britannia* on September 15, 1898, and on January 14, 1900, he was gazetted midshipman in *Canopus*, in which he served for three years. He passed for Acting Sub-Lieutenant, won five " firsts," and in January 1905 was promoted to be Lieutenant with seniority of March 10, 1904, his twentieth birthday. He served in the submarines for six months, and then joined *King Edward VII.*, the Flagship of Sir Arthur May. In 1906 he joined *Vernon* to specialize in torpedo work. He afterwards served in H.M.S. *Talbot, Formidable, Superb, Dreadnought,* and *Indefatigable.* He joined the last-named in 1913, and was First-Lieutenant and Torpedo-Lieutenant when she was sunk off Jutland on May 31, 1916.

Of Wilson's football career it may be said at once, he was thorough and enthusiastic first and last. He played for his Naval College XV. in 1903-4 and 1907-8, and was Captain of it during the two last years, when they played 33 and won 28 matches, losing but 4 and drawing 1. Points scored, 944 against 115. This XV. also won the Kent County Cup in 1908. He was Captain of the United Services XV. in 1908 and 1909, and played for the Navy *v.* Army at Queen's in 1907-8 and 1913. It is probable that 1908 and 1909 were his two best years, and in them he played for Scotland *v.* England and *v.* Wales respectively. He was a grand forward, one of the busy sort, always to be found somewhere near the ball, and never shirking his bit in the tight work for the sake of splashing about in the open and drawing the plaudits of the easily satisfied. Apart from the Rugby game Wilson was considered a good all-round man, as indeed his record proved him to be. He was a specially good oarsman and boat sailor, winning, among many other boat races, Lord Charles Beresford's Cup for Midshipmen's sailing races. His elder brother, Major Harry S. Wilson, 1st Munsters, was killed in action in

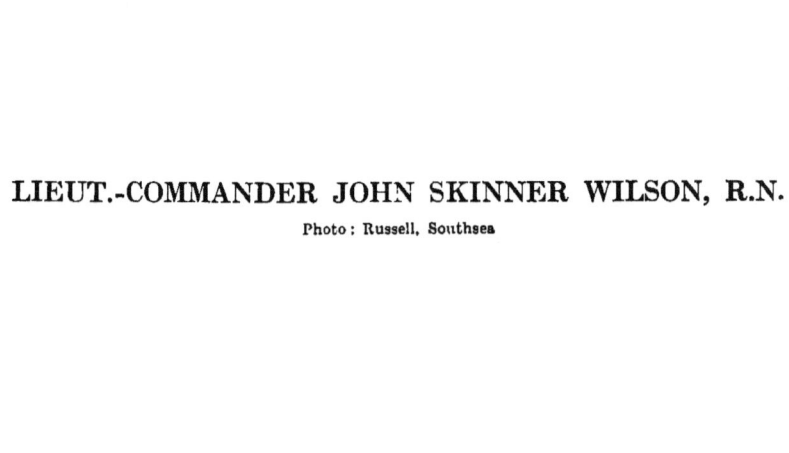

LIEUT.-COMMANDER JOHN SKINNER WILSON, R.N.
Photo: Russell, Southsea

CAPTAIN ERIC TEMPLETON YOUNG
8th Scottish Rifles

Photo: Brown, Falkirk

France, and his younger brother is a Captain in that grand regiment, the 42nd, the Black Watch.

ERIC TEMPLETON YOUNG

CAPTAIN ERIC TEMPLETON YOUNG, the Cameronians, 8th Scottish Rifles, fell in action on Gallipoli on June 28, 1915, aged 23. He was educated at Cargilfield from 1902–6; at Fettes College from 1906–10, where he was in the XV. in 1909–10; and at Magdalen College, Oxford, from 1910–13. He played occasionally for Oxford University, but not against Cambridge. He played for Scotland in the pack against England in the last International match played on British soil—that in March 1914, at Inverleith. Captain Young's home was at Crutherland, East Kilbride, Lanarkshire. He joined the Territorial Army in 1911, and was promoted Captain in August 1914. After training at Falkirk, he went to the Front in May 1915, and was reported missing, since presumed killed. Of him a brother officer wrote: "He was a man of most sincere and straightforward character, absolutely downright, and one of the most fearless. He took great interest in his men, and was much loved by them."

THE END.

www.ingramcontent.com/pod-product-compliance
Lightning Source LLC
Chambersburg PA
CBHW052039220426
43663CB00012B/2380